Facilitating Reflective Learning

To our grandchildren
who continue to inspire us

SECOND EDITION

Facilitating Reflective Learning

Coaching, mentoring and supervision

Anne Brockbank
and Ian McGill

KoganPage

LONDON PHILADELPHIA NEW DELHI

First published in Great Britain and the United States in 2006 by Kogan Page Limited
Second edition 2012

Apart from any fair dealing for the purposes of research or private study, or criticism or review, as permitted under the Copyright, Designs and Patents Act 1988, this publication may only be reproduced, stored or transmitted, in any form or by any means, with the prior permission in writing of the publishers, or in the case of reprographic reproduction in accordance with the terms and licences issued by the CLA. Enquiries concerning reproduction outside these terms should be sent to the publishers at the undermentioned addresses:

120 Pentonville Road	1518 Walnut Street, Suite 1100	4737/23 Ansari Road
London N1 9JN	Philadelphia PA 19102	Daryaganj
United Kingdom	USA	New Delhi 110002
www.koganpage.com		India

© Anne Brockbank and Ian McGill, 2006, 2012

The right of Anne Brockbank and Ian McGill to be identified as the authors of this work has been asserted by them in accordance with the Copyright, Designs and Patents Act 1988.

ISBN   978 0 7494 6507 0
E-ISBN   978 0 7494 6508 7

British Library Cataloguing-in-Publication Data

A CIP record for this book is available from the British Library.

Library of Congress Cataloging-in-Publication Data

Brockbank, Anne, 1943–
    Facilitating reflective learning : coaching, mentoring and supervison / Anne Brockbank, Ian McGill. – 2nd ed.
        p. cm.
    Includes bibliographical references.
        ISBN 978-0-7494-6507-0 – ISBN 978-0-7494-6508-7   1. Employees--Coaching of.
2. Mentoring in business.   3. Reflective learning.   4. Organizational learning.
I. McGill, Ian.   II. Title.
    HF5549.5.C53B76 2012
    658.3'124–dc23

                                                                                    2011052737

Typeset by Graphicraft Ltd, Hong Kong
Printed and bound in India by Replika Press Pvt Ltd

CONTENTS

ACKNOWLEDGEMENTS

Once again we express our appreciation of our colleagues, mentors, coaches, clients, participants on our courses, friends and family, all of whom have contributed to this book in their own individual ways. In particular we are grateful to the reviewers of our first edition, Jenny Rogers and Lise Lewis, who gave important guidance in preparation for this second edition.

We are grateful to our academic colleagues, Professor Yvonne Hillier of Brighton University and Professor David Megginson of Sheffield Hallam University for their valuable and incisive guidance. We recognize the role of our colleagues at City University where much of the material has been tried and tested. In addition, we acknowledge the contribution of the Masters students who participated in the Mentoring Coaching and Supervision module from 1995 to 2005 for the challenges and development they provided.

We extend our appreciation to our mentoring and coaching clients and for the insights we have gained through our relationships with them which support many of the ideas we present here. In our preparation and training of mentors and coaches for corporate clients we have been made aware of the variety of contexts in which mentoring and coaching activities are carried out.

We are grateful to Gerard O'Connor for his provision of diagrams in Chapter 10 and Dr Alison O'Connor who advised us in our initial discussions about the map of mentoring and coaching approaches.

We appreciate the role of our case study authors and contributors in illustrating many of our ideas, including: Alison Lyon and Eve Bazely of NCH, the children's charity; Jan Kay and Les MacDonald for the First Nation case; Patricia Easterbrook and Claire Siegel for the Professional Awarding Body case; Helene Donnelly, Forensic Paper Conservator and Founder of Data & Archival Damage Control Centre; Dorothea Carvalho, Director, Chartered Institute of Logistics and Transport; and Robert Clasper-Todd, Training Manager, Addaction.

In addition we would like to thank Nathalie Tarbuck of Two Minds Together for permission to include her coaching evaluation form in Appendix 6.

Our own experience of mentoring and coaching has influenced the content of the book and we acknowledge our debt to our past mentors and coaches, who have influenced and inspired our endeavours. These include Anne's violin teacher Helen Hogg, her private mathematics tutor David O'Connor, her trainer/supervisor Eunice Rudman and academic mentor, Professor Gary Davies, as well as Ian's teachers T Broadhurst, Mrs E Cox, and tutors Brian Thomas and Jack Greenleaf.

We also recognize the support of the editorial team at Kogan Page, including Helen Kogan, Martina O'Sullivan and Sara Marchington, who have enabled us to bring the book to publication.

Anne Brockbank (**Anne.Brockbank@mailbox.ulcc.ac.uk**) and
Ian McGill (**Ian.McGill@mailbox.ulcc.ac.uk**)

How to use this book

The revised edition is for those who practise mentoring or coaching as well as for those clients[1] who are interested in the mentoring and coaching process and wish to make best use of their experience as clients. We include coaches or mentors in training as well as those experienced in the field who may wish to review their practice.

The book may also be useful for those responsible for staff and management development in organizations who are involved in creating mentoring and coaching programmes. The revised situational framework for coaching and mentoring may help clarify how such programmes can be used for organizational transformation.

Our experience in the field as coaches and mentors, as well as designers of mentoring or coaching programmes for corporate clients, is the basis of this book, as is our experience of designing and running postgraduate programmes. We seek to build a theoretical base for professional practice which supports individual learning as well as organizational learning and change.

Readers who are more interested in practice than theory may choose to leave aside Chapters 2 and 3 in Part One and go straight to definitions and models of coaching and mentoring in Part Two, possibly returning to the chapters dealing with theory later (see Figure 0.1). Readers who are new to mentoring and coaching theory may want to absorb the material in Parts One and Two before moving on to our reports of practice in Part Three, which takes the reader into the different contexts for mentoring and coaching. Part Four deals with accreditation, diversity, ethical standards and the need for supervision.

The terminology of mentoring and coaching in the literature has been confused and remains confusing. Sometimes the words are used interchangeably with little or no agreement on their meaning. Academics have tended to position coaching as an activity which aims at performance only, meaning a minor adjustment to behaviour, whereas they have linked mentoring to a transformational learning outcome, where the learner experiences a total change in how they view the world. However, the recent expansion of coaching as a developmental method insists that coaching aims at transformation as a learning outcome, and mentors are simply company advisers

FIGURE 0.1   How to use this book: alternative routes

START HERE

↓

Part One: How coaching and mentoring support reflective learning
Chapter 1: The revised situational framework

↓   ↓

Theory to practice route	Practice to theory route
Part One: Chapter 2: Learning theories for coaching and mentoring Chapter 3: Reflective dialogue and learning	
Part Two: What is the difference between coaching and mentoring? Chapter 4: What is mentoring? Chapter 5: What is coaching? Chapter 6: Mentoring models Chapter 7: Coaching models	**Part Two: What is the difference between coaching and mentoring?** Chapter 4: What is mentoring? Chapter 5: What is coaching? Chapter 6: Mentoring models Chapter 7: Coaching models
Part Three: Coaching or mentoring in each quadrant Chapter 8: Performance Chapter 9: Engagement Chapter 10: Development Chapter 11: The systemic quadrant	**Part Three: Coaching or mentoring in each quadrant** Chapter 8: Performance Chapter 9: Engagement Chapter 10: Development Chapter 11: The systemic quadrant
	Part One: Chapter 2: Learning theories for coaching and mentoring Chapter 3: Reflective dialogue and learning
Part Four: The reflective practitioner: accreditation, ethics, diversity and supervision Chapter 12: Accreditation, ethics and diversity Chapter 13: Why supervision? Theories, sources and models Chapter 14: Conclusion	**Part Four: The reflective practitioner: accreditation, ethics, diversity and supervision** Chapter 12: Accreditation, ethics and diversity Chapter 13: Why supervision? Theories, sources and models Chapter 14: Conclusion

↓

END OF ROUTES

or even inexpensive tutors. Organizational programmes, unless clearly defined, have the potential for disappointment for mentors, coaches and clients alike.

We aim to clarify the meaning of the terms mentoring and coaching by relating them to the following questions:

- Whose purpose? Is the purpose of the coaching or mentoring owned by the employer, the organization, the coach, the mentor or the client?
- What process? Is the process didactic, impositional or humanistic?
- Which learning outcome? Is the likely outcome performance, adjusted behaviour or transformation?

Mentoring and coaching may be clearly defined by taking into account the purpose, the process and the potential learning outcome in a coaching or mentoring contract.

Part One is about theory. We set out the origins of our work in a theoretical account which underpins our practice. Alongside theory we declare the values with which we approach mentoring and coaching. In Chapter 1 we assert that the process of mentoring or coaching has one clear purpose, the learning and development of an individual. This process involves change, which may be one of modest improvement or of radical change where the outcome may be transformational. Thus we present a framework of approaches to mentoring and coaching which identifies the activities by their purpose, process and hence their learning outcome. Because each mentor or coach will have their own belief system, it is crucial that they take time to examine this, however embedded it might be, and make this known to prospective clients. We identify four categories of mentoring or coaching:

- *Performance* mentoring or coaching, where objectives may be imposed as in performance management.
- *Engagement* mentoring or coaching, where persuasive methods may be used to align personal aims with organizational objectives.
- *Developmental* mentoring or coaching, where the individual's own desires take centre stage and may or may not harmonize with the stated aims of the organization. The outcome may be transformational.
- *Systemic* mentoring or coaching, where an organization sets out to transform itself through a programme of development for its people.

Chapter 1 is designed to set these four categories in the context of the purpose, the process used and the learning outcome of the activity. This chapter seeks to clear up some of the confusion around the terms by categorizing coaching or mentoring as an activity for performance, engagement or development, depending on the purpose, the process or method used, and the learning outcome which is implied in the definition. We continue Chapter 1 with the view that mentoring and coaching do not operate in a value-free or neutral form. Both parties to the process are influenced by their social and organizational context. Mentor, coach and client are all influenced by how power factors of class, race, gender, role, identity and relative opportunity impact on learning.

In Chapter 2 we discuss how coaching and mentoring can support reflective learning in each of the four categories of mentoring and coaching above. This chapter introduces the reader to single and double loop learning and the significance of emotion in relation to learning, immunity to change, psychology in learning, social and organizational learning and levels of learning.

Chapter 3 builds on the previous chapter by addressing the significance of reflective dialogue for mentoring and coaching. We examine the notion of dialogue and the importance of working interactively as a means to seek improved performance as well as personal development for the client.

In Part Two, in Chapters 4 and 5 we describe how mentoring and coaching are defined by a wide range of writers, practitioners and academics. We examine here the importance of cross-cultural issues by reference to relationships between coaches or mentors and clients who differ in gender, race or ethnicity.

In Chapters 6 and 7 we examine the available models for use in different coaching and mentoring situations, including our own NEWW model.

Part Three is about practice and here we explain the four different types of coaching or mentoring mentioned above.

Chapter 8 discusses coaching and mentoring in the performance quadrant. Coaching is the most common method used in organizations for performance management. The coaching starts from a definable goal, which may or may not be owned by the client, and proceeds to methods of achieving that goal.

In Chapter 8 we discuss the basic skills which you will need if you are acting as a performance coach or mentor. By this we mean an activity which is primarily for the purpose of improvement. A company seeking to improve its customer complaints record may use coaching or mentoring for this. In this quadrant, mentoring or coaching does not seek to disturb things or enable transformation as described in Chapter 2, but seeks to improve performance without altering the underlying system. The skills described in this chapter are listening, restatement, summary, questioning and feedback. Many readers are equipped with further skills and we discuss these in Chapter 9. Chapter 8 presents the minimum level of skill for working in the performance quadrant.

Chapter 9 discusses mentoring or coaching for engagement, a popular choice of developmental activity in organizations, illustrated by our case studies. In particular, we explore the impact of programmes and the benefits in terms of organizational development. The skills needed in this quadrant are contracting, listening, questioning, primary empathy, summary and feedback.

In Chapter 10 we explore developmental coaching and mentoring, which enable the client to generate their own goals as well as their own method of achieving them. We locate the skills needed as a developmental coach or mentor. By this we mean coaching or mentoring which aims to achieve reflective learning and transformation. A company seeking to launch a culture change may use internal managers for this, or an organization wishing to develop key personnel may use external practitioners. Developmental coaches or mentors seek to enable their clients to question the taken-for-granteds (tfgs) in their work environment, recognize the prevailing discourse and transform their view of the world, as described in Chapter 2. A developmental practitioner, while attending to day-to-day performance, seeks, through reflective dialogue, to challenge their client to look beyond their immediate horizon and transform their view of the system in which they live and work. The skills appropriate here include coach and mentor presence, high levels of listening, restatement, advanced empathy, summary, questioning, feedback, challenge, immediacy and confrontation.

Chapter 11 explores how an organization may use mentoring or coaching to transform itself, through systemic change. The chapter includes a discussion about the expanding field of team coaching, what it means, who does it and how effective it is. Existing research is compared to case study material to reveal the special group skills needed for team coaching.

In Part Four we address the importance of mentors and coaches being accredited and having supervision in order to ensure quality and maintain safe conditions and boundaries for clients.

In Chapter 12 we discuss methods of accreditation, ethical codes and diversity. We examine the boundary between coaching, mentoring and therapy. At present, much of coaching and mentoring practice draws on therapeutic sources, and practitioners may be justifiably unsure of where to draw the line. This chapter clarifies the position.

Chapter 13 describes supervision theory, sources and models. We review existing and well-tried supervision models before recommending the FIT model – a simple approach ensuring that all three domains of learning are covered when supervising coaches and mentors (Harris and Brockbank, 2011). This is especially important as many practitioners have been trained to ignore, deny or dismiss the emotive domain, often the most powerful route to development and change (Brockbank, 2009). Many supervision models map against the passage of time and chart changes or stages in the relationship from its beginning to its end, but tend to be silent on how to structure each session. Our recommended model is holographic in that it offers supervisors a plan for a single session or a programme to be used over a long time period.

The concluding chapter (14) emphasizes the importance of identifying which quadrant the coach or mentor is working in, and this applies to coaches, mentors, clients, managers, supervisors and sponsors. We reiterate how the double hermeneutic may operate to achieve organizational transformation, as when individuals opt for radical change themselves, they have the power to influence such change in their organizations.

Note

1 For ease of definition, throughout the book we use the term client to include mentee, coachee, protégé and learner, except where we are quoting or discussing the work of another author.

PART ONE
How coaching and mentoring support reflective learning

The revised situational framework

The situational framework arose from our frustration with the confusion about what coaching is, what mentoring is, and which is best. The argument still rages. Mentoring has been described by Helen Colley as 'a practice that remains ill-defined, poorly conceptualized, and weakly theorized, leading to confusion in policy and practice' (Colley, 2003: 13). Mentors are rarely trained, often coming from respected senior ranks in communities and organizations. Coaching describes a wide range of activity, from sports tuition to life coaching which echoes therapy. Coach training can sometimes be achieved 'in three days' (Pointon, 2003).

Mentoring or coaching has one clear purpose, the learning and development of an individual, a process which involves change for the individual client and potentially for the organization in which they work. When coaching and mentoring are seen as reflective learning opportunities for change, it is possible to be clear about the terms we use to describe that change. Briefly, the name of the activity is less important than its purpose and what is actually happening, as this will influence the kind of learning outcome.

The situational framework is a map of change, which identifies the purpose, process and learning outcome of particular approaches in the mentoring and coaching field. Ownership of purpose and learning outcome are the two important dimensions in which a coach or mentor is working. These two dimensions give four areas, and the four quadrants of the map are described in detail below. The map is based on the work of sociologists Gibson Burrell and Gareth Morgan (1979), the philosopher Rolland Paulston (1996) and educationalist Ann Darwin (2000).

What is coaching? What is mentoring? There are as many answers to these questions as there are practitioners, and it depends on the situation. The situational model clarifies the confusion about the two terms, and ensures that when practitioners offer coaching or mentoring they and their clients are clear about what is meant. Are corporate clients seeking improved performance or do they want transformation, either individually or for the organization? The situation can be identified by these three questions:

- **Who owns the coaching or mentoring purpose?** Is it the organization or the individual, or both?
- **What process is to be used?** Is it directive, non-directive, purely cognitive, behavioural and does it include empathy?
- **Which learning outcome is sought as a result of the coaching or mentoring?** Improvement (with no change in the status quo) or transformation?

These situational factors, shown in Figure 1.1, will dictate the nature or type of activity on offer, regardless of whether it is called coaching or mentoring.

FIGURE 1.1   Situational coaching or mentoring

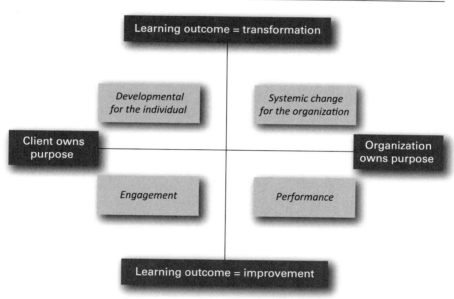

SOURCE: © 2010 Dr Anne Brockbank

The situational framework in Figure 1.1 shows two dimensions: ownership of purpose and learning outcome:

From left to right: This is the ownership of purpose dimension, from individual ownership on the left to organizational ownership on the right.

From bottom to top: Learning outcomes range from improvement with no radical change to complete transformation at the top.

Ownership (from right to left)

When the organization dictates the objectives of a coaching or mentoring programme, the employee is less likely to own objectives for themselves. Such a programme will emphasize imposed objectives with less consideration of the personal and social world of the learner.

Where employees resist meeting imposed objectives, a social control mechanism comes into play and this is described as engagement mentoring or coaching. Here employees receive coaching or mentoring which seeks to persuade them to align their own objectives with organizational aims.

These objectives, based on a perceived objective reality, may use personality profiles and learning styles inventories because they assume a set of fixed qualities. Typical inventories categorize individuals as 'activist', 'reflector', extrovert, introvert etc.

When the individual owns their purpose, the social and emotional world of a learner is acknowledged as part of the developmental process, as well as strategies for achieving that purpose. Such mentoring or coaching uses truly reflective dialogue to stimulate the desired transformation for the client and the process is developmental. Ownership of purpose implies with it the ability to take responsibility for progressing personal objectives, so is needed in flatter, more democratic organizations.

Learning outcome (from bottom to top)

Improvement as a learning outcome suggests that essential factors in the organization remain unchanged; indeed, for induction the process informs about 'how things are done around here'. The power structure in the workplace remains unaltered by new ideas and the taken-for-granteds (tfgs) remain unchallenged behind what is described by Vivienne Burr as the prevailing discourse (Burr, 1995). Such mentoring or coaching has been described by Ann Darwin as the recycling of power (Darwin, 2000) because of its tendency to replicate existing power relations.

Transformation as a learning outcome suggests that either employee or organization (or both) is radically changed as a consequence of learning and development. To achieve transformation it is necessary to challenge the tfgs within a system or the working environment, and this is known as the prevailing discourse, explained on page 16. For individual transformation, mentoring or coaching invites learners to identify the prevailing discourse in which they work and consider its impact on them, as well as their contribution to it. This allows employees to look beyond their power horizon (Smail, 2001), their perceived limit of action, which is explained on page 18.

We look now at what happens in each quadrant.

The four quadrants

The quadrants are defined by ownership of purpose and learning outcome, as well as the process used in coaching or mentoring, ie the situation defines the coaching or mentoring type used.

The performance situation: The organization seeks improved performance from staff and may use directive coaching/mentoring programmes to achieve this. The purpose here is owned by the organization and the method may be 'tell', which is appropriate for an induction situation or apprenticeship programme. In addition, the organization needs to manage the performance of its employees through effective line management. Performance coaching seeks to align the activities and objectives of all employees to business objectives and goals. When resistance is likely, coaching or mentoring initiatives may be presented to staff with the performance intent masked. When Helen Colley researched mentoring programmes she named this kind of masking as engagement, so this is known as engagement mentoring or coaching (Colley, 2003).

The engagement situation: Engagement mentoring or coaching seeks to persuade the employee to adopt the objectives of the organization, or align their own objectives with the organization's mission. The use of non-directive coaching techniques, such as active listening and empathy, to address resistance and 'engage' staff has been described, rather negatively, as 'sugar-coating' (Howe, 2008). Line managers are most likely to deliver engagement coaching, although increasingly external practitioners are involved in engagement work. Research shows that engaged employees are more productive and this affects organizational performance (Gallup, 2010).

The developmental situation: The individual seeks change or transformation for themselves through internal or external coaching or mentoring, and their purpose may or may not be aligned with the organization's objectives. Developmental coaching or mentoring assumes that clients define their own goals, while offering the potential for challenge and transformation, through a dialogue in all three domains of learning, namely thinking, doing and feeling. Such a dialogue, known as reflective dialogue, which includes their emotions as well as the other two domains of learning – knowing and acting – has the potential to lead to transformational learning.

The systemic change situation: The organization seeks to transform itself as a system, through individual developmental coaching or mentoring by internal personnel or external practitioners. This may be supported by strategic mentoring where board members work with senior managers off-line, or team coaching. For the organization to transform itself systemically, the dimensions of individual ownership and organization ownership must move towards each other, and ideally converge. Attempts to transform an organization through performance coaching or mentoring are doomed to failure as the criteria for deep, significant transformative learning include access to the emotional domain, connectedness and agency. Connectedness refers to a relationship which supports learning, and agency means that individuals or teams take ownership of their goals.

The situational framework for coaching and mentoring addresses some of the confusion about the terms and how they are used, by identifying what factors influence the learning outcomes of the activities. Ownership of purpose and the process used affect learning outcomes as well as the tfgs in the environment. Four types of coaching or mentoring are described: performance, engagement, developmental and systemic, the last referring to organizational transformation, which is likely through the engagement and developmental route and less likely through simple improvement by performance management, and this is shown in Figure 1.2.

How can an organization transform itself through coaching or mentoring?

FIGURE 1.2   Situational coaching or mentoring: the route to organizational transformation

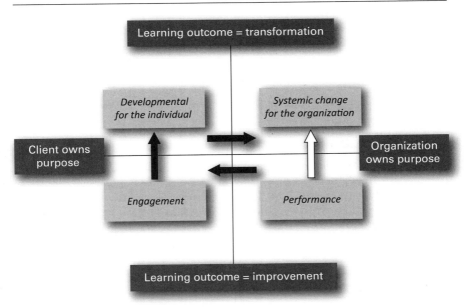

SOURCE: © 2010 Dr Anne Brockbank

As Figure 1.2 shows, coaching and mentoring activity in the performance quadrant, within a performance management structure, while important for addressing corporate goals, is likely to lead to improvement, a laudable aim, but without changing the organization. Therefore this is unlikely to take the organization directly to systemic change (shown by a white arrow in the diagram). The route to organizational systemic change lies first through performance management, then to staff engagement with aligned objectives, then to development for individual transformation with individually owned objectives, and thence to organizational transformation. This route is shown by black arrows in the diagram and refers only to the development of employees which is relevant to organizational change. Many employees are likely to be pursuing individual development activities outside their work context, a point well noted 30 years ago by Tom Peters (Peters and Waterman, 1982).

Performance

Performance mentoring or coaching focuses on efficiency and objective targets or standards, very much needed in day-to-day work. The approach assumes an objective real world, aiming at improved performance, and, in order to maintain the status quo, tends to suppress challenge and questioning by the learner, employee or client. The focus on tangible and imposed objectives emphasizes the task, and ownership is sought but not required. For instance, the necessity to maintain the existing system leads mentors to socialize their clients, ensuring that existing values and norms are preserved, thereby 'guaranteeing' career advancement. So this approach ensures grooming for career advancement, recycled power relationships and less diversity, resulting in 'a successful core of white middle class successors to organizational hierarchies' (Darwin, 2000: 205). So for many individuals the imposed objectives are easily aligned with their own for improved performance.

Where the purpose is improved performance, ie how to do the job better, then coaching is a favourite method for performance management where imposed objectives may not be easily aligned with individual desires. Hence the primacy in performance coaching of questions and empathy (if it exists at all) as a secondary skill. The approach tends to reinforce existing power relations and even overtly and/or covertly reproduce social inequalities, and relies on the prevailing discourse. We discuss the prevailing discourse on page 16. The performance coach serves the perceived 'needs' of the organization or society by ensuring (without necessarily realizing this) that power structures remain intact and the tfgs continue to inform the prevailing discourse, regardless of the career advancement of the client.

Coaching of apprentices can be identified as improvement, as are some modern mentoring programmes which are in reality cheap teaching schemes. This fits with those of our clients who were using a coaching or mentoring programme to replace or enhance expensive external training for qualifications needed by their employees, as in our case study in Chapter 8. Where such a direct approach is undesirable or ineffective, a non-directive stance is recommended to facilitate engagement of employees, so that they are persuaded to align their objectives with those of their employing organization. This takes us to the engagement quadrant.

Engagement

Engagement mentoring or coaching recognizes the subjective world of the learner, and uses a non-directive approach to maintain the status quo. Organizations seeking to create an engaged workforce may use mentoring or coaching programmes which are broadly humanist in their approach in order to minimize opposition. We discuss such a programme in Chapter 9. While the mentoring or coaching couple are 'engaged', ie there is a relationship, usually facilitated by using empathy, nevertheless the power horizon remains invisible to them. We discuss the power horizon on page 18. The idea of engagement mentoring includes interventions responding to disaffection and social exclusion – 'positive action' or 'community mentoring' aimed at supporting young people from oppressed groups, eg young men from black and Asian communities. In her description of engagement mentoring, Colley (2003: 151) suggests that 'it seeks to reform young protégés "dispositions" in line with employers' demands for employability' and that for their mentors 'it seeks to engender devotion and self-sacrificing dispositions in mentors through its discourse of feminine nurture'. Colley uses 'feminine' here to characterize the tendency in her mentors to over-care for their protégés. Dispositions are the habitual unconscious ways of thinking and feeling; ways of being – habitual states – are named 'dispositions' by Bourdieu (quoted in Grenfell and James, 1998) because they are believed to 'dispose' individuals to do/think/feel in particular ways. They are our unconscious tendencies, inclinations and habits, developed over a lifetime, often revealed in psychological tests.

Engagement coaching has some factors in common with performance coaching in that the desired outcome is improvement without radical change, and to achieve this employees are offered a humanistic style of helping which includes empathy. The method is used in contexts where imposed objectives are not acceptable and the alternative method of persuasion is applied. Employees are said to be 'engaged' when they have aligned their objectives with the purposes of the organization. This type of approach is used mostly by line managers in organizations and features in the journal *Coaching at Work*. This is not quite as devious as it sounds. Many employees are able to assess what they are being asked to do, compare this with their own needs and desires and become engaged with organizational aims. The non-directive approach, recommended for coaching at work, with skilled managers, can deliver employee engagement, as it acknowledges the employees' own feelings and purposes as well as those of the organization.

Developmental approach

Developmental coaching or mentoring acknowledges the subjective world of the client, respects their experience and generates ownership of their objectives, by using a Rogerian approach which enables them to move to potential transformation (Rogers, 1983). By working with the individual's social reality, which may include oppression and varieties of discriminatory behaviour, the client is enabled to realize their personal power, taking responsibility for their own learning and development as well as challenging the tfgs in their environment. In addition, a reflective dialogue which includes high levels of empathy facilitates deep, double loop learning for clients. Developmental mentoring or coaching (which may also be called executive coaching) offers the client a chance to identify the prevailing discourse and challenge it, through reflective dialogue. In this recognition of their socially constructed world there are opportunities for transformation for both individuals and organizations. Developmental mentoring or coaching is usually (but not always) found in private arrangements, often quite separate from the workplace, where a professional mentor or coach works with their protégé or client over time, to an agreed contract. For developmental mentoring or coaching the necessary and sufficient conditions are the ownership of goals by the learner and the potential for transformation through a reflective dialogue, which includes high levels of empathy.

Systemic approach

Systemic mentoring or coaching seeks to promote the transformation of a company, an organization, or an institution within society. Here the aim is to transform the organization through complete restructuring or culture change programmes. In many such programmes the subjective world of the client may be ignored and change is sought through rational argument and persuasion. As readers will know, this approach is doomed to failure, as many are. The systemic intent can be addressed by beginning with performance management, essential for efficiency, then working in the engagement quadrant as objectives are aligned, then following through the development quadrant with one-to-one developmental mentoring or coaching where the purpose is to enable the individual to work with their beliefs and feelings to transformation, and in the fullness of time to become part of a larger changed system.

We complete this chapter with an explanation of the terms 'prevailing discourse' and 'power horizon' used in the definitions above.

The prevailing discourse

Discourse is how we talk about talking. The idea of a prevailing discourse comes from social constructivist ideas, which challenge the presumption of objective reality and focus on language as the medium through which learners construct new understandings (Burr, 1995). Learning contexts, like mentoring or coaching, are themselves socially constructed, so that 'we create rather than discover ourselves' and we do this through engagement-with-others through our discourse (Burr, 1995: 28). The powerful role of discourse lies in its taken-for-granted nature. The prevailing discourse in any system is tfg and invisible to its users, as the 'givens' of a prevailing discourse are often never examined and may only be revealed when named. An example of an invisible prevailing discourse is the executive washroom, where only those above certain grades are admitted and this is accepted without question by those excluded. Other examples are the casual sexism of remarks like 'Calm down, dear' and 'Don't worry your pretty head', often only recognized when the prevailing discourse is identified and named for what it is by those at whom it is directed.

How does a prevailing discourse become established?

The prevailing discourse is defined as 'a set of meanings, metaphors, representations, images, stories, statements etc that in some way together produce a particular version' of events, person or category of person (Burr, 1995: 48). Examples of how such discourse is used can be seen in terms like 'attitude problem', 'downsizing', regulating, on-message, global-ization, unionized, eco-warrior and, as above, 'executive washroom'. Hence, as learners, we exist in a system which is not value-free, where power is exercised that can influence our progress and affect our development.

Developmental mentoring and coaching, through reflective dialogue, seeks to offer clients an alternative discourse. This has the potential to challenge the taken-for-granted assumptions (tfgs) of the prevailing dis-course in which clients are embedded. The context of empathic acceptance and challenge without judgement (itself an alternative discourse) allows the client to recognize their emotional response and reconsider some of the givens of their situation, and gives them the option to seek improvement or transformation.

Developmental mentoring and coaching begin from the client's owner-ship of their goals, and allow for environmental effects to be acknowledged. This enables clients to access their potential and challenge what limits them. Developmental mentoring or coaching is at its best when the client is able to challenge the tfgs in which they are living and working. An example of this is 'presenteeism', the practice whereby employees believe that working long hours over their working day makes them more productive and will get them promotion. Where a client is struggling with their work/life balance, the realization that 'presenteeism' is nothing more than a tfg may lead them to transform their approach to work.

As we learn we are ever-changing, responding to and influencing our environment, through interaction with others. Smail maintains that 'our environment has much more to do with our coming-to-be as people than we do as authors of our own fate' (2001: 23) and introduces the idea of a power horizon.

The power horizon

In organizational life the pattern of work and control of employees require them to perform specific and regulated roles. An important consequence of this is the cult of individualism, where the individual is identified as the source of disorder and the only resource for curing it, making the individual solely responsible for outcomes in the workplace. While recognizing the importance of individual responsibility at work, the dogma of individualism may lead to a work environment where employees feel helpless, confused and stressed. Why should this be?

Where individualism is the only theory available, the social context, with all its power, is largely ignored and kept invisible, particularly to those who are powerless. This is known as a 'power horizon' (Smail, 2001: 67) and is kept in position by offering a version of objective reality as truth, known as the prevailing discourse, a version which keeps the sources of power invisible.

The idea of a power horizon which is always just out of our sight suggests a prevailing discourse which maintains it in position, not unlike the unfortunate hero in the film *The Truman Show* who was unaware that his life was actually a TV show. The power horizon divides our nearby real-life experience at work from the distant power effects exerted by larger political and social factors, keeping the latter invisible (Smail, 2001: 67). The individual's power horizon, through the prevailing discourse, ensures that distant power effects are out of sight, leaving the individual no option but to concentrate on closer agents who are often themselves powerless and held within their own power horizon. An example of this is a client's perception of her manager as 'difficult' when he makes demands, while the manager is himself struggling to meet targets set by his superior, who is responding to board-level panic, a consequence of share price insecurity. The client's power horizon ensures that she attends primarily to her manager, without 'seeing' the more distant causes of her difficulty.

Developmental mentoring or coaching has the potential, through reflective dialogue, to expand the power horizon for an individual, enabling them to see, often for the first time, where the source of their difficulty or frustration lies. This is achieved by acknowledging the individual's feelings and experience, recognizing their goals and challenging the prevailing discourse in their organization, as well as the standard strategic support from their coach or mentor in the knowledge and action domains.

Chapter summary

In this first chapter we have presented the revised situational framework, which illustrates the route to organizational transformation. Performance and engagement coaching or mentoring are needed for corporate and business success. However, for organizational transformation there must be activity in the developmental quadrant, where individuals are offered coaching or mentoring opportunities with the potential, through reflective dialogue, for radical change. Thereafter, with coaching and mentoring in strategic and corporate change programmes, often including team coaching, there is hope of organizational transformation.

02 Learning theories for coaching and mentoring

The tendency in writing about coaching and mentoring is to set out how to do it and to practise it without considering the theory which underlies our practice. Since coaching and mentoring are about learning, it is necessary to focus on learning theories in order to inform and understand our practice.

Coaching and mentoring have not developed their own theoretical base and have tended to borrow from related disciplines such as psychology and psychotherapy. However, as the purpose of coaching and mentoring is learning, development and change, these are the fields where we can find suitable material for a theory of coaching and mentoring.

In this chapter we consider the following learning theories as constituting a theoretical base for coaching and mentoring:

- deep and surface;
- single and double loop;
- emotion in learning;
- immunity to change and defensive reasoning;
- psychology of learning;
- learning and the body;
- social activity learning;
- ownership and autonomy;
- individual learning and the organization.

In Chapter 1 we presented four approaches to mentoring and coaching:

- Performance mentoring or coaching, which aims at improving the performance of employees. The goals/objectives of the organization are a given.

- Engagement mentoring or coaching, which recognizes the subjective world of the client and uses a non-directive approach to enable the socialization of the client into the organizational world.

- Developmental mentoring or coaching, which acknowledges the subjective world of the client, respects ownership of the individual's goals and invites an examination of embedded power structures which inhibit learning.

- Systemic mentoring or coaching programmes which seek to promote the transformation of an organization through systemic change.

What are the implications for learning of these four different approaches to mentoring/coaching?

There is no science or theory of learning which embraces all the activities involved in human learning. Most of what we do, think, feel and believe is learnt, so the field of activities is wide and varied. The behavioural psychologist tends to identify learning in changed behaviour, while cognitive psychologists seek for change in the mind of the client as evidence that learning has taken place. Traditional academic learning has tended to emphasize learning as exclusively a mental process, whereas progressive approaches to learning assert that clients must also be active and learn by doing. Recent progressive ideas include emotional elements in learning and recommend that all three domains of learning are considered, that is, **doing, thinking and feeling,** for deep and significant learning (Brockbank *et al*, 2002; Brockbank and McGill, 2007; Brockbank, 2009). The significance of emotion has been neglected in learning theory and modern neuroscience emphasizes its importance.

So why is the emotional domain important for learning? The rationale for extending the domains of learning to include emotion can be found through our exploration of learning theories below.

Deep and surface learning

Early researchers categorized different levels of learning (Marton *et al*, 1993). Moving from basic to more complex forms, they identified:

1 a quantitative increase in knowledge;

2 memorizing;

3 acquisition of facts or routines etc which can be retained and used when necessary;

4 the abstracting of meaning;

5 an interpretation process aimed at understanding reality;

6 developing as a person.

Levels 1–3 are often characterized as *surface* learning, which implies cognitive learning measured in terms of recall, retention and remembering. These are utilized in performance mentoring/coaching.

Levels 4–6 are often characterized as *deep* learning, where the learner is making connections with any spoken or written discourse such that the person feels themselves to interact and be an *agent* of the learning. These are utilized in engagement and development mentoring/coaching.

With adults, surface learning is taken as a given and acquired when necessary, as in performance coaching or mentoring for improvement. In the engagement or development quadrant, *reflection* upon their experience is essential for deep and significant learning. We are using the term reflection in two senses. Firstly, the *process* or means by which an experience, in the form of thought, feeling or action, is considered, while it is happening or subsequently. Secondly, deriving from the first, the creation of meaning from this consideration, which may lead to looking at things as other than they seem, ie to transformation in how we see the world. We explore reflection further in Chapter 3, and simply offer here our definition of *reflective* learning:

> an intentional process, where social context and experience are acknowledged, in which clients are active individuals, wholly present, engaging with others, and open to challenge, and the outcome involves transformation as well as improvement for both individuals and potentially for their organization.
>
> (Brockbank *et al*, 2002: 6)

For mentors and coaches our definition indicates that there are several important factors to consider in what we know about learning. We consider some of them now.

Single and double loop learning

The terms single and double loop learning were first used by Argyris and Schön (1996) to distinguish between learning for improving the way things are done, and learning that creates a different view of the situation or a different way of seeing the world. Single loop learning, while it achieves immediate improvement, leaves underlying values and ways of seeing things unchanged. Improvement learning may involve reflection on the given task but is not likely to change it. Double loop learning is learning where assumptions about ways of seeing things are challenged and underlying values are changed (Brockbank and McGill, 2007). Double loop learning, in questioning 'taken-for-granteds' (tfgs), has the potential to bring about a profound shift in underlying values by cracking their paradigms or 'ways of seeing the world[1]' as:

> In order to see how ideas different from ours exist in their own legitimate framework, it is necessary to leap out from our shell of absolute certainty and construct a whole new world based on some other person's ideas of reality, other assumptions of truth. (Daloz, 1986: 228)

Single loop learning or day-to-day learning, for improvement, meeting goals and altering practice on the basis of experience, enables progress to be made. This is an important rationale for performance management. The concept of effective single loop learning has been described graphically in a well-known diagram by Kolb (1984), where goals are set on the basis of theory, action is taken and, on the basis of this experience, and reflection, a new action or plan is devised. For day-to-day learning the loop is productive and the employee gains competence and confidence, ie this is reflective learning for improvement. The process is illustrated in Figure 2.1.

FIGURE 2.1   Single loop learning

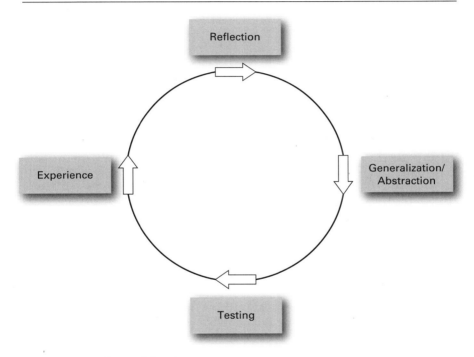

SOURCE: Adapted from Kolb (1984)

Single loop learning has been identified by Stacey (1993) as typical of what is known as 'ordinary management', which:

- translates the directives of those higher up in the hierarchy into goals and tasks;
- monitors the performance of the task in terms of goal achievement;
- ensures that staff are motivated to perform the task;
- supplies any skills or efforts that are missing;
- articulates purpose and culture, so reducing uncertainty.

Ordinary management is important because 'No organization can carry out its day-to-day tasks effectively, no organization can continue to build on and take advantage of its existing strengths, unless it practices ordinary management with a high degree of skill' (Stacey, 1993: 306). Hence the justification for single loop learning in day-to-day work. Performance mentoring and coaching are characterized by single loop learning as their outcome, and they mirror ordinary management in their objectives. Work in the engagement quadrant adopts persuasive methods to achieve the above.

What about developmental mentoring and coaching? We refer now, with permission, to Peter Hawkins' original diagram to illustrate double loop learning in Figure 2.2.

The arrows in the lower circle indicate day-to-day functioning in single loop learning. When conditions are favourable, in reflective dialogue, assumptions or tfgs are questioned, and the client may swing out of the lower-circle orbit and begin to traverse the upper circle in double loop learning mode. The client has 'come outside of their box'. The option remains of returning to the single loop when appropriate, perhaps to test a new theory in the normal way, in order to achieve improvement with a new understanding. The single loop orbit is contained and can be traversed within, say, an action plan, setting goals within a given cycle of activity or achieving a level of understanding within a professional field. The double loop orbit would occur when reconsidering the whole project with a view to major change, or even reconsidering an organization's purpose, structure or culture, ie learning for systemic change. Such an outcome is characteristic of what is known as 'extraordinary management' where:

- new knowledge is created when the tacit is made explicit and crystallized into an innovation, that is, a *re-creation* of some aspect of the world according to some new insight or ideal;

- innovative organizations... accept the paradox and use their informal organization, such as mentoring or coaching, as the tool for destroying old paradigms and creating new ones that lead ultimately to concerted action;

- when they operate informally rather than using formal structures in the organization, people are likely to achieve extraordinary management.

Stacey describes extraordinary management as double loop learning:

> Extraordinary management is concerned with how managers *smash the existing paradigm* and create a new one... create the chaos required to destroy old patterns of perception and behaviour... create new paradigms of perception and behaviour. (Stacey, 1993: 337, original italics)

For the individual, developmental mentoring and coaching are characterized by the transition from single to double loop learning. This enables the

FIGURE 2.2 Double loop learning

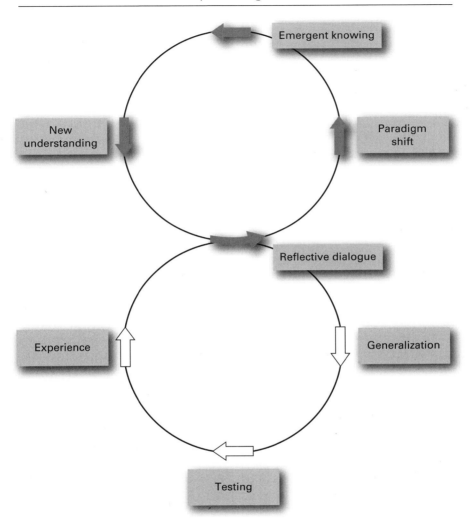

SOURCE: Adapted from an original idea by Peter Hawkins (1997)

client to move beyond their existing way of seeing the world, with the support and challenge, using reflective dialogue, of their mentor or coach.

What is needed to enable the client to shoot out of the single orbit and traverse the exciting and potentially disturbing orbit of double loop learning? If we were to pursue our analogy of orbits and trajectories, the answer suggests that what is required is *energy* to fuel the 'burn' of a changed trajectory. Where is the source of this energy to come from? There is evidence that emotion supplies the required fuel for double loop learning.

Emotion in learning

The evidence suggests that 'emotion and motivation are inherently connected' (Giddens, 1992: 201) and that double loop or transformative learning can be triggered by strong emotion, through trauma or 'peak' experiences (Brookfield, 1987: 7). The learner fuels energy from their emotional being, giving rise to expressions like 'passion to learn', 'hunger for truth', 'thirst for knowledge', which recognize that the double loop trajectory may be reached when fuelled by emotional energy (Brookfield, 1987). More recent writings suggest that emotional factors are essential for learning and decision making in every sphere of human endeavour (Lehrer, 2009; Zander and Zander, 2000).

Using empathy in order to access the affective domain will harness the emotional energy to support the learner who chooses to go into the double loop 'orbit'. The qualities needed for a practitioner to support double loop learning have been acquired by many coaches and mentors, often as a result of the influence of Carl Rogers who expressed the goal of education as 'the facilitation of change and learning' (Rogers, 1983: 120) which rests upon 'qualities that exist in the personal *relationship* between the facilitator and learner' (Rogers, 1983: 121).

In addition, the process of questioning and challenging can stimulate strong emotions, disturbance, distress and also joy and exhilaration (Brookfield, 1987: 8). We are told that a certain degree of energy or excitement is necessary for learning to occur, so that a crisis may generate transformative learning.

How can mentors or coaches enable their clients to access their emotions? The capacity to deal with emotion appropriately, known as emotional intelligence (EQ), together with IQ, is a predictor of future success in business (Dulewicz and Higgs, 1998: 42–45). EQ has been defined as: 'the ability to understand and reflectively manage one's own and other people's feelings' (Mayer, 1999: 49), and those who are emotionally adept are those who: 'know and manage their own feelings well and who read and deal effectively with other people's feelings' (Goleman, 1995: 36). We identify this latter ability as empathy in Chapters 9 and 10.

Emotion holds the key to a higher level of learning, through reflective dialogue, because emotion offers a gateway to the energy and power needed to countenance alternative discourses and challenge prevailing ones (Brockbank, 2009). Traditional learning and business have devalued the affective domain and valorized the cognitive (Fineman, 1993). Research findings in neuro-psychology explain what happens when the emotional world is cut off from learning (Rock and Schwartz, 2006; Lehrer, 2009; Zander and Zander, 2000). The power of material from the emotional brain to dominate the rational pre-cortex has been established through modern scanning technology (Rock and Schwartz, 2006). When the emotional domain is included in learning then transformation is possible. The idea that developmental learning can occur where emotional material is ignored, while favoured in many rationalist contexts, fails to appreciate the nature of the changes which take place when meaning is transformed through reflection.

What is needed for *a transformation of perspectives*, based as they are on cultural codes, is a process involving 'a critique of assumptions... by examining their origins, nature and consequences' (Mezirow, 1994: 223). The recommended method for such learning to occur is dialogue, as 'dialogue is central to human communication and learning' (Mezirow, 1994: 225). The chances of such a critique being achieved without generating emotion are remote, and, where emotion is denied or suppressed, transformative learning is unlikely.

In order to recognize the existence of emotion in learning situations we turn again to Argyris and Schön (1996), as they identify the phenomenon of defensive reasoning and its role in immunity to change.

Immunity to change and defensive reasoning

The tendency to overlook the obvious, the tfgs in life, is inherently human. Some of the tfgs form quite powerful defences, known as defensive reasoning, which are difficult and painful to dislodge. As clients, the prospect of really looking at what is taken for granted in our work, and analysing our defensive reasoning, is threatening on four counts:

- We may lose control.
- We may not win.
- We may not be able to suppress negative feelings.
- We may not be rational.

For managers trained in the Western rational system, such threats are real and powerful, and they resort to defensive reasoning in order to protect against these threats, maintaining comfort and, in the process, cloning another generation of managers in their own image. For managers to engage in reflection they need to be confident in themselves and able to tolerate doubt and uncertainty about their decisions. A manager who can face up to the possibility that they might have so-called irrational feelings, and express them, is prepared to display their vulnerability. This is done by naming what is taken for granted in the work context, and staying with the discomfort which may be engendered by such naming. An example is the recognition that a punitive appraisal system is demotivating employees and a commitment to replace it with a developmental programme. Needless to say, such moves can generate differences in the organization, and this may lead to conflict. Where conflicts occur, the political process in organizations rarely offers facilitation for resolving differences, thereby inhibiting organizational development and potential transformation.

Argyris and Schön (1996: 78) offer a method of analysing the tfgs in our work, which transfers well to the mentoring or coaching situation, known as the left-hand side of the page method. Here the client revisits or antici- pates a problematic event. The page is divided into two columns and the facts of the story are entered on the right-hand side. In the left-hand column the client is invited to note the thoughts and feelings associated with each stage of the story. The content of the left-hand column is highly illuminating, as strong feelings are revealed which are not likely to be spoken aloud. When clients become aware of some of their left-hand-side material they are at the cusp of double loop learning.

Developmental mentors or coaches acknowledge the left-hand side of their client's material and, through reflective dialogue, offer them opportu- nities for double loop learning. The process is helped by attending to the three domains of learning, ie feeling as well as thinking and doing. If the learning process is limited to one of the three domains, the others are affected and learning is not so effective. To accommodate the full range of human potential, development should address all three domains of learning, ie thinking, feeling and doing. The two-column method has been built on by Kegan and Lahey (2009) in their analysis of the dimensions of immunity to change. Their x-ray method begins with three columns detailing:

- goals or visible commitments;
- what I am actually doing or not doing;
- hidden competing commitments.

Working on these first three columns uncovers the fourth column, ie some of the underlying assumptions which contribute to the immunity, and this can occur both individually and collectively. Analysis of an individual's x-ray reveals the strong emotions which may be attached to competing commitments and assumptions, and Kegan and Lahey report the realization of one of their clients as follows:

> What I've come to realize is the function of emotion in this work... the organization ruthlessly suppresses all emotion... we need to find ways to reverse this dynamic of suppressing emotion... this is what the four column work helps us to do.
>
> (Kegan and Lahey, 2009: 79)

These authors remind us that immunity to change is a well-developed de- fence mechanism (see page 30) which keeps dread at bay, and the coach or mentor involved will need to have competence in the emotive domain. We discuss working in the emotive domain with empathy in Chapters 9 and 10.

Mentoring or coaching that concentrates on one or two out of the three domains will be less effective. An effective process should seek to 'tease out' learning in the missing domains, monitoring the balance between the three domains and guiding our questioning or explorations to cover all three as fully as possible. In particular, as a coach or mentor you may have a tendency to avoid the emotional content of learning, and this would disadvantage your client as: 'An emotional content to learning is inevitable, because learning begins in that part of the brain' (Rose and Nicholl, 1997: 31).

For example, where a client is discussing an aspect of their work and their coach notices some negative body language, uncovering how the client is feeling may assist their development. Eric Jensen in *Brain Based Learning and Teaching* (1995) suggests that 'all learning involves our body, our emotions and our attitudes'. We discuss learning and the body further below on page 31. We now address some of the psychology which underpins learning in mentoring and coaching.

Psychological principles of learning

The humanist approach to learning is used in engagement and development coaching and mentoring. The approach recognizes the power in every human being to learn in a self-directed way, finding the appropriate method and medium for whatever they desire to learn. The method begins from the following beliefs:

1 People are OK – fundamentally good.

2 A person is a whole person.

3 Human beings are driven to change and grow.

4 The 'abundance' model rather than the 'deficiency' one is suitable for personal development.

5 Humans operate with a spiritual dimension.

Engagement mentoring or coaching uses this non-directive and respectful approach to work with employees in a way that encourages and stimulates learning. However, the learning sought in engagement work is aligned to the objectives of the organization, which may or may not accord with the dispositions of the individual concerned.

On the other hand, developmental mentoring and coaching require trust in the client and confidence in the client's capacity for development. Developmental mentors and coaches hold the belief that clients are fundamentally sincere and desire to change and develop. In addition, humanist principles of learning emphasize the importance of being authentic rather than being impersonal, and we discuss coach and mentor congruence in Chapter 10.

Carl Rogers (1983) described the conditions for deep learning and development as person-centred, a statement which grows from the humanistic belief in the 'actualizing tendency' of human beings, the striving towards growth and development present in every person. What psychological climate in a learning relationship makes possible the release of the individual's capacity for learning and development? Rogers offers three conditions for a person-centred climate:

- congruence, ie genuineness, realness, sharing feelings and attitudes rather than opinions and judgements;
- unconditional positive regard, ie acceptance and 'prizing' of the other;
- empathy, ie understanding of the other's feelings, experience and attitudes and communicating that understanding.

All three qualities call for a high degree of emotional intelligence in that to be congruent implies a willingness to express feelings; unconditional acceptance relies on managing competing emotions; and empathy is the key skill for handling emotional material. Coaching or mentoring for development emphasizes emotion and seeks to tap the energy available there, offering the potential for transformative learning through access to the many facets of learning which may be hidden in traditional approaches.

We must not leave psychological principles of learning without mentioning defence mechanisms, which, like boundaries, are not strictly part of a humanistic approach, coming as they do from traditional psychology. The typical defence mechanisms that are likely to appear in mentoring or coaching relationships are the following:

- *denial* – unconsciously being unaware of what is happening;
- *displacement* – unconsciously expressing a feeling to the wrong person;
- *projection* – unconsciously sending away aspects of the self to another;
- *identification* – unconsciously taking on aspects of another;
- *introjections* – unconsciously becoming what an important other says;
- *transference* – unconsciously projecting aspects of self onto another based on past experience.

For many, the idea of defence mechanisms is not relevant to mentoring or coaching. However, there is plenty of evidence that defence mechanisms are alive and well in such relationships, as transference is now understood to be 'an entirely natural occurrence in any relationship... a form of projection... involving archetypal material' (Jacoby, 1984: 19). We discuss and explain defence mechanisms in detail in Appendix 5, and move now to another mainly unconscious aspect of learning.

Learning and the body

In this section we aim to explore a hidden dimension in modern learning theory – the body. First we introduce the idea of two selves, identified by Gallwey (1974), and discuss how they interact in a learning situation like mentoring or coaching. Then we discuss methods to empower the emotional brain, and support transformational learning through mentoring and coaching.

The two selves

This idea came from Tim Gallwey's (1974) analysis of his tennis clients who he noticed 'talked to themselves'. This usually silent dialogue is common to most adults. The 'I', or self 1, seems to give instructions while 'myself', or self 2, seems to perform the action (Gallwey, 1974: 13).

When a typical dialogue between self 1 and self 2 is analysed, what emerges is a self 1, the thinker, which does not trust self 2, the doer, although self 2, because it includes the unconscious mind and nervous system, hears everything, forgets nothing and is anything but stupid. When people struggle to improve their performance (be it tennis or giving presentations or delegating) by thinking too much and trying too hard, self 1 sabotages the innate competence of self 2 to do the job. The thinking activity of self 1 interferes with the natural 'doing' activity of self 2. In a mentoring or coaching situation an understanding of the effects of this internal dialogue assists both parties to identify barriers to learning and development. The skilled mentor or coach will enable their client to articulate the inner dialogue and submit it to rigorous inspection and evaluation so that judgemental self-talk like 'I'm just no good as a manager' and 'I'll never do it' can be recognized as interference from self 1 and addressed in the mentoring or coaching relationship.

How did self 1 get to be so dominant? The Western way of understanding the mind separated it from the body, as totally unconnected and different. Modern neuroscience has established that this is not the case, and that the mind and body are linked by continuous electrical and chemical communication (Rothschild, 2000; McGilchrist, 2010; Lehrer, 2009). In addition, because the mind differed from the body (thought to be a site of sinfulness), it was believed to be innately superior. Western educators have not caught up with science and still operate as though the mind can be addressed by directly ignoring the body and is the superior partner in learning and behaviour. Hence self 1 has been led to believe that it can order self 2 about and that self 1 should decide what happens without reference to self 2. Needless to say, self 2 asserts itself and we find ourselves behaving in ways we don't understand and are sometimes ashamed of. Modern person-centred approaches to learning and development have the potential to reverse this and reconnect self 1 and self 2.

To address the tendency of self 1 to destructively criticize and undermine self 2, Gallwey recommends that: first, we persuade self 1 to trust self 2 to do what is asked of it, and relax its surveillance of self 2; second, we instruct self 2 with images rather than words. How can this be done in coaching and mentoring?

It is sometimes necessary to revise the destructive core beliefs embedded in self 1, which informs self 2. The brain learns in order to survive. When under threat or perceived threat, the brain takes us into a trance-like state where only the core beliefs are relevant. The influence of this on advanced or transformative learning is obviously powerful, as effective reflective dialogue is a challenge to just those core beliefs which are lodged within self 1. The calming of our self 1 enables us to 'hear' our self 2 and we discuss how to access self 2 below.

How can self 1 relax its control of self 2? Some people use meditation to practise quieting their conscious mind by deep relaxation and concentration on an object or word, which disallows the 'buzzing' of stressful thinking. Letting go of judgements and negative thoughts is associated with a quieter, calmer mind. Positive thinking techniques seek to replace negative thoughts with positive ones, but, because these are judgements too, they agitate rather than quiet the mind. The state of stillness we seek has been called 'mindfulness' as the mind is full of the present, excluding the judgements and fears, concentrating on the here and now. Mindfulness is 'about being aware of what is happening in the present, on a moment by moment basis. It is an intentional becoming aware of our bodies and minds and the world around us whilst not making judgements about what we like or don't like in what we find there' (Landale, 2005; Siegel, 2010). A mindfulness example can be found in a brief guide by two general practitioners (Ridgeway and Manning, 2008).

How are we to instruct self 2? It seems likely that when the client in a mentoring or coaching relationship can access their self 2 and visualize what they want to achieve, success is more likely. Research at Harvard University provided satisfactory proof of this when people who visioned themselves doing exercise alone produced measurable decreases in weight and improved health measures (Crum and Langer, 2007). The two selves described above are equivalent to the thinking brain and the emotional brain. How can the mentor or coach enable their client to access their emotional brain and quieten the self 1 for long enough for this to happen? The relationship forged between mentor or coach and client will support the process, as the couple learn to trust and respect each other. The person-centred approach implicitly promotes communication which values the messages from self 2, and builds a gentle but solid relationship.

Learning as a social activity

Deep learning is likely to be achieved by clients who take responsibility for their own learning, and are motivated by their own learning ambitions, as in developmental approaches to mentoring and coaching. Hence the importance of the ownership dimension in coaching and mentoring. When clients themselves are consulted about their learning they are revealed as active responsible adults who are capable of sharing their meanings and justifying their understandings. The socially constructed nature of knowledge has been explored at length elsewhere (Berger and Luckmann, 1966; Brookfield and Preskill, 1999) and we discuss this further below. The social systems in which a client is embedded will dominate learning as 'no human thought is immune to the ideologizing influence of its social context' (Burr, 1995: 21). The workplace has its own ideology, often invisible to clients. However, the existence of the social and thus the learning context can be used to enable development through recognition of others as sources of knowledge, and reflective dialogue offers a method for doing this. The cultural, emotional and value contexts of learning can vary considerably, and this highlights the importance of raising such issues for consideration in mentoring and coaching designs. The learning contexts of mentoring and coaching are themselves socially constructed in three ways:

- By learners who create meaning through their interactions with each other (Kim, 2001; Kukla, 2000). 'We create rather than discover ourselves' and we do this through engagement-with-others.

- By the coaching and mentoring discourse, which defines the context and may (or may not) enable clients to access their potential and challenge what constrains their learning.

- By the learner who both influences and is influenced by their experience and the environment. This is known as the 'double hermeneutic' (Giddens, 1991, 1993).

This last item has implications for organizational transformation and we allude to this again in Chapter 11.

The prevailing discourse, discussed in Chapter 1, produces a particular version of events, or category of person. Identities are constructed through discourse; for example, how intelligent someone is judged to be may relate to their physical appearance and to how they are allowed to talk without interruption. The operation of discourses is not power-neutral, but rather they are imbued with power relations which impact on how people are defined and whether they are granted a voice, resources and decision-making powers. The individual is not a given, but is continuously constructed through the social relationships and discourse of the organizational or family culture in which he or she is embedded. This is nicely put by Maturana and Varela as 'We who are flesh and blood people are no strangers to the world in which we live and which we bring forth through our living' (1987: 129).

The learning context can also be defined by the concepts and 'taken-for-granteds' of the prevailing discourse, and its acronym, tfgs, has been utilized by learners as another code for the prevailing discourse. There is still a tendency to make assumptions in organizations about 'the way things are done around here'. The discourse itself promotes particular power relations by naming and then silencing unwelcome voices as 'political'.

The social nature of learning offers opportunities for the client to reflect upon their learning not just alone, but with others. Being able to undertake reflection alone is necessary but not sufficient. The tendency to self-deceive, collude and be unaware is ever present. When others are present the client has potentiality for challenge which may not be available alone. As meaning is created in relation to others, reflection and the creation of meaning are inevitably a social process. The context in which such reflection occurs is the learning relationship.

The learning relationship is one that can occur formally or informally, explicitly or implicitly. When people in an organization find themselves in an enabling learning role, like mentor or coach, the stance they create with the client(s) is crucial. Without explicit recognition of the interaction as a relationship, in working with these conditions we may be less effective. In the case of performance management the coach may treat their client as detached and passive. This is a very limited form of relationship, inhibiting learning, but can be sufficient for the behavioural change needed in performance management. In recognizing the interaction as constituting a relationship between mentor or coach and client we are saying that the learning outcome of the interaction comes through their connection. Julie Hay has described such a relationship in the development quadrant as a developmental alliance which depends on genuine connection and she asserts that it 'will not work properly unless those involved believe that it is normal for people to want a close connection with each other' (Hay, 1995: 47).

Learner ownership and autonomy

The question of a learner's autonomy was investigated by Ryan and Deci (2000) in their motivation research about intrinsic and extrinsic motivation. Using self-determination theory, based on the idea of organismic development, the research found that 'contexts which are supportive of autonomy, competence and an experience of relatedness for the learner, will foster greater internalization and integration than contexts which thwart satisfaction of these needs' (Ryan and Deci, 2000: 76). Although the researchers do not acknowledge Carl Rogers' work, their organismic theory draws on his definition of the human personality in terms of the organismic self and its development under conditions of worth (Rogers, 1951). Ryan and Deci, using a self-determination continuum from amotivation, through extrinsic motivation, to intrinsic motivation, identified autonomy and competence as conditions which facilitate intrinsic motivation and well-being. On the other hand, extrinsic motivation, with conditions of control, non-optimal challenge and lack of connectedness, was associated with lack of initiative and responsibility as well as less well-being and ill-health. Their findings suggest that the conditions under which people learn has important implications for those concerned with education and development, such as coaches and mentors.

Additional work by Deci and Ryan (2000) explored the concept of goals, another concept in learning theory which confirms many of the ideas given above. They conclude that extrinsic rewards, goals or evaluations can undermine the three essential psychological needs, ie autonomy, competence and connectedness, leading to a decrease in creativity, poor problem solving and an absence of deep conceptual processing (Deci and Ryan, 2000: 234). Goals imposed by others lead to the lowest levels of intrinsic motivation. Indeed, imposed goals have been described very negatively, as 'thought which imposes is violent' (Isaacs, 1999: 68). Obviously the weight accorded to the three psychological needs of autonomy, competence and connectedness will depend on cultural contexts, and the balance will be culturally defined.

Individual learning and the organization

As we noted in Chapter 1, many writings on learning and development at work start from the idea that the individual is responsible for their own development, and this suggests that their progress is a product of their own motivation, commitment and drive. Some assessment tools, for example learning style questionnaires, assume a neutral context, as if all clients were the same gender, class and race and the notions of diversity, status and relative opportunity did not exist. As discussed in Chapter 1, there is also a tendency to ignore the impact of social context, ie discourse, culture and ideology, on clients.

If the client feels powerless in a learning relationship, then there will be a lack of trust. Lack of trust means that the client will not feel able to trust the learning context, or any enabler of learning in that context. Given that reflective learning will involve feelings or emotion in addition to thinking and action, a lack of trust will inhibit any display of emotion or vulnerability and therefore openness to learning. When we really learn, particularly that which is potentially developmental, we lay ourselves open to uncertainty and can feel (temporarily) unstable. For the feelings that uncertainty can engender we need conditions of safety that ensure those expressed feelings are not taken advantage of. Determining who is part of the learning relationship will be important, and it is therefore inappropriate in the developmental quadrant to match clients with their line manager. It may also be considered less than ideal in the engagement quadrant.

Enlightened organizations will generate development programmes likely to deliver managers and others with the high-level skills needed to support reflective learning, and these will be the coaches and mentors of the future. While emphasizing the need for taking organizational responsibilities seriously, it is important that the responsibility of the client remains just that, the individual's responsibility to manage their own learning, while keeping in sight 'the greater good', that is, the needs of the organization as a whole.

Levels of learning

When individuals learn, they may improve their performance and they may also transform themselves. This has been described as not only doing things right, but also, more challenging, doing the right things (Flood and Romm, 1996: 10). In addition, an organization whose members are capable of reflecting on the learning process, ie learn about learning, is likely to develop, prosper and survive. We can identify these three levels as improvement, transformation and learning about learning:

- **Improvement:** Reflective learning will deliver improvement, as employees process their work, assessing and reconsidering for improved performance, that is, 'doing things right'. Performance and Engagement coaching or mentoring support improvement.

- **Transformation:** Reflective learning for transformation offers the potential for clients to move one step further and reconsider their work in strategic terms, questioning and challenging existing patterns, thereby opening the door to change, creativity and innovation, that is, doing the right things. Developmental coaching or mentoring support transformation.

- **Learning about learning:** We also offer the idea of a further level of reflection, which can only occur as a consequence of the first two, and that is reflective learning about learning. This entails an individual or organization standing back from its improvements and changes, and seeking to identify 'how we did that' so that this knowledge can be transferred to future situations. Systemic change is supported by learning about learning.

Reflective learning for improvement is a necessary component for organizational success but it is no longer sufficient for organizations, which hope to survive in a world continually subject to change. The ever-changing market environment demands learning that can keep up, developing and creating ever-new ideas and products, while keeping in mind the organization's responsibilities to its stakeholders. The increasingly globalized economy, along with the rapidity of social change, also impacts upon the public and voluntary sectors. In order to stay in the race, the organization needs to collectively stop and reflect, critically, on the organization's purpose. Reflective learning for development occurs when clients are enabled to pause and reconsider, preferably with others, the nature of what they are doing. This means more than re-examining the task in hand. It means re-examining the rationale behind what is being done. When such a dialogue with others is enabled throughout a system, the organization collectively reflects, reconsiders, and ultimately transforms itself from within.

Chapter summary

This chapter has summarized some of the learning theories which are relevant in coaching and mentoring. Learning can be perceived in a variety of ways: new knowledge and understanding; a change in behaviour; or a revision of attitude. As a consequence, mentoring or coaching may lead to improvement in performance, greater engagement, or transformation, and then perhaps to learning about learning itself. Learning outcomes have been found to be influenced by ownership, autonomy, the social context and discourse, as well as emotion and defences. When clients dare to traverse the double loop by confronting their taken-for-granteds (tfgs), they may transform their view of the world. A learning environment which nurtures single and double loop learning, and offers clients a chance to reflect on their learning, demands high-level skills in those enabling learning, either formally or informally. A clever organization builds on such individual transformation, and indeed will encourage and enable it to happen through executive mentoring or coaching. The complex power of discourse and culture is recognized by such an organization, and development programmes including mentoring and coaching are likely to reflect this. We move now to explore how best to achieve the reflection needed for all types of learning through reflective dialogue.

Note

1   Here 'world' is used to denote the realities of an individual, group or organization.

03 Reflective dialogue and learning

We now connect learning theory to practice through the use of reflective dialogue, the basis of successful mentoring or coaching. We differentiate reflective dialogue for learning from everyday dialogue, and explore how it leads to the different levels of learning. Reflective dialogue is compared with internal dialogue and intentional dialogue is recognized as part of the mentoring and coaching process.

Reflective dialogue is an exchange between coach or mentor and client that promotes learning. The theory set out below provides the underpinning that reveals mentoring or coaching as a valid and relevant approach to learning and development. The aim here is to show how dialogue itself contributes to learning and development. The second aim is to distinguish learning that leads to improvement from learning that leads to a transformation of one kind or another. It is important to explain the particular meaning we give to dialogue and how dialogue within a mentoring or coaching relationship can differ from other forms of interaction. We distinguish dialogue as that which takes place between people, or *interpersonal*, from internal dialogue, inside individuals, so *intrapersonal*. We also distinguish intentional dialogue from casual chat.

Day (1993) discusses reflection for professional development, often presented in reflective learning logs. He concludes that when reflection is done through journals or logs, ie **intra**personal, learning outcomes are limited to 'carrying out tasks more and more efficiently, while remaining blind to large issues of the underlying purpose' (Griffiths and Tann, 1991 cited in Day, 1993: 86). This description parallels the single loop learning discussed in Chapter 2 and contrasts with double loop learning where for professional learning 'individuals will no longer be able to remain locked into their own unquestioned and unquestioning value system' (Day, 1993: 86). Self-reflection is insufficient for professional development because 'reflection will need to be analytic and involve dialogue with others... confrontation by self or other must occur' (Day, 1993: 86).

Dialogue does occur quite naturally between people, in the form of a conversation or discussion. Dialogue in the form of discussion, where the speaker's intention is to hold forth in order to convey their knowledge, is unlikely to lead to some new understanding. This form of dialogue is often characterized by one party claiming to be expert holding forth to another who may not be. For the receiver, what is received may be significant, but the mode is primarily one-way.

Dialogue has been explored by the physicist David Bohm (1996), who contrasts dialogue with the word 'discussion'. For him discussion really means to break things up:

> It emphasizes the idea of analysis, where there may be many points of view, and where everybody is presenting a different one – analysing and breaking up. That obviously has its value, but is limited, and it will not get us very far beyond our various points of view. Discussion is almost like a ping-pong game, where people are batting the ideas back and forth and the object of the game is to win or to get points for yourself. (Bohm, 1996: 7)

On the other hand, Bohm offers a definition of true dialogue as a process where:

> meaning is not static – it is flowing. And if we have the meaning being shared, then it is flowing among us... (Bohm, 1996: 40)

Why is there a need for dialogue? Intrapersonal reflection is needed as much as interpersonal but the latter is largely absent in learning environments. Intrapersonal reflection is often a fertile ground for deep re-collecting of thoughts and potentially even feelings and actions. The potential for collusion is one counter-argument to lone reflection as adequate for high levels of reflection. The idea of the lone and isolated learner is a powerful concept and there are reports of transformative learning occurring as a result of such lone activity. Indeed, Descartes withdrew from all human contact to generate his famous 'cogito ergo sum' and libraries are traditionally silent to maximize the study process, dominated as it has been by thought. However, without a reality check humans have been found to be prone to error (Damasio, 1995).

The promotion of dialogue has come from unexpected sources in the persons of David Bohm (a physicist) and William Isaacs (a businessman), and their work has supported the idea of dialogue as a method which supports not just individual learning, but has important implications for organizational learning. Bohm (1996) and Isaacs (1994, 1999) identified some very good reasons for using dialogue for learning, particularly where adversarial methods have been the norm. They have established the crucial necessity of trust and safety for learning and the difficulty for intellectually driven individuals to suspend beliefs and begin the process of honest enquiry.

This is a useful point at which to introduce the notion of 'separated' and 'connected' knowing, originally set out in Belenky *et al* (1986) and developed further in the writing of Tarule (Goldberger *et al*, 1996), a sequel to Belenky. Separated knowing leads to:

> a kind of dialogue that values the ability to pronounce or 'report' one's ideas, whereas [connected knowing] values a dialogue that relies on relationship as one enters meaningful conversations that connect one's ideas with another's and establish 'rapport'. (Belenky *et al*, 1986: 277)

Separated knowing is very similar to Bohm's didactic discussion. Connected knowing is that which suggests the creation of that flow of meaning suggested by Bohm (Bohm, 1996: 40). It is appropriate here to introduce the work of Belenky *et al* (1986), who are central to our concepts of learning and development.

Stages of learning

Mary Belenky and her colleagues wrote *Women's Ways of Knowing* in 1986. The original research behind their book was undertaken to bring attention to the 'missing voices of women in our understanding of how people learn'. Prior to their work a scheme of personal learning and development in adults was conducted by Perry (1970) and he only recorded the results amongst Harvard men. Belenky and her colleagues argued that this represented a major failure in not examining closely women's lives and experience. Their project was both an extension of Perry's work and a critique of his scheme.

They undertook research with a group of 135 women of different ages, ethnic and class backgrounds from urban and rural communities and with varying degrees of education, not just higher education. They included high school dropouts as well as women with graduate or professional qualifications. This was itself a breakthrough given that most research in this area at the time was restricted to white, middle-class groups, often male. They intentionally sought a diversity of backgrounds in order 'to see the common ground that women share, regardless of background' (Belenky *et al*, 1986: 13). Their aim was stated thus: 'Let us listen to the voices of diverse women to hear what they say about the varieties of female experience' (Goldberger *et al*, 1996: 4). Five perspectives emerged:

1 **Silence** – a position of not knowing in which the person feels voiceless, powerless and mindless.

2 **Received knowing** – a position at which knowledge and authority are construed as outside the self and invested in a powerful and knowing another from whom one is expected to learn.

3 **Subjective knowing** – in which knowledge is personal, private and based on intuition and/or feeling states rather than on thought and articulated ideas that are defended with evidence.

4 **Procedural knowing** – the position at which techniques and procedures for acquiring, validating and evaluating knowledge claims are developed and honoured. Within this sub-head they also described two modes of knowing:

- **separated knowing** – characterized by a distanced, sceptical and impartial stance towards that which one is trying to know (reasoning against another position);

- **connected knowing** – characterized by a stance or belief and an entering into the place of the other person or the idea that one is trying to know (reasoning with another position).

5 **Constructed knowing** – a position at which truth is understood to be contextual; knowledge is recognized as tentative, not absolute; and it is understood that the knower is part of what is known and has a share in constructing it. In their sample of women, constructed knowers valued multiple approaches to knowing (subjective and objective, connected and separate) and insisted on bringing the self and personal commitment into the centre of the knowing process. (Goldberger *et al*, 1996: 4–5)[1]

The first learning stage of silence, where women had yet to discover their mind, is a position of powerlessness. Many mentoring programmes seek to rescue people perceived to be in this position and an example of this is given in The First Nation case study on page 240.

The second stage of received knowing is reminiscent of 'received wisdom', the term which suggests the presence of a prevailing discourse, and here performance coaching and induction mentoring can be found.

When the third stage of subjective knowing is reached, where the subjective world is recognized for the first time, through primary empathy, then mentors and coaches are edging towards engagement mentoring, although their performance agenda is likely to remain in place.

The fourth stage, described as procedural knowledge, was realized in two forms: separated and connected. Researchers found that the connected mode was more typical of female conditioning, while the separated mode was akin to men's. The separated strategy, known as 'the doubting game', is characterized by the objectification of the other (Elbow, 1998). Traditional training tends to engage in separated knowledge, discussions often become adversarial interactions, and 'it's not personal' is something to be proud of. Coaching and mentoring that lack empathy can be recognized as 'the doubting game'.

Connected knowing, which can be described as the 'believing game' (Elbow, 1998), is achieved through empathy, being without judgement and coming from an attitude of trust, and is quite the opposite of separated knowing. However, connected knowing differs from simple subjectivism as it is 'the deliberate imaginative extension of one's understanding into positions that initially feel wrong or remote' (Belenky *et al*, 1986: 121).

There is no reason to suppose that connectedness is the preserve of women only, and connected knowing is available to men as well as women. The principle of connectedness is essential to developmental mentoring or coaching as it involves the client as a whole person, rather than a recipient of facts and figures, and acknowledges their hopes and desires, as well as offering a mutuality of understanding. This has been confirmed by the findings reported by Deci and Ryan (2000).

Connected knowing prepares learners for their fifth and final stage of development, the adoption of constructivist approaches to knowledge. For the constructivist, 'all knowledge is constructed, and the knower is an intimate part of the known' (Belenky *et al*, 1986: 137). In this category of learning, there is passion and participation in the act of knowing which, as a philosopher, Sara Ruddick knew only too well: 'instead of developing arguments that could bring my feelings to heel, I allowed my feelings to inform my most abstract thinking' (Ruddick, 1984: 150). Constructivist learning is characterized by empathy and connectedness, so relationship is a key ingredient in what is a completely holistic stance towards knowledge and learning. The components of constructivist knowledge are those which lead to a recognition of relationship in learning, ie connectedness to another, as above, advanced empathy and awareness of feelings, all characteristics of high-level developmental mentoring or coaching.

For Belenky *et al* (1986) the use of the terms separated knowing and connected knowing is intrinsic to their work. We want to explain these terms more fully for they are a valuable way of understanding mentoring and coaching relationships, based as they are on particular forms of dialogue.

Separate[2] and connected knowing

Connected knowing means that the mentor or coach suspends judgement in an attempt to understand the client's ways of making sense of their experience. In the words of Elbow (1998), they 'play the believing game', asking questions like:

> 'What do you see?... Give me the vision in your head.'
> 'That's an experience I don't have. Help me to understand your experience.'
> (Elbow, 1998: 261)

The mentor or coach is seeking to understand where the client is coming from and what it means to the client as 'knower' of that experience.

In contrast, when conducting a dialogue through separate knowing, the mentor or coach will relate in a different way to the client. They will, in Elbow's words, 'play the doubting game' (1998: 148), looking for flaws in the client's reasoning, examining the person's statements with a critical eye and insisting that the client justify every point they make. It tends to be an adversarial stance – the mode of discourse is implicitly argument. Performance mentoring and coaching are typified by separate knowing. With connected knowing the dialogue is about understanding what the person is saying – their experience, and this is more typical of work in the engagement or developmental quadrants. The mode of discourse is 'one of allies, even advocates, of the position they are examining' (Clinchy, 1996: 208).

Developmental mentoring or coaching is a relationship where understanding how their client is 'coming from in their experience' is significant in enabling the client to work with that experience. '"Playing the believing game" becomes a *procedure* that guides the interaction with other minds. It is not the *result* of the interaction' (Clinchy, 1996: 209). In other words, I do not necessarily have to agree with the person's stance, but I suspend my judgement in order to understand them.

Connected knowing as a procedure

Clinchy refers to connected knowing as originally a serendipitous discovery when they undertook the research leading to their publication, *Women's Ways of Knowing* (Belenky *et al*, 1986):

> Connected knowing was originally a serendipitous discovery. We did not ask the women we interviewed to tell us about it; they did so spontaneously, and from their comments we constructed the procedure as a sort of 'ideal type'.
>
> Clinchy (1996: 205)

This coincides with the authors' own experience. As we have worked with clients, we have learnt, with some reflective dialogue (!), that empathic interactions have dramatic learning outcomes. Empathy, which leads to an increased understanding of the client's experience rather than attempting to 'knock it', causes clients to shift their understanding of their worlds without having to be convinced by the 'rational' arguments of another. A very ordinary example will be given here.

In an early mentoring session one of the authors listened to his client wishing to sort her work priorities. She brought a long jumbled list of things she was attempting to do currently in her work.

As a separate knower, I might have challenged the list and no doubt sought to get her to order the list according to some logic and criteria. In fact I listened to her explanation of what she was doing and not doing, and offered her empathy by re-stating her expression of frustration, blockages, and ambivalence towards her work. The purpose here, rather than seeking clarification, was simply to ascertain what she found important and how she felt about it all. At the end of our session she had done some sorting but there was a sense of the unfinished about it. Slowly, at our subsequent meetings the list became a recognition of something wider and deeper – her recognition of a shift in the direction of her career. We could not have foreseen this and it would have been inappropriate at an earlier stage to have drawn that conclusion.

As our experience in mentoring and coaching developed we realized that getting into the world of our client through empathy was not only effective from their standpoint, it was also, in Clinchy's words, a useful *procedure* to adopt to enable the learner to understand her world and to work from there.

Connected procedure as a means of transformation

The procedure we are adopting in our work is a shift in culture by moving away from the prevailing discourse in the worlds of work that we live in – be it business, education or training. In reflective dialogue there is an explicit aim through the process to get into the world of our client. This does not mean a subjective immersion in that world. It is to try to understand where the other is coming from. The emphasis here is on the word try. It is not easy or natural. Clinchy quotes the anthropologist Clifford Geertz (1986) here:

> Comprehending that which is, in some manner or form, alien to us and likely to remain so, without either smoothing it over with vacant murmurs of common humanity,... or dismissing it as charming, lovely even, but inconsequent, is a skill we have arduously to learn and having learnt it, work continuously to keep it alive; it is not a natural[3] capacity, like depth perception or the sense of balance, upon which we can complacently rely. (in Clinchy, 1996: 209)

In early mentoring or coaching sessions, it is easy to seem to get into the client's world and there may be a temptation to make assumptions about that world and to base interventions upon those assumptions without check-ing if they are accurate. Having made assumptions about the other's world, we may then proceed to ask questions that detract from her world on the basis that I now know her world. In fact the dialogue may be nearer my world than that of my client. Also, coaches and mentors may be afraid of getting into their client's world, especially if it is painful and emotional. Here is another ordinary example from one of the authors' supervision work.

> When reviewing the work of a supervisee recently, through a video-recording, I was struck by the coach's inability to offer empathy, as their client recounted a work colleague's betrayal. Instead the coach engaged in the 'doubting game' and implicitly dictated how their client should behave towards their colleague. In supervision he realized that he had 'escaped' from emotional discomfort into separate mode.

We should emphasize that getting into the client's world through connected knowing does not mean that we are acritically accepting that world. This would mean a subjectivism which would suggest that we accept whatever the client says as a valid view of the world. The point for the connected knower is to understand their world, not necessarily to accept it.

Understanding what the learner expresses doesn't mean that we have to agree. Geertz (1986) explains this as:

> understanding in the sense of comprehension, perception and insight needs to be distinguished from 'understanding' in the sense of agreement of opinion, union of sentiment, or commonality of commitment… We must learn to grasp what we cannot embrace. (in Clinchy, 1996: 217)

To be really heard as a client in connected knowing terms is to be affirmed and validated and this is achieved by the coach or mentor 'swinging boldly into the mind' of their client. Clinchy (1996: 218) suggests that by 'swinging boldly into the mind of another', two perversions of connected knowing are prevented. The first, known in the United States as the 'Californian fuck off', is typified by a response like: 'well given your background, I can see where you're coming from', is simply patronizing and is a totally negative response. The second is like the assumption made above with a quick response like 'I know how you feel', when in fact they have little idea or quite the wrong idea. Worse still is the favourite question from coaches or mentors, 'How does that make you feel?', when it is obvious how their client is feeling, and all that is needed is primary or advanced empathy, explained in Chapters 9 and 10.

The relatedness that arises when connected knowing occurs has echoes in a story we have of a week-long workshop introducing facilitation methods to senior government personnel in China. Following the first day, when we arrived at the start of subsequent days, we would ask the participants for their overnight thoughts. This process, our normal practice, was designed to address any feelings or reflections about the previous day and was useful in grounding the workshop at the beginning of the day. We asked on the third morning for overnight thoughts. One of the participants told a story to us and his colleagues.

He had telephoned his partner late the previous evening and she had relayed to him her upset at how she had been treated very negatively by her manager that day despite undertaking all that had been required of her. Our storyteller asked questions essentially about what had happened and by using empathy he showed that he understood how she felt. She worked through on the phone her feelings about the event and created her own picture about the interaction with her manager, and our participant told us that this was the first time he had ever done this with his partner. Usually on hearing her woes he would have launched into giving her solutions. He was surprised by his change in behaviour, which he attributed to the work he was doing at the workshop. He had swung boldly into the mind of his partner without being judgemental and endeavoured to understand her world of work and the relationship with her manager, a good example of connected knowing. Moreover, as a consequence of his stance, she took ownership and responsibility for her issues and how she would resolve them.

We can now summarize the story so far. As a mentor or coach, you enter into a dialogue with your client. The dialogue that you engage in can be termed one of separate or connected knowing, depending on which quadrant you are working in. For performance coaching or mentoring you are likely to work, without empathy, largely in separate mode. In the engagement and development quadrant, you will endeavour to enter your client's world in order to understand where they are coming from. It is a procedure to enable you to enter the world of your client and possibly to learn from it as well. The form the dialogue takes represents a cultural shift from that prevailing in many work situations. We now explore how this dialogue enables reflection and reflective learning.

Reflection and reflective dialogue

There are many definitions of reflection, and they tend to say what reflection is but not how to do it. For instance:

> reflection is a generic term for those intellectual and affective activities in which individuals engage to explore their experiences in order to lead to new understandings and appreciation (Boud, Keogh and Walker, 1985: 3)

or reflection is:

> the process of internally examining and exploring an issue of concern, triggered by an experience, which creates and clarifies meaning in terms of self, which results in a changed conceptual perspective. (Boyd and Fales, 1983: 100)

Both these definitions assume an intrapersonal dialogue and we discussed the limitations of this above. Our definition not only describes what reflection is but also how to achieve it, by engaging with another:

> We define reflective learning as an intentional process, where social context and experience are acknowledged, in which learners are active individuals, wholly present, *engaging with another*, open to challenge, and the outcome involves transformation as well as improvement for both individuals and their organization. (Brockbank *et al*, 2002: 6)

We maintain that while intrapersonal reflection is effective, and may offer opportunities for deep learning, which may or may not be shared with another, *it is ultimately not enough to promote transformational learning.* On the other hand, providing for interpersonal reflection in reflective dialogue-with-another, in a mentoring, coaching or supervisory relationship, guarantees that learners are challenged, that double loop learning is an option and that the transformational learning which results from dialogue is a real potential outcome.

What is reflective dialogue? Reflective dialogue is intentional. Naturally occurring dialogue may reflect the power differences in a situation and this can inhibit learning. A dialogue with a client which takes the form of a monologue about how things should be done, with which they are obliged to agree, is unlikely to promote reflective learning for improvement or transformation! In addition, the casual conversation at the water fountain does not carry the requisite safety needed for reflective dialogue leading to transformative learning.

We identified the characteristics of reflective dialogue (Brockbank and McGill, 2007) as dialogue which 'engages the person (who is in dialogue) at the edge of their knowledge, sense of self and the world'. Intentional dialogue provides the safety for voicing the realities of their world, and ensures that the implications for themselves and their learning are attended to by means of what has been called 'inclusion' (Buber, 1965). Inclusion demands a relationship between two people and an event which is lived through from the standpoint of the other.

Intentional dialogue has a purpose, which is clear to both parties. Hence the process is agreed from the start. Reflective dialogue engages the learner's realities and subjective experience, giving space for the learner to consider and reconsider, without haste. This form of discourse we referred to earlier as 'connected knowing', as against 'separate knowing' where the dialogue seeks to analyse and itemize rather than to understand and connect with the learner (Goldberger *et al*, 1996).

In addition, intentional dialogue supports the perturbation or disturbance which may occur when existing assumptions are challenged, and deals with the emotional material flowing from such challenges. The engagement with another at the edge of awareness, although sometimes painful and possibly difficult to maintain, may generate new learning, forged from the discomfort and struggle of dialogue, which emerges as the reflective learning we seek as an outcome of the mentoring or coaching relationship.

The importance of reflective dialogue for individual learning is understood at all three levels of learning, described in Chapter 2. These are reflective learning for improvement (single loop), as in performance or engagement, through reflective learning for transformation (double loop), to our third level of learning, that is, where the learner goes one step further to consider and reflect upon how the single and double loop learning was achieved, in other words, reflective learning about learning (Argyris and Schön, 1996: 20).

Reflective dialogue mirrors these levels of learning as follows.

Levels of reflective dialogue

Dialogue-with-another offers opportunities for reflective learning at all three levels.

1 Improvement

Here the employee is at the received stage of learning described on page 40. Reflective dialogue informs them and may also lead to a reconsideration of how things are being done, and how things can be improved. For example, in a coaching session a retail employee considers how customers are directed to the correct department, and devises a more effective method. This places it in the performance quadrant of our map in Chapter 1. With the addition of primary empathy the dialogue moves into the subjective stage of learning and has the potential to create the connection which takes it into the engagement quadrant of our map. For example, in a mentoring session an employee may consider a range of different methods to increase customer movement in a store with the aim of increasing sales.

2 Transformation

Here the client carries assumptions and dispositions and is in potential connected mode. Reflective dialogue offers the possibility of engaging at the edge of their assumptions and beliefs, reconsidering the taken-for-granteds (the tfgs) in relation to self-generated goals, and, through advanced empathy, leads to potential transformation. This places the dialogue in the development quadrant of our map. For example, in a coaching or mentoring session a client may discuss how staff could meet and greet customers in a completely new approach to customer service. This real practice example revealed, when empathy was present, that employees actually felt rather intimidated by customers.

3 Learning about learning in organizations

When improvement or transformation has occurred, reflective dialogue can take learning one step further, so that clients learn about learning itself, from their experience as reflective learners in mentoring or coaching relationships. For example, the realization that a particular method of production is economically sound but environmentally damaging may lead to altered methods, a transformation perhaps. In addition, mentors, coaches and clients may choose to identify what factors enabled the realization to emerge and the change to be implemented, that is, the client reflects upon their reflective learning. Consideration of what issues were considered in dialogue and how they were processed would enable clients to pinpoint the key elements of their learning for future reference, and this applies to organizations too. A dialogue at this level can be placed in the systemic quadrant of the map in Chapter 1.

How dialogue can lead to organizational transformation

The social and political context of learning is more likely to be revealed when emotion is part of a dialogue, as this will influence the degree of autonomy experienced by the learner. When agency, as the potential of individuals to act, is accessed through dialogue, this allows the third way for power to be exposed for what it is (Lukes, 2005). Expression of emotion may enable learners to recognize the constraints of social systems in which they work, as well as acknowledging their desires, ambitions, respect, pride and dignity, so often missing in organizational life. When the gate of the emotive domain is opened, many other facets of learning may be revealed and accessible, a process likely to offer material for challenge.

The affective domain provides a route to some of the factors which are known to influence learning and others which remain mysterious. For example, emotive material in dialogue has the potential to uncover how learners are affected by gender, race, class, hierarchy, power, culture, age etc. The multidimensional nature of learning is hidden when the affective domain is silenced and constructive challenge is less likely. This explains the failure so far of initiatives to develop high-level learning in educational, social, corporate and other work environments. The emerging drive to include reflective dialogue in learning situations through methods such as mentoring and coaching is recognition that a different approach to the current separate learning is needed for growth and success in a variety of enterprises.

So, to conclude, definitions of reflective practice venerate the process of reflection, urging professionals to engage in it, before, during and after their practice, with a view to improvement, transformation and, hopefully, learning about the learning process (Schön, 1987). Such definitions often imply self-reflection, and this, we suggest, seriously limits the quality of learning achieved. Hence the value of a developmental mentor or coach who engages in this connected form of dialogue with their client.

What do we dialogue about?

The material for dialogue in the coach or mentor–client relationship is often about the content of work, the tasks and processes which form the work we do. To reflect on the task we begin from a description of what is being or is going to be done. To reflect on the process we work with a description of how the task is being done or is going to be done. The content of dialogue is dictated by the client in developmental mentoring and coaching (but may not be with performance coaching or mentoring), who brings material from a current, past or future project, and it is likely to cover the three domains of learning:

- doing;
- feeling;
- thinking.

Doing and thinking are familiar areas for modern organizations. The commitment to emotional literacy is less significant and here, we maintain, the key to effective learning lies. Leading edge organizations are increasingly including emotional intelligence in their management development programmes. We noted above that a dialogue which gets below the surface to 'defensive reasoning', in Argyris's term, is likely to stimulate double loop learning and enable the tfgs to be questioned and challenged. Such dialogue may incorporate and stimulate emotion and feeling for both learners and dialoguers. In developmental mentoring or coaching relationships the dialogue should be followed by a reflective learning review, and this ensures learning at levels 1, 2 and 3 taking the form of questions and comments about what has been described. Reflection can occur at three levels as before:

1 Reflection for improvement, where mentors and coaches will analyse and discourse with the learner about what has been described (the task) and how (the process), a model often found in good performance management as well as engagement work. We offer ideas for such a dialogue in Chapters 8 and 9.

2 Reflection for transformation, where coaches and mentors need to proceed with care, and here the learning relationship and trust are crucial. Examining the tfgs in a process uncovers material which may be uncomfortable and destabilizing, so mentors and coaches need to have skills in the emotional arena, be comfortable in it, and have a clear grasp of appropriate boundaries in the workplace. Typical relationships for transformative learning include one-to-one mentoring or executive coaching in the development quadrant.

3 Reflection for understanding the learning process may be an additional aim. This level is appropriate for continuous personal development (CPD) records, supervision or organizational change. A step back from the two earlier processes is required, and consideration is given to how the reflective learning was achieved, whether it was for improvement or transformation. This can be done as part of the mentoring or coaching review session. The implications for radical change and organizational transformation, if a critical mass of personnel are engaged in this level of reflective dialogue, would place it in the systemic quadrant.

Chapter summary

This chapter has compared the benefits of intrapersonal and interpersonal dialogue and described what is needed for interpersonal reflective dialogue. Three levels of learning related dialogue to the learning outcomes of coaching and mentoring in our map in Chapter 1. A dialogue in separate mode without empathy is likely to be used for performance management. A dialogue with the addition of empathy in limited connected mode is likely to be used for engagement. For developmental mentoring or coaching the reflective dialogue process demands structured time, space, clear boundaries, tolerance of uncertainty and competence in dealing with emotional material for the relationship to prosper for the client and stimulate transformational learning. The three levels of dialogue include the possibility of organizational learning through systemic reflective dialogue.

Notes

1   This summary of the five perspectives is drawn from Goldberger *et al* (1996) rather than the original (Belenky *et al*, 1986). The summary is essentially the same except that the later version is probably intended to be more accessible to the reader. In Goldberger *et al* (1996) the original authors and invited contributors explore how the theory introduced in Belenky *et al* (1986) has developed and shifted over the years.

2   The original term in the Belenky research was 'separated'. In the later review of their work Goldberger *et al* used the term 'separate'.

3   In the original quotation, Geertz uses the term 'connatural'. We take this to mean the same as 'natural'.

PART TWO
What is the difference between coaching and mentoring?

The meaning of these terms is contested by practitioners worldwide. For instance, many organizations, including Harvard University, state that mentoring is for whole person development to potential transformation, whereas coaching is for day-to-day improvement. On the other hand, many others, including international coaching organizations, maintain that coaching is the whole person development tool and mentoring is for passing on knowledge to juniors. This book is an attempt to clarify the situation. However, for readers who are mystified by the difference the next four chapters may help. This part of the book describes how coaching and mentoring are described and practised in various different contexts, for different purposes and with sometimes very different outcomes. In addition, there are two chapters which provide a brief outline of available models for mentoring and coaching.

What is mentoring?

04

We aim to clear up some of the confusion around the term mentoring by placing definitions on the situational map given in Chapter 1. They may be categorized as:

- performance,
- engagement, or
- developmental,

depending on:

- the purpose,
- the process, and
- the learning outcome,

which is implied in each definition. In addition, we review what are considered potential barriers to mentoring, and identify aspects of dysfunctional mentoring.

The definitions reveal a range of understandings of mentoring. Caruso (1992) reported that 'mentoring help' functions were:

1 learning technical skills and knowledge;

2 learning current job;

3 learning organizational culture;

4 learning organizational policies;

5 preparation for a future job.

Following Chapter 1 we can recognize this as a *performance* or *engagement* approach, and it has been described as an old-fashioned model of mentoring (Darwin, 2000). The advantage of such an approach is that it makes evaluation possible, as success is measured by how far these objectives have been achieved.

However, mentoring has also been defined as a *developmental* relationship 'between two people with learning and development as its purpose' (Megginson and Garvey, 2004: 2). In addition, mentoring is primarily for the protégé as 'the protege's dream' (Caruso, 1996) is central to mentoring. This refers to the term 'dream' in the Levinson and Levinson (1996) publication, *The Seasons of a Woman's Life*, quoted in full on page 64 below.

Acronyms in this chapter mean as follows:

EMCC   European Mentoring and Coaching Council

ICF   International Coach Federation

CIPD   Chartered Institute of Personnel and Development (UK only)

We now examine each of the three approaches under consideration and, primarily as independent practitioners, we admit our preference for the developmental approach.

Performance mentoring

We define performance mentoring as 'an activity between mentor and client with a prescribed purpose which may or may not be assented to by the client, using a directive process, and the learning outcome is improvement'. Performance mentoring is typically used for induction, and aims for individual improvement without radical change in the work context. The approach is usually hierarchical and the process has been described as the 'recycling of power' (Darwin, 2000), and is clearly evident in this description of a mentor written nearly 30 years ago:

> A good enough mentor is a transitional figure who invites and welcomes a young man into the adult world. He serves as guide, teacher and sponsor... The protégé has the hope that soon he will be able to join or even surpass his mentor in the work they both value. (Levinson *et al*, 1978: 323)

Note: The assumption then was that the workforce was all-male.

The performance intention, ie grooming the junior to adapt and conform to the work context, within a hierarchical structure (older mentor with more power than client), is revealed in this description of mentoring:

> A relationship between a young adult and an older, more experienced adult, that helps the younger individual learn and navigate in the adult world and the world of work. (Kram, 1988: 2)

In addition, performance mentoring programmes may be used to support employees who are seeking to gain a qualification, and here again the mentoring has improvement as its learning outcome. The process is typically didactic, emphasizing the transmission of knowledge, and is typified by advice-giving and direction.

This is confirmed in the CIPD factsheet where mentoring is described as 'a technique for allowing the transmission of knowledge, skills and experience' (CIPD, 2010b). The ICF now takes a similar line on mentoring, as follows:

> Mentoring... can be thought of as guiding from one's own experience or sharing of experience in a specific area of industry or career development, is sometimes confused with coaching. (**http://www.coachfederation.org/about-icf/overview/**, accessed July 2011)

In the joint code of conduct published by the EMCC/ICF, mentoring is described as:

> a transfer of skill or knowledge from a more experienced to a less experienced person through learning dialogue and role modelling, and may also be a learning partnership between peers. (EMCC/ICF Joint code, 2011)

The recycling of power has echoes in the historical roots of mentoring, which lie in the Greek myth of Ulysses, who in preparation for his lengthy sea voyages entrusted his young son Telemachus to the care of his old friend Mentor (alias Athena in some versions of the story). Thereafter the name has been identified with a more experienced person who forms a relationship with a less experienced person in order to provide them with advice, support and encouragement (Megginson and Clutterbuck, 1995) and the mentor role has been mythologized to one of nurture and self-sacrifice (Colley, 2003).

Kathy Kram

Kathy Kram (1988) identified two broad functions within mentoring. Firstly, career functions, including sponsorship and coaching, which enhance career advancement (of the client). Where career functions are the primary focus, which is often the case in formal mentoring programmes, the model tends to be knowledge based, instrumental and carefully controlled, ie performance. Secondly, psychosocial functions, including friendship, counselling and role modelling, were identified as enhancing a sense of competence, identity and effectiveness in a professional role. The benefits of career functions come largely from the experience, seniority and organizational ranking of the mentor, who is able to help the protégé to 'navigate effectively in the organizational world' (Kram, 1988). When psychosocial functions are actively present the purpose is different and we discuss this under 'Engagement mentoring' below.

Megginson and Clutterbuck

The earliest mentoring research in the UK was carried out by David Megginson and David Clutterbuck (Megginson, 1988; Clutterbuck, 1991). The difference between mentoring in US contexts and the equivalent in UK contexts was identified by them (Megginson and Clutterbuck, 1995). The UK approach replaces the sponsorship element in the US context with career support but limits this to professional development. The psychosocial functions identified in Kram's US research are replaced by personal development functions. In addition, the details vary as shown in Table 4.1.

TABLE 4.1   US and English/European approaches

The US approach	The English/European approach
Career functions	*Professional functions*
Sponsorship	Career development but not sponsorship
Exposure-and-visibility	Sharing knowledge (connection with study)
Coaching	Improve performance through coaching
Protection (source of the term protégé)	
Challenging assignments	
Psychosocial functions	*Personal functions*
Role modelling	Work-related 'counselling'
Acceptance-and-confirmation	Social contact typified by distance and English reticence
Counselling	Friendship

UK and European business mentors are more likely to be offline and more experienced rather than more powerful. Where only career functions or professional functions are present, the mentoring is performance related and this is typical of many mentoring programmes, where the purpose is linked to induction and corporate objectives.

Eric Parsloe

Parsloe and Wray (2000), using a broad definition of mentoring as 'a process that supports and encourages learning to happen', identify three types of mentor:

corporate – in a business context;

qualification – as part of an educational process;

community – as support for disadvantaged or oppressed groups in society.

The improvement model of learning offered by Parsloe and Wray (2000: 25) positions corporate and qualification mentoring in the performance quadrant and offers an appropriate model for robust environments where the mentoring objective is performance and the desired outcome is improvement (Parsloe and Wray, 2000: 117).

Darling and nursing

In a nursing context, performance purposes can be detected in the classification by Morton-Cooper and Palmer (2000) as shown in Table 4.2.

TABLE 4.2   Classification of mentoring types

Type	Nature
1. *True mentoring relationships* (i) Classical mentoring – informal (primary mentoring). A natural, chosen relationship. Purposes and functions are determined by the individuals involved. An enabling relationship in personal, emotional, organizational and professional terms.	- Self-selection of individuals, persuasive influences; attraction with a shared wish to work together. - No defined programme. - Less specific purposes and functions as set by the individuals, circumstances and context. - No explicit financial rewards for mentors. - Probable duration 2–15 years.
(ii) Contract mentoring – formal (facilitated mentoring/secondary mentoring). An artificial relationship created for a specific purpose that is essentially determined by the organization. Some elements of mentor function, with focus on specific helper functions.	Programmes are identified by: - clear purposes, functions, defined aims or outcomes; - selected individuals with assigned mentors, forced matching or choice of mentors from mentor pool; - explicit material rewards; possibilities of financial incentives for mentors; - probable duration 1–2 years.
2. *Pseudo-mentoring relationships* (quasi-mentoring/partial mentoring/sequential mentoring) Mentoring approaches in appearance only – as offered by academic involvement in thesis preparation, orientation and induction programmes.	- Focus on specific tasks or organizational issues of short-lived duration. - Guidance from several mentors, for short periods. - Relationships do not demonstrate the comprehensive enabling elements of the true classical model. - Specified clinical placements. - Probable duration 6 weeks to 1 year.

SOURCE: Morton-Cooper and Palmer (2000: 46)

The definition of contract mentoring places it in the performance quadrant with pseudo mentors and minor mentors (discussed below). Contract mentoring by its nature will be semi-formal or formal and is performance in purpose, seeking for conformation and adaptation to existing structures and norms. The method is likely to be instructional and advice driven, especially where qualification or accreditation is the aim, and this places contract mentoring firmly in the performance quadrant of our mentoring map. The processes adopted in mentor selection, choice and support structures, mentor training and skills differentiate true mentors from pseudo mentors.

Darling (1984) also identifies mentor types in the nursing context, in terms of three components: attraction, action and affect. First, attraction, meaning admiration and/or a desire to emulate the mentor; second, action, meaning that the mentor invests time and energy for and on behalf of their protégé; and thirdly, affect, meaning that the relationship has an emotional component, ie the couple respect and like each other, and the mentor offers encouragement and support as well as challenge.

A minor mentor is defined by Darling (1984) as having fewer than three of these components present; for instance, a mentor who is admired and invests time and energy but is unconnected emotionally to their client is likely to be a minor mentor, as the relationship is focused on prescribed outcomes, which are not informed by a close emotional bond. Some minor mentors fit the engagement quadrant and we discuss these below.

Other researchers

Carruthers (1993) suggests, as above, that performance mentor relationships are those which emphasize only the professional development of the client, without an emotional bond or the presence of psychosocial functions.

Norman Cohen (1995) identified six principles for adult mentoring in US business or government contexts, as follows:

relationship emphasis – building rapport and trust;

information emphasis – offering tailored advice;

facilitative focus – introducing alternatives (TAANA v TINA[1]);

confrontive focus – to offer challenge;

mentor model – to motivate;

protégé vision – to encourage initiative.

This model, with its single loop emphasis, lies within the performance quadrant. However, the focus on trust and relationship edges it into the engagement field, and while the confrontive focus leaves a door open to the developmental corner, the presence of advice leaves it indisputably as a performance perspective. The scale provides for 55 specific mentor behaviours clustered into the six categories and Cohen provides a self-assessment questionnaire for potential mentors to rate themselves on the six principles. An adaptation of this questionnaire was used in the CILT case study reported in Chapter 9.

E-mentoring

When the mentoring relationship is conducted electronically, by e-mail or other method, the term e-mentoring has been coined. E-mentoring, using asynchronous e-mail or synchronous chat software to communicate, is being adopted by an increasing number of organizations with global reach, because of its practical advantages for geographically distant mentoring couples (Hall, 2005). Can learning be achieved electronically? The method is in its early stages, and outcomes from similar programmes suggest that learning for improvement can be achieved by the use of virtual classrooms and e-mail coaching and support, an approach known as a blended solution (Brockbank *et al*, 2002).

Bierema and Merriam offer a definition of e-mentoring as:

> a computer-mediated, mutually beneficial relationship between a mentor and a protégé which provides learning, advising, encouraging, promoting and modeling, that is often boundaryless, egalitarian, and qualitatively different than traditional face-to-face mentoring. (2002: 214)

Is e-mentoring in the performance quadrant?

There is plenty of evidence to support the generation of significant relationships online, with support for the idea that the medium itself generates intimacy (McKenna and Bargh, 1998). Hence mentoring online exists and has the potential to be developmental but the evidence to date suggests otherwise.

The naivety of the 'boundaryless' claim made in the quotation above is supported by Russell (2001), who suggests that e-mentoring may perpetuate 'cultural imperialism' where existing cultural values are replaced by values from the far from egalitarian 'adviser'. Alternatively, the potential of e-mentoring to reach marginalized populations is reported by Burgstahler and Nourse (1999), as the anonymity provided online gives courage to protégés.

The benefits of e-mentoring have been stated by Andrew Cardow as 'the elimination of noise due to personal bias' and 'only precise, simple and clear instructions were given to the protégé from the mentor' (Cardow, 1998: 35). Although e-mentors reported giving guidance and instructions, the relationship was described as non-hierarchical, which seems unlikely. Also, the issue of conveying empathy electronically is ignored as 'both the protégé and mentor are part of the same institutional field', which unfortunately is not a guarantee of empathy being present, electronically or otherwise (Cardow, 1998: 37; Anthony, 2000). We discuss the significance of empathy in mentoring and coaching in Chapters 9 and 10. There is evidence that online relationships generate higher levels of disclosure (Anthony, 2000) but, as with face-to-face relationships, this will depend on the mentor's degree of responding skills, such as empathy, restatement and summary, also discussed in Chapters 8–10.

We conclude, therefore, that, in general, e-mentoring is performance related in intent and in practice, with improvement as the desired outcome and mentoring online being deployed for economic rather than developmental reasons. Can e-mentoring be developmental?

We have found no evidence of e-mentoring which resembles developmental mentoring with transformation as a learning outcome. Why should this be? We believe that the participants in e-mentoring programmes, both mentors and protégés, are primed for performance outcomes, whatever they may say about their method. The process is cheap and does not entail commitment in time and space to another individual, so it must seem attractive to busy managers who prefer to keep a distance between themselves and potential protégés. There is no reason why potential developmental mentors should not use technology to support their relationships with protégés, and when this occurs there will be evidence of transformative outcomes achieved online.

Engagement mentoring

We define engagement mentoring as an agreed activity, where the purpose is prescribed (which the client may or may not be made aware of), which takes a humanistic stance that respects the client's subjective world, and the learning outcome is improvement, leaving underlying values and systems unchanged.

Engagement mentoring describes mentoring in the quadrant where the individual is persuaded to align their goals with those of the organization, using a non-directive method, which respects the employee in nurturing ways. However, the intention is improvement in performance. We identify the characteristics of engagement mentoring in a variety of corporate programmes (some are described in our case studies in Chapter 9), where the purpose is improvement and the approach utilizes a nurturing or non-directive approach. The stated objectives of such programmes include development of particular skills related to the business concerned, induction, transitions or change initiatives which may be problematic or meet with resistance. These objectives mirror the goals of 'employability' initiatives, where aims for young clients include 'to sign on to the values and ethos of the business and to fit into its organizational structure, culture and work ethics' (Colley, 2003: 25).

Helen Colley (2003) reports her in-depth study of one mentoring scheme, 'New Beginnings', for 'disaffected' youngsters mentored by volunteer university undergraduates. Engagement mentoring is the term first used by Colley to describe an intervention responding to disaffection and social exclusion. Engagement mentoring projects targeted groups of young people 'at risk' of disengaging or already disengaged from formal systems of education, training and employment. The programmes explicitly seek to re-engage young people with these systems in preparation for entry to the labour market. Other versions of engagement mentoring are the business/education partnerships and community mentoring (see Parsloe and Wray above) programmes focusing on oppressed groups.

What about engagement mentoring in a business context?

Engagement mentoring can be seen as a key aspect of staff and management development (Whitely, Dougherty and Dreher, 1991), as it is an integral part of a properly defined human resource strategy which must be concerned with the development of people in the most effective manner (Keep, 1992).

Formal and informal mentoring have increasingly been seen as part of a human resource strategy in which organizations seek to develop their human resources in a way that leads to competitive success (McKeen and Burke, 1989; Wright and Werther, 1991; Cunningham and Eberle, 1993). This understanding is associated with a 'soft' management style which is concerned to develop abilities, competencies and concepts in people, and to facilitate and encourage their use, rather than creating a performance system of control and extrinsic motivation. Research findings reveal that employees may engage with a range of aspects of their working environment: at high levels with the job itself, the line manager, and colleagues; at moderate levels with the organization so that only 'the money gets you up' (CIPD, 2010c). Engagement mentoring at high levels will prepare the ground for a developmental mentoring programme.

In Kram's research, when psychosocial functions are present the mentoring experience can include emotion and development for both parties. Psychosocial functions rely on the quality of the interpersonal bond between mentor and client, and the degree of trust which exists within the relationship. Factors identified by Kram, which influence psychosocial bonding, include mutual liking, respect, exclusivity, counselling skill and the desire for friendship intimacy (Kram, 1988). The presence of psychosocial functions, which includes empathy, differentiates engagement and developmental mentoring from performance mentoring.

Developmental mentoring

We define true developmental mentoring as 'an agreed activity between mentor and client, where goals are generated by and for the client, where the process is person-centred and the learning outcome is transformation'. We reiterate the need for high levels of empathy for developmental work.

For many clients their development will challenge the underlying values and systems in their organization.

We will now examine typical definitions of mentors and mentoring in terms of their purpose, process and learning outcome. Let us consider the nature of a 'true' mentor, described as follows:

> A true mentor fosters the young adult's development by nourishing the youthful Dream and giving it her or his blessing, believing in the young woman, helping her to define her newly emerging adult self in its newly discovered adult world, and creating a space in which she can move towards a reasonably satisfactory life structure that contains the Dream. (Levinson and Levinson, 1996: 239)

In this near-perfect definition of developmental mentoring, the 'dream' refers to lifetime hopes held in early adulthood, and nourishing the 'dream' ensures that the client's goals are their own. The process has person-centred characteristics, and the learning outcome is identified as the transformation into a 'satisfactory life structure that contains the dream'.

The Harvard view of mentoring is clearly a developmental one, following Kram's research, including both career and psychosocial functions, with coaching as just one small aspect of the mentoring skills set. The Harvard mentor guides and supports their protégé, who generates their own long-term learning goals, with an emphasis on listening, and is never their line manager (Harvard, 2004).

The different understandings of what mentoring is (versus coaching) are revealed in a recent Harvard publication where mentoring is described as follows:

> 'the scope of mentoring is vastly greater than coaching, which is, itself, a small subset of mentoring' which is 'not limited to the development of some narrow set of skills or behaviours but addresses the whole person and his or her career'. Effective mentoring is believed to build personal and institutional bonds, enhance job satisfaction and well-being. (Harvard, 2004)

In the UK nursing profession a mentor is described as:

> Someone who provides an enabling relationship that facilitates another's personal growth and development. The relationship is dynamic, reciprocal, and can be emotionally intense. With such a relationship, the mentor assists with career development and guides the mentoree through the organizational, social and political networks. (Morton-Cooper and Palmer, 1993: xix)

The purpose of the relationship described here is the development of the client, hence the goals can be assumed to be the client's own. The presence of emotion suggests a person-centred approach, and the learning outcome, if and only if the goals are the client's own, is likely to be developmental, placing the definition in the developmental sector.

Morton-Cooper and Palmer (2000) classify mentor types, given in Table 4.2 on page 59, which shows true mentoring as 'Classical mentoring, a naturally-chosen, personal and emotional enabling relationship in an organizational and professional context'.

Classical mentoring may be identified as developmental, where 'naturally chosen' implies that the client will generate their own goals, the relationship suggests a person-centred approach and the learning outcome has the potential for transformation. However, the organizational and professional context may influence ownership of goals. For readers seeking to launch a contract mentoring programme, Morton-Cooper and Palmer (2000) offer a clear continuum from formal through semi-formal to informal, so that protégés can be aware of the type of mentor they will end up with (Figure 4.1).

FIGURE 4.1   Mentoring: the continuum of informality and formality

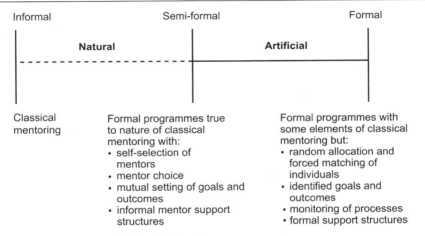

SOURCE: Morton-Cooper and Palmer (2000: 69)

Contract mentoring programmes which aim to stimulate true developmental mentoring rarely address the issue of whose purpose is being served and hence may regress into performance or engagement mentoring mode. Where contract mentors insist on clients generating their own goals the developmental quality is preserved. Clutterbuck (1998) supplies a list of 'must haves' for a successful contract programme (page 102) which includes training for everyone concerned, ie mentor, protégé and line manager, as well as ongoing support for mentors, an identified need in mentor research (Brockbank, 1994; Brockbank and Beech, 1999).

Darling's typology as discussed earlier uses three components: attraction, action and affect. A major mentor is defined as having all three necessary components and this (Darling, 1984) suggests that major mentors have the potential to be placed in the developmental quadrant, because the relationship enables the purpose and learning outcome to be agreed collaboratively between the mentor and their client. Similar findings exist in education and business where Carruthers (1993) suggests that mentoring relationships are developmental in intent if they can be described as those which address the owned professional and personal development of the client, and an emotional bond exists between the mentoring pair.

Julie Hay

Julie Hay (1995) has done a thorough job of untangling the variety of mentoring meanings and formats available, and she recommends using the term 'developmental alliance' rather than the more confusing term 'mentor'.

Hay defines a developmental alliance as follows: 'A relationship between equals in which one or more of those involved is enabled to: increase awareness, identify alternatives, initiate action, and develop themselves' (Hay, 1995: 3). The client here is enabled to generate their own goals, the relationship suggests a person-centred approach, and the 'develop themselves' indicates the potential learning outcome as transformation. Hay (1995) makes a sharp distinction between developmental alliances and a typically performance mentoring scheme in business where the mentor is a senior manager who is expected to develop protégés within corporate norms or functions, and whose career prospects will depend on how successful they are. On the other hand, in a mentoring scheme which promotes developmental alliances, the organization trusts the mentor (who may not be senior) to develop staff for their own benefit and that of the organization. The difference in values here can be seen in the respect for the individual shown in the latter. Hay's approach emphasizes the quality of a relationship which recognizes and values the subjective, adopts humanistic values and, because of its person-centred approach, promotes transformation. A developmental alliance depends on genuine connection and she asserts that it 'will not work properly unless those involved believe that it is normal for people to want a close connection with each other' (Hay, 1995: 47).

The Hay approach (Hay, 1995) also establishes the skill set needed for developmental mentoring, and is not afraid to admit that they are common to other activities like coaching and counselling. This is illustrated in Figure 4.2.

The long-term focus of Hay's definition includes a process she calls 'bonding' to differentiate it from coaching, counselling and traditional mentoring (Figure 4.3). We discuss the overlap between mentoring and counselling in Chapter 12.

Andy Roberts

Andy Roberts of the Birmingham College of Food Technology & Catering Science reviewed the mentoring literature across a variety of disciplines (Roberts, 2000) in order to uncover its essential attributes. His motive can be summed up in his comment that 'if no definitional agreement exists [about mentoring] how do we know we are talking about the same thing?'

FIGURE 4.2   Overlaps in mentoring, coaching and counselling

SOURCE: Hay (1995: 60)

(Roberts, 2000: 150). The result of his findings revealed that the essential attributes of mentoring (ie those without which mentoring is not mentoring) were identified as:

a process;

an active relationship;

a helping process;

a teaching-learning process;

reflective practice;

a career and personal development process;

a formalized process;

a role constructed by or for a mentor.

And the contingent attributes of mentoring were identified as:

role modelling;

sponsoring;

coaching.

FIGURE 4.3   Different perspectives

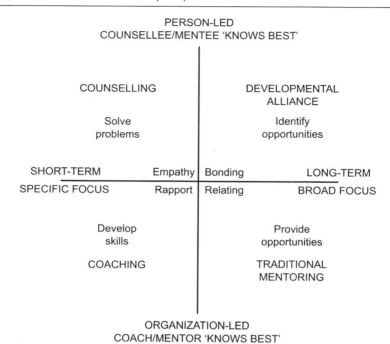

PERSON-LED
COUNSELLEE/MENTEE 'KNOWS BEST'

COUNSELLING

Solve
problems

DEVELOPMENTAL
ALLIANCE

Identify
opportunities

SHORT-TERM   Empathy | Bonding   LONG-TERM
SPECIFIC FOCUS   Rapport | Relating   BROAD FOCUS

Develop
skills

Provide
opportunities

COACHING

TRADITIONAL
MENTORING

ORGANIZATION-LED
COACH/MENTOR 'KNOWS BEST'

SOURCE: Hay (1995: 62)

On the basis of these findings Roberts offers a definition of mentoring as:

> A formalized process whereby a more knowledgeable and experienced person actuates a supportive role of overseeing and encouraging reflection and learning within a less experienced and knowledgeable person, so as to facilitate that person's career and personal development. (Roberts, 2000: 162)

We place this definition within the developmental quadrant as ownership of goals and the potential for transformation are present, with their suggestion of reflective dialogue, but it may also support a performance or engagement equilibrium outcome.

Summary

The range of mentoring activity in organizations is wide and Sue Cross (1999) summarizes the variety of purposes to which mentoring is put in the modern 'learning organization'. These include:

counteracting the stress of restructuring (engagement);

initiating new staff (performance);

enhancing performance (performance);

developing new skills (performance);

refreshing motivation (engagement);

exploring potential (developmental);

changing direction (developmental);

breaking new ground for under-represented groups (engagement or developmental).

This list covers mentoring in all of our three quadrants, the performance, engagement and developmental. Cross is adamant that mentoring is different from being a friend or colleague because 'mentoring is neither mutual nor spontaneous. It is planned, contrived and one-way' (Cross, 1999: 230), echoing our requirements for reflective dialogue in Chapter 3. She does not exclude the possibility of peer or co-mentoring but does emphasize that 'during the actual process, the roles of mentor and protege are clearly defined and mutually exclusive' (Cross, 1999: 230).

When we review how definitions 'fit' our four approaches to mentoring, the focus of business in performance mentoring is apparent, with the protégé's desires being less important than corporate objectives. In engagement mentoring we see the use of empathy at primary level, to bring protégé and organizational aims together. Where developmental mentoring is adopted, with the client generating their own objectives, and the mentor is using advanced empathy, there is the possibility of individual transformation. With sufficient individual development comes the possibility of systemic organizational change.

Barriers, obstacles and myths in mentoring

Morton-Cooper and Palmer (2000) have supplied a list of mentors' disabling traits, based on what are called 'destructive minds' (Heirs and Farrell, 1986). They describe three such minds as:

- first, the rigid, stereotypical mind with set values and ideas, found in bureaucratic organizations, so a danger in the public service sector;
- second, the ego mind, self-interested and self-important, unable to share but typically entrepreneurial so a danger in business; and
- third, the Machiavellian mind, devious and calculating, obsessed by power and politicking, a danger anywhere.

Morton-Cooper and Palmer have placed these mentor traits within two axes: enabling/disabling and facilitation/manipulation (Figure 4.4).

The destructive minds mentioned above are best avoided if possible, as they can 'infect' their protégés. Darling (1986) develops this idea, and

FIGURE 4.4   Enabling/disabling traits

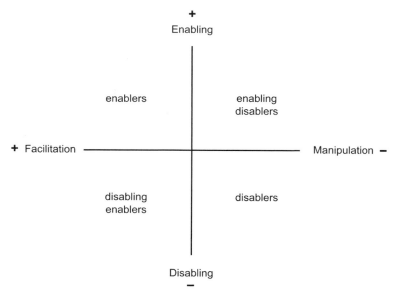

SOURCE: Morton-Cooper and Palmer (2000: 58)

identifies a gallery of 'toxic' mentors based on her interviews with nurses. These include avoiders, dumpers, blockers and destroyer/criticizers, and their related behaviours of refusing, nagging, belittling, undermining and withholding. She describes them as follows:

- avoiders who are neither available nor accessible;
- dumpers who place protégés into new and challenging roles and then abandon them;
- blockers who thwart the protégé's needs either deliberately or unconsciously;
- destroyer/criticizers who 'tear down' their protégé in private or in public, undermining them.

Antidotes for toxicity are provided in the form of contracts and straight talking and of course, ultimately, divorce (Darling, 1986).

Kram defined organizational obstacles to mentoring as follows:

1 a bottom-line results reward system as this will take a narrow evaluative focus without recognizing mentoring activity and benefits;
2 design of work which minimizes interaction as this excludes natural mentoring as part of the working day;

3 lack of performance management systems where mentoring couples are unable to identify a baseline for the protégé's development;

4 culture of the organization – if it is anti-learning or indifferent there will be no interest in developing staff;

5 assumptions, attitudes and lack of mentoring skills in senior staff.

It seems likely that such obstacles are still present in today's organizations.

Kram also identifies some of the myths of mentoring (current in 1988) and we comment in today's terms:

1 *That the primary beneficiary is the protégé as the mentor gains nothing from the process.* In fact, not only does the mentor often bask in the reflected glory of the protégé's success, but may learn about other parts of the business, and may be gently challenged by different and more youthful ideas. We refer to such an outcome in the NCH case study in Chapter 10.

2 *That the mentor relationship is always a positive experience for both parties.* Research has shown (Brockbank, 1994; Beech and Brockbank, 1999) that it is possible for both parties to feel disappointed and let down by the process.

3 *That mentor relationships look the same in all work settings.* This chapter suggests that mentoring varies depending on the quadrant in which the activity is taking place even if this is not made explicit.

4 *That mentor relationships are readily available to those who want them.* The prevalence of engagement mentoring for the purposes of empowering the disadvantaged suggests otherwise and there is evidence that gender and race influence opportunities for mentoring which we discuss under diversity in Chapter 12.

5 *That finding a mentor is the key to individual growth and career advancement.* The quadrant will dictate the effect of having a mentor, as will the approach adopted, and we discussed this above.

General difficulties or issues likely to arise in mentoring couples include gender, race, power and age, and we discuss these under diversity in Chapter 12.

Carruthers (1993) lists some of the negative consequences of some mentoring, known as the Matthew and Salieri effects. The Matthew effect, named after the favourite disciple of Jesus Christ, occurs when high flyers or gifted students get mentors, but the less gifted or disadvantaged don't. This emphasizes the gap between them and may lead to jealousy between colleagues. The Salieri phenomenon is based on Mozart's manipulative mentor, Antonio Salieri, who tried (without success) to keep Mozart's genius from being publicly recognized (Carruthers, 1993: 19).

There can be negative or even destructive consequences in dysfunctional mentoring for engagement or development, as reported by Colley (2003) and Scandura (1998). In particular, the element of choice for both mentor and protégé is crucial, as well as confidentiality and professional discretion, which should feature in any mentoring training.

Chapter summary

We have reported the various definitions of mentoring which exist by grouping them under the quadrants in our map in Chapter 1. Currently there is dramatic disagreement about what is and is not mentoring. Our experience indicates that in certain contexts the term mentoring is acceptable while the term coaching is not, and vice versa. Academic, voluntary and traditional organizations tend to favour the term mentoring, especially for engagement purposes. Corporate organizations favour the term for induction and 'tell' purposes. For readers who are quite understandably confused by the plethora of definitions, we recommend that they use the term their corporate or individual client chooses and then establish which quadrant is desired. This ensures that the contract is clearly performance, engagement or development and reduces the risk of misunderstanding and disappointment.

Note

1   TAANA – the acronym means There Are Always Numerous Alternatives – arose as a reaction to the Thatcherite expression TINA – There Is No Alternative (Halfpenny, 1985).

What is coaching?

05

Naming a coaching activity replicates the difficulty with the term mentoring discussed in the last chapter, ie the confusion in definition. We seek to clear up some of the confusion about the term by categorizing coaching as:

- performance,
- engagement, or
- developmental,

depending on:

- the purpose,
- the process or method used, and
- the learning outcome,

which is implied in each definition.

We explore what is meant by coaching in each quadrant and how it is currently practised. We also consider how coaching may be understood in different cultures. Although we recognize the necessity for performance coaching and the need for engagement coaching, our preference and most of our professional work involves developmental coaching in one form or another.

The dictionary definitions of coaching include the terms instructor, teacher, trainer, giving instructions, as well as professional adviser. A typical internet site suggests that 'the name allegedly recalls the multi-tasking skills associated with controlling the team of a horse-drawn stagecoach' (Wikipedia, 2005). US college sports teams have always had their own coaches and, more recently, coaches emerged who were non-experts in the specific technical skills of their clients, but who nevertheless ventured to offer inspiration to their clients. Current practice in performance coaching focuses on non-directive questioning and helping clients to analyse and address their own challenges rather than offering advice or direction.

The International Coach Federation defines coaching as:

> partnering with clients in a thought-provoking and creative process that inspires them to maximize their personal and professional potential.

The EMCC/ICF joint definition of coaching offers:

> 'coaching is facilitating the client's learning process by using professional methods and techniques to help the client to improve what is obstructive and nurture what is effective, in order to reach the client's goals.'
>
> Coaching can also be described as: 'Coaching is partnering with clients in a thought-provoking and creative process that inspires them to maximize their personal and professional potential.'

However, the UK's Chartered Institute of Personnel and Development (CIPD) factsheet includes job performance and defines coaching as 'developing a person's skills and knowledge so that their job performance improves, hopefully leading to the achievement of organizational objectives' (CIPD, 2010b).

This definition is remarkably similar to the statement in the performance management survey carried out by the CIPD where performance management is defined as 'about helping people to understand how they contribute to the goals of organizations and ensuring that the right skills and effort are focused on the things that really matter to the organization and will make an impact on organizational performance' (CIPD, 2011b).

Coaching by line managers or external practitioners is believed by organizations to be one of the most effective methods of supporting learning and development, and this trend continues (CIPD, 2011a). For this purpose line managers may be offered coaching training.

A typical question when line managers are offered coaching training is 'Why do coaching? Can't we just tell them what to do?' That is certainly an optional approach to learning, and teaching or telling is included in the dictionary definition of coaching so managers naturally ask this question. The idea of non-directive coaching may not be attractive to a busy manager. Let's take a simple example of learning how to make tea.

Table 5.1 shows how much we remember as learners.

TABLE 5.1   How much we remember as learners

20%	Of what we read	It's on the packet
30%	Of what we hear	Being told to do it
40%	Of what we see	Shown how to do it
50%	Of what we say	Saying you'll do it
60%	Of what we do	Doing it
90%	Of what we see, hear, say and do	All of the above

SOURCE: Rose and Nicholl (1997: 142)

The telling approach has low levels of immediate recall about fact or skill and this does not improve over time (see Table 5.2). Even being shown the skill does not improve recall. The combination of being shown, being told, talking about it and actually doing it improves the situation dramatically.

TABLE 5.2   Learner recall

	Told	Told and shown	Told, shown and experienced
Recall after 3 weeks	70%	72%	85%
Recall after 3 months	10%	32%	65%

SOURCE: Whitmore (1996: 18)

Clearly, being told or shown does not enable learning in terms of recall, and Whitmore (1996) recommends actually doing the activity in question. So effective coaching will need to do more than tell and show. At this point it would be useful to identify what sort of learning is being sought here. Is the desired learning the sort that is memorable or recallable? What learning outcome is intended with coaching? Improvement or transformation? We recall the four coaching approaches under examination in this book:

- performance coaching, where the intended learning outcome is single loop or improvement and the methods may be directive and advice driven;
- engagement coaching, where the intended learning outcome is also single loop or improvement but the method is humanistic and relationship driven;
- developmental coaching, where the intended learning outcome is double loop or transformation and the method is humanistic and relationship driven;
- systemic programmes of coaching, which aim to transform the organization.

With this in mind, we can identify how the available definitions reveal their purpose, the process involved, and the desired learning outcome. How do the available definitions of coaching fit into these approaches? The answer will depend on whose purpose is being served and we discuss below the purpose of coaching for an organization and for an individual, including the intended learning outcome.

Performance coaching

With factual learning, which can be recalled at will and when it directly relates to the organization's purpose, a teaching approach is sufficient, with instructing and training as the process with the learning outcome single loop, a classic case of learning for improvement (Brockbank, McGill and Beech, 2002). For many practitioners this would not be considered coaching at all, but we include it as we have recent experience of such programmes in organizations. We have identified this as performance coaching, as there is an objective goal to be achieved, with little or no exploration of the client's personal world. The approach may be part of performance management and the relationship is often a line relationship.

Coaching programmes in organizations which aim to support staff to achieve a minimal qualification or competence level are performance programmes in that their purpose is an increase in qualified staff, the process is directive and rather like teaching, and the learning outcome is improvement. Michael Carroll (2004) refers to such coaches as first generation coaches and they are represented by the statement 'I have been there – I can help you get there'.

Here the earlier dictionary definition of teaching, tutoring, instructing is valid as the purpose is transfer of factual material. The first generation coach is the expert who can advise others and give direction to the client. As Gore Vidal said, 'there is no human problem which could not be solved if people would simply do as I advise' (cited in Carroll, 2004). So the purpose is transmission, the process is teaching or telling and the learning outcome is single loop and limited to improvement.

Thus the purpose of coaching is declared in general terms but the all-important ownership of that purpose is often unstated. For instance, many define coaching as a process to improve performance, develop skills and maximize potential. A coach is someone who 'works with the learner to help them achieve goals, solve problems, learn and develop' (Caplan, 2003 cited in Hawkins and Smith, 2006: 21) – this without clarifying whose goals.

McLeod declares that coaching is: 'the use of silence, questions and challenge to assist a coachee toward a defined work-based target' (McLeod, 2003: 9), but whose target?

The process has been described as follows:

> a structured two-way process in which individuals develop skills and achieve defined competencies through assessment, guided practical experience, and regular feedback. (Parsloe, 1995: 1)

We are not told who defines the competences here.

There is an implicit assumption that these are organizational goals, targets and competences, and that they are one and the same as those of the employee being coached.

Peltier (2001) recommends that the manager-as-coach should observe and assess their staff, and offer feedback and guidance as well as potential reward in order to effect behavioural modification through reinforcement. Despite the negative connotations of the method, it is useful for measuring and evaluating the coaching process. The benefits of observation/assessment/feedback, in combination with a recognition of the cognitive elements in staff behaviours, can lead to coaching which is problem solving and solution focused, and this meets the aims of performance management. Problems arise where staff have expectations of coaching which go beyond these and expect personal, even emotional support in their endeavours. We recommend that these points are clarified by managers, so that there is clarity of intent, agreement about process and realistic expectations about outcomes.

We note that coaching initiatives which are performance in intent may be presented differently, with the performance intent under-emphasized, when resistance is likely or there is tension between organizational goals and individual goals. Such coaching we term engagement coaching.

Engagement coaching

When there is a desire in the organization to improve performance in an unpopular activity, a teaching or telling approach is unlikely to be successful, which is why humanistic approaches have been popularized. Colley's work informs us here as she highlighted how such approaches are used to mask the performance agenda at work (Colley, 2003). Engagement coaching seeks to persuade the client to adopt the learning objectives of the organization or system. The method is used for downsizing, culture change and restructuring programmes where the coaching purpose is not owned by the individual and there is likely to be resistance to change. No wonder such coaching is described as an 'art': 'coaching is the art of facilitating the performance, learning and development of another' (Downey, 2002: 15).

What is missing from the definition is the desired learning outcome. In engagement coaching the hidden agenda is improved performance by persuading staff to adapt to their surroundings and adjust their behaviour in line with organizational objectives.

The engagement coaching approach is a process which recognizes the value of relationship in learning and change. The method has been described as participative (Quinn, 2000: 14), as the coach invites the client to explore a limited range of potential choices within their subjective world.

Engagement coaching includes Carroll's second generation coach who is characterized by the statement 'I may or may not have been there – I create the learning environment' (Carroll, 2004). Here the coach has begun to step away from the action, and is quizzing the client about their learning needs.

Modern sports coaches work away from the pitch rather than on it. The participative strategy commits to a 'win–win' outcome and is equivalent to the sports analogy, a favourite in the literature (Whitmore, 1996; Gallwey, 1974; Parsloe and Wray, 2000). The purpose is established in advance, by the team's trainer, even if the goals are shared. So the purpose is improvement, the process is humanistic and the learning outcome is single loop. The ultimate purpose here is engagement with the organization's mission, rather than individual transformation, and hence we identify such coaching as engagement coaching.

Coaching in the engagement quadrant is usually carried out by line managers, often within a performance management framework. Coaching then becomes part of the line manager's duty to develop their human resources in a way that leads to competitive success (Warren, 2005; Clutterbuck and Megginson, 2005). The nurturing and non-directive element calls for the skill of empathy and many managers have difficulty with empathy – we discuss this in Chapter 8. The recent coaching guide published by the CIPD notes that line managers are most likely to deliver coaching, and includes among the core characteristics of non-executive coaching:

short term;

individual and organizational goals;

time-bounded;

provides feedback;

non-directive. (Jarvis, 2004: 17)

We note here the item 'individual and organizational goals' as if they are the same. The tension between individual and organizational goals because of the legal rights of proprietors in preference to those of employees, in private-sector organizations, has been noted by Coopey (1995), and the nature of engagement coaching where the organizational goals are promoted using humanistic methods resolves some of that tension. However, the manager's dilemma remains, as they are asked to direct performance towards organizational goals while being non-directive.

The non-directive style of engagement coaching is evident in this fuller description, where both purpose and process are declared:

> Coaching is unlocking a person's potential to maximize their own performance. It is helping them to learn rather than teaching them. (Whitmore, 1996: 8)

For many business practitioners the concept of non-directive coaching has been described as a myth, through either lack of time or lack of skills.

Engagement coaching focuses on specific skills and behaviours which serve to progress the objectives of the organization. Some of these may coincide with the personal goals of the individuals concerned. The engagement coach aims to align these individual goals with those of the organization, and the crucial extra skill used here is empathy. This builds trust and connection, supports the development of particular abilities and encourages their use, rather than creating a performance system of command and control.

What is the recommended approach for engagement coaching?

The humanistic approach utilized by non-directive coaches is almost always based on the ideas of Carl Rogers. His name, however, is notably absent from the coaching literature and coaches may not even be aware that they are using his core conditions in their work. In spite of his rigorous research into personal change and learning, he is seen as being a 'touchy-feely' therapist, out of touch with the hard realities of business. The so-called 'soft skills' needed for this approach, particularly empathy, are not much in evidence, although they are known to be associated with individual and organizational learning and improvement (Cooper, 1997).

We draw on the work of Rogers to identify the necessary and sufficient conditions for enabling learning, which can be applied to the engagement context, the coach and the individual concerned (Rogers, 1983).

1 Learning is affected by the *context* in which it occurs, ie the vision and values of a company or organization will influence the learning process.

2 Learning is affected by the *stance* of the individual learner and their dispositions.

3 Learning is affected by the *stance of those* who seek to facilitate learning, *their* dispositions.

1 The context affects learning, so mission statements reveal the value that an organization places on learning and development. In practice, the organization can prescribe learning as performance by limiting coaching to identified improvements or offer a broader canvas through executive coaching.

2 The stance of the individual affects their learning. Where there is a history of fear and mistrust, learning is unlikely to happen (this is all too common in the workplace). Where the individual is unwilling to take risks, their development is unlikely to be transformation, whereas openness and disclosure will enable the paradigm shift described in Chapter 2.

3 The stance of the coach as a facilitator of learning has been researched by learning theorists. For deep, holistic and intrinsic learning which results in worthwhile and significant change, a humanistic, person-centred approach is recommended (see Brockbank and McGill, 1998, 2007).

Rogers (1983) offered some principles of learning which guide the potential coach:

- Human beings have a *natural potentiality* for learning, a natural curiosity and they also experience the ambivalence associated with the accompanying pain of any significant learning.
- People learn when the subject has *relevance* and meaning for them. More relevance also affects speed of learning.
- Learning which involves change in *self-perception* is threatening and tends to be resisted. Such learning is more easily achieved when external threats are minimized.
- Significant learning is achieved by doing and action. Learning is *facilitated* when the learner participates in the learning process.
- *Self-initiated* learning which involves the whole person, feelings as well as intellect, is most lasting and pervasive.
- Independence, creativity and self-reliance are facilitated when *self-evaluation* is primary and evaluation by others is secondary.
- The most useful learning in the modern world is learning about the *process* of learning itself. (Brockbank *et al*, 2002)

Rogers (1983) insists that the key to effective learning is the relationship between the coach as facilitator of learning and their client as 'the facilitation of significant learning rests upon... qualities that exist in the personal relationship between the facilitator *(ie the coach)* and learner' (Rogers, 1983: 121, our italics).

What are these qualities?

- Acceptance and trust of the learner, ie a belief that the other person is fundamentally trustworthy, and this means living with uncertainty as they might make a mistake.
- Congruence, ie self-disclosure, a willingness to be a person rather than a role, to be and live the feelings and thoughts of the moment.
- Empathic understanding of the learner's world, and this must be communicated (silent or invisible empathy isn't much use).

We discuss these qualities in more detail in Chapter 10. When a coach holds such attitudes and qualities, they revolutionize learning: 'giving freedom and life and the opportunity to learn' (Rogers, 1983: 133), although Rogers recognizes the difficulties here:

> the person-centred way... is something that one grows into. It is a set of values, not easy to achieve, placing emphasis on the dignity of the individual, the importance of personal choice, the significance of responsibility, the joy of creativity. It is a philosophy, built on the foundation of the democratic way, empowering each individual. (Rogers, 1983: 95)

The primacy of a person-centred approach in any coaching which recognizes the subjective world of the client is confirmed by a useful statement of criteria for coaching given by Flaherty: 'coaching must allow for people to change, to become more competent, and to become excellent at performance' (1999: 21). Hence approaches which suggest that people have fixed attributes deriving from personality tests or learning styles would make engagement coaching impossible.

So how do ideas about coaching use Rogers' principles?

Jonathan Passmore in his industry guide, targeted primarily at coaches in the workplace, defines coaching as:

> A collaborative, solution-focused, results-oriented and systematic process in which the coach facilitates the enhancement of work performance, life experience, self-directed learning and personal growth of the coachee.
>
> (Passmore, 2010: 10 citing Grant, 1999)

Here we have every aspect of coaching being served at once: a performance approach for improved performance, a collaborative approach for engagement, and a developmental approach for personal growth. For line managers or internal coaches this is a 'tall order' (Brown and Hirsch, 2011), as 'organizational sponsors have their own views about what needs to be delivered from coaching' (Passmore, 2010: 2).

Julie Starr emphasizes that coaching at work seeks engagement by describing it as a conversation:

> The coach intends to produce a conversation that will benefit the other person using 'listening, questions and reflection'. (Starr, 2008: 5)

We argue in Chapter 2 that truly significant and transformative learning demands that there is client ownership of goals, and the process is again characterized by a humanistic stance which recognizes both the subjective world of the learner and the social context. We have called this developmental coaching, to which we now turn.

Developmental coaching

Developmental coaching works with clients to define their own goals, while offering the potential for challenge and transformation through high levels of empathy. A developmental coach may work at all levels, from improvement through engagement to transformation.

Carroll (2004) identifies such a coach as third generation: 'Professional facilitators of learning at different levels'. Coaching becomes developmental when the relationship supports trust, the focus is decided by the client, who becomes responsible for their own learning and development, and the process, through empathy, recognizes the client's world, and leads to potential transformation.

The learning may include factual material, and improving performance, as for performance or engagement, as above, but the characteristic of the developmental coach is their ability to support the client through double loop learning to transformation. A developmental coach is able, when and where appropriate, to adopt the processes of performance and engagement coaching as part of their approach. However, the developmental purpose is personal and professional development, promoting the client's own desires; the developmental process is humanistic; and the learning outcome is transformation.

Developmental coaching can last a lifetime: 'Coaching is a powerful alliance designed to forward and enhance the lifelong process of human learning, effectiveness, and fulfilment' (Whitworth *et al*, 1998: 202).

A very clear statement of the principles of developmental coaching is given by Jenny Rogers (2004), who offers six principles which follow the humanistic philosophy almost exactly and echo the core conditions of Carl Rogers as follows:

- The client is resourceful.
- The coach's role is to spring loose the client's resourcefulness.
- Coaching addresses the whole person – past, present and future.
- The client sets the agenda.
- The coach and client are equals.
- Coaching is about change and action. (Rogers, 2004: 7–8)

Indeed at its most effective:

> Coaching is an art in the sense that when practised with excellence, there is no attention on the technique but instead the coach is fully engaged with the coachee and the process of coaching becomes a dance between two people moving in harmony and partnership. (Downey, 1999)

One crucial component of coaching which is developmental is the ability of the coach to conduct a reflective dialogue with their client as this offers the potential for double loop learning and transformation. The key element here is the degree of empathy that is present. We discuss the conditions for reflective dialogue in Chapter 3 and we discuss the skills needed in the developmental quadrant in Chapter 10.

Peltier (2001) confirms that executive coaching uses Rogerian principles without necessarily recognizing them, emphasizing the importance of relationship and the core conditions given above. Where it is accepted that unconscious factors influence behaviour, as established recently (Cramer, 2000), the developmental coach is able to consider the effect on his or her client's learning of defence mechanisms, without, of course, pathologizing them. Such an approach to coaching includes recognition of anxiety and defensiveness, and the toleration of conflict, while promoting choice and authenticity for the client.

The systemic quadrant

Where the organization is able to offer coaching to staff in order to promote their own development and this is believed by both parties to be for the benefit of the organization, then developmental coaching may happen. However, the usual coach-and-line-manager arrangement is unlikely to promote developmental coaching because the relationship is hierarchical, and the client may not disclose what their development needs are within a power relationship with their senior who can 'hire and fire'. For developmental work the coach will need to be outside the remit of the line, and ideally outside the organization itself, and these are often known as executive coaches. The risk for the organization is that support is being provided without control, so that executive coaching may prepare a client to leave the organization rather than benefiting it.

Further risks in executive coaching have been identified by Berglas (2002) and Williams and Irving (2001). For CEOs, executive coaching offers quick and easy solutions, with 24 per cent listing external coaching as one of the most effective methods of development for their people (CIPD, 2011a). However, Berglas believes that 'in an alarming number of situations, executive coaches who lack rigorous psychological training do more harm than good' (2002: 87). He mentions the propensity for 'unschooled' coaches to exploit the powerful hold they develop over their clients. Indeed, the practice of executive coaching has been described as 'an unregulated, unstructured and (potentially) unethical process' (Williams and Irving, 2001). Typically, practitioners with a business background focus on the business context and may be unaware of the psychological state of their client. Alternatively, coaches with a background in psychology tend to focus on the inner life of their client and forget the business context. The consequence of such unbalanced work is not likely to be beneficial to the client or sponsor. We discuss the guidelines for regulated coaches in Chapter 13.

Can an organization transform itself? A coaching strategy which aims for a critical mass of developed employees is likely to lead to systemic change and organizational transformation. Indeed, the ICF recognize the impact that a coaching programme may have on the bigger picture, be it the organization or society itself.

The ICF defines coaching as:

> partnering with clients in a thought-provoking and creative process that inspires them to maximize their personal and professional potential. ICF envisions a future in which coaching will be an integral part of society and ICF members will represent the highest quality in professional coaching.
> (**http://www.coachfederation.org/about-icf/overview/**, accessed July 2011)

This definition, providing that the client generates their own goals, conforms to developmental coaching, with implications for the systemic quadrant. The ICF competences include many developmental skills, which include systemic awareness.

Surface and deep structures

A particular idea based on the work of Noam Chomsky, which is useful for all levels of coaching, is the idea of deep structures and surface structures in language. Surface words and sentences are incomplete or distorted versions of deep but un-articulated statements, and the coach may offer their client the opportunity to recover the deep structure in order to communicate more effectively. An example is given below:

Surface structure	'It's not fair – nobody ever tells me anything'
Deep structure	'I have not been informed about the work rota'
	'X has not informed me'
	'This happened last month'
	'I feel unjustly treated'
Coach question and empathy	Can you tell me who 'nobody' is?
	What does ever mean?
	It feels unfair to you

We discuss surface and deep structures in Chapters 8 and 10.

Transcultural issues in coaching

Coaching across cultures, global coaching, has been described as a more creative form of coaching because it 'challenges your cultural assumptions and propels you beyond your previous limitations to discover creative solutions that lie outside the box' (Rosinski, 2003: xix). Traditional coaching can fall into the trap of ethnocentrism, ie the assumption that one's own culture is a true representation of reality. Coaching in an ethno-relative way, on the other hand, recognizes and accepts difference, adapts and integrates by accepting different frames of reference simultaneously and moving outside the coach's comfort zone (Rosinski, 2003: 30). Using a cultural orientations framework, Rosinski offers global coaches a model for practice which attends to six dimensions:

- Sense of *power and responsibility*, which can be based on control, harmony or humility.

- *Time management*, which can be based on an idea of time as scarce or plentiful; one at a time or multi-task; and focus on the past, the present or the future.

- *Identity and purpose*, an important dimension which can be individualistic or collectivist; and focused on being or doing.

- *Territories* or boundaries can be either protective or shared.
- *Organizational arrangements*, which encompass hierarchy or equality; universalist or particularist; seek for stability or change; and is competitive or collaborative in style.
- *Communication patterns*, which may be formal or informal; affective or emotionally neutral; direct or indirect; and be coded or explicit.
- *Modes of thinking*, which may be deductive or inductive and analytic or systemic.

Perusing these dimensions brings into question some of the coaching definitions given above, as they may appear unilaterally Eurocentric or Western in their approach. In addition, there is the glaring absence of gender issues, with some rather masculine concepts in evidence. The role of emotion in cultural matters is also invisible in this framework and is more evident in Barna's list of barriers below.

Global coaching is defined as 'the art of facilitating the unleashing of people's potential to reach meaningful, important objectives' (Rosinski, 2003: 4), which neatly sidesteps the issues of whose purpose or objective is met by the coaching, whose potential is in question, and how 'meaningful' and 'important' are to be understood. Without such information the intended learning outcome remains a mystery.

Where coaching is an intercultural encounter, there are likely to be barriers to effective communication between coach and client. The coach carries responsibility for ensuring that these barriers are minimized and may like to take the online Implicit Association Test (IAT), which measures your instinctive responses to images of persons of colour, available at **www.understandingprejudice.org.lat**.

Barna (1997) has identified six cultural barriers and we list them below:

- Anxiety due to feeling like a stranger or outsider in a different culture.
- Assuming similarity instead of difference.
- Ethnocentrism – negatively judging aspects of another culture by the standards of one's own.
- Stereotypes and prejudice – judgements made about others on the basis of their ethnic or gender membership.
- Non-verbal misinterpretations as non-verbal expressions vary from culture to culture and can easily be misunderstood.
- Language – the Sapir–Whorf hypothesis that culture is controlled by *and* controls language. (Barna, 1997: 50)

We add here some DO's and DON'T's in transcultural communication, based on work from the Tavistock intercultural centre in London, for coaches who may find themselves giving offence without meaning to, and perhaps not realizing what has given the offence:

Do	Don't
Do be aware that in some communities it may not be the custom to shake hands, especially a woman.	Don't underestimate the influence of your own cultural background in your perceptions and the way you behave.
Do avoid use of racial and ethnic terms like 'coloured', 'Afro-Caribbean' and 'half caste' as they are liable to give offence. Alternatives may include 'black' 'African-Caribbean' and 'mixed race'.	Don't ask someone what their 'Christian' name or 'surname' is but do ask what their 'personal' or 'family' name is.
Do appreciate how cultural differences in body language can cause misunderstanding and conflicts, eg touching, putting an arm around someone may cause offence.	Don't assume that breaking eye contact is a sign of dishonesty or disrespect. In some communities it may be the opposite.
Do be sensitive to using terms of endearment that may cause offence to some individuals from minority ethnic communities, eg 'love' or 'dear'.	Don't assume that when members of an ethnic minority raise their voices they are losing control or becoming aggressive.

For additional discussion about difference we refer the reader to our discussion of diversity in Chapter 12.

Chapter summary

We have clarified that performance coaching has its place, but sponsors, managers and employees should be made aware of its limitations. We have categorized engagement coaching as often performance coaching in disguise, using a humanistic approach with empathy to achieve a 'don't rock the boat' purpose. Again we recommend that such programmes come clean about their intended outcomes in order to minimize disappointment. Executive coaching is identified as developmental, with a clearly defined transformation purpose using humanistic person-centred methods based on the work of Carl Rogers. We recommend that clients or contractors ensure that coaches are properly trained and accredited if possible and we discuss these matters in Chapter 12.

In addition, practitioners who emphasize a solution-focused method may consider that: 'since emotion is the key element of motivation, any coaching method that misses emotions ... is flawed' (McLeod, 2003: 9).

Hence our insistence that, while performance coaching may underplay emotions, engagement coaching requires at least a minimal degree of empathy, while developmental coaching demands high levels of empathic skill to produce the learning outcome we call transformation. Where high degrees of empathy are present, coaching is capable of transcending cultural difference, and some guidance in transcultural issues completed this chapter.

06 Mentoring models

Existing and well-tried mentoring models can be used for work in performance, engagement and development situations. A model provides structure to enable coaches and mentors to conduct individual sessions and to structure a series of sessions. The NEWW model included in this chapter shows how to structure a session, together with guidance for new mentors.

Traditional mentoring models conform to the definitions of mentoring for development which we described in Chapter 4. For developmental mentoring there are many models available, starting with Kathy Kram in the 1980s. Traditional developmental mentoring models map against the passage of time and chart changes or stages in the relationship from its beginning to its end, but tend to be silent on how to structure each session.

The developmental models summarized in the chapter are those by Kathy Kram, John Carruthers, David Clutterbuck, David Megginson, Lois Zachary and Julie Hay. We also mention the Torbert model of leadership, and Watkins' First 90 Days for transition mentoring. We include a brief account of writings about unconscious elements in mentoring relationships.

Definitions of mentoring given in Chapter 4 by the ICF and the UK's CIPD tend towards transmission and advice, being suitable for induction or improvement purposes in the performance and engagement quadrants. The six mentoring functions provided by Norman Cohen have been found to work well here as well as our own NEWW model.

Kathy Kram

Kathy Kram conducted research in a US business context and identified four phases in developmental mentoring which replicated the stages found by Levinson *et al* 20 years before. The phases of a mentoring relationship were identified as: initiation, cultivation, separation and redefinition (Kram, 1988; Levinson *et al*, 1978). We show these phases in Figure 6.1.

FIGURE 6.1   Kram's stages of the mentoring relationship

Phase	Definition	Turning points*
Initiation	A period of six months to a year when the relationship begins and becomes important to both managers.	– Fantasies become concrete expectations. – Expectations are met; senior manager provides coaching, challenging work, visibility; junior manager provides technical assistance, respect and desire to be coached. – There are opportunities for interaction around work tasks.
Cultivation	A period of two to five years when the maximum range of career and psychosocial functions are provided.	– Both individuals continue to benefit from the relationship. – Opportunities for meaningful and more frequent interaction increase. – Emotional bond deepens and intimacy increases.
Separation	A period of six months to two years after a significant change in the structural role relationship and/or in the emotional experience of the relationship.	– Junior manager no longer wants guidance but rather the opportunity to work more autonomously. – Senior manager faces midlife crisis and is less available to provide mentoring functions. – Job rotation or promotion limits opportunities for continued interaction; career and psychosocial functions can no longer be provided. – Blocked opportunity creates resentment and hostility that disrupt positive interaction.
Redefinition	An indefinite period after the separation phase when the relationship ends or takes on significantly different characteristics, making it a more peerlike friendship.	– Stresses of separation diminish, and new relationships are formed. – The mentor relationship is no longer needed in its previous form. – Resentment and anger diminish; gratitude and appreciation increase. – Peer status is achieved.

*examples of the most frequently observed psychological and organizational factors that cause movement into the current phase
SOURCE: Kram (1988: 49)

The phases cover:

- initiation – the start-up;
- cultivation as the mentor uses all the career and psychosocial functions described in Chapter 4;
- the separation phase as the relationship alters because of changes in one or both mentor and protégé or the organizational context forces a change;
- redefinition when the relationship ends or is defined in a new and different way.

The idea of phases suggests that mentor relationships end eventually, although many mentoring stories talk of lifelong relationships and the redefinition phase defines a different relationship. The chosen model for mentoring will need to take phases into account.

The phases in mentoring have been compared to the stages in a person's life (Levinson *et al*, 1978). If we relate these to the stages of life, initiation is the stage where we are helpless and vulnerable, so mentoring needs to support the fledgling nature of client learning. Cultivation is the 'getting to know you' stage of childhood where congruence and honesty will nurture a robust relationship for learning. Separation is the inevitable stage of moving away to independence, so painful for parents, but essential for growing up. This may take the form of the client taking more responsibility and being proactive in the relationship, while the mentor needs to take a back seat. This can be a tricky time for mentors in senior positions who feel 'cast off' by their client, but acceptance of the inevitable leads to a healthy redefinition where both parties respect each other as equals in terms of learning outcomes. Most models ignore the unconscious processes and intimacy which occur in a mentoring relationship, and our recommended model addresses these invisible but powerful factors in mentoring couples.

John Carruthers

Carruthers' developmental mentoring model shows the stages through which both mentor and client pass, as the mentor's influence wanes and the protégé's personal power increases (see Carruthers, 1993), with the power balance moving gradually from the mentor to become wholly with an autonomous protégé:

$$M \to \to Mp \to \to MP \to \to mP \to \to P$$ (Carruthers, 1993: 21)

Key:

M = mentor has most influence
p = protégé dependent
m = mentor influence wanes
P = protégé going through stages to self-confidence and autonomy

FIGURE 6.2   Kubler-Ross change curve

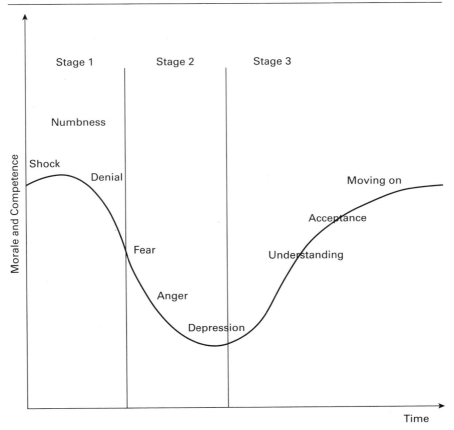

SOURCE: Kubler-Ross (1991)

Carruthers identifies these stages in the mentoring relationship as:

M: Formal, where a protégé is dependent on the mentor's guidance.

Mp: Cautious, where a protégé is likely to begin to feel confident in completing tasks with the support of M.

MP: Sharing, where the protégé's opinion is respected as much as the mentor's.

mP: Open, where both recognize the expertise of the other and this is openly acknowledged.

P: Beyond where the relationship evolves into a friendship of equals.
(Carruthers, 1993: 82)

The transition curve based on the grief stages pioneered by the psychologist Elisabeth Kubler-Ross (Figure 6.2) reflects Carruthers' model as the protégé

FIGURE 6.3 Dimensions of mentoring

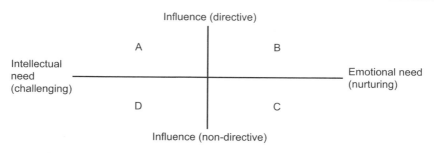

SOURCE: Clutterbuck (1998: 8)

moves from denial and resistance; an 'unlearning' of old habits and facing up to the prospect of changing them; through a middle stage where the protégé is experimenting and is likely to feel confused; to the incorporation stage where the protégé is confidently taking on new ways of working. The original model included a bargaining stage.

David Clutterbuck and David Megginson

David Clutterbuck's model (1998) draws on two dimensions, the directive/non-directive axis and the need axis, which runs from intellectual to emotional, a truly Cartesian measure, separating as it does the mind from the body (Ryle, 1983). Within Figure 6.3 four sectors correspond to four roles in assisting learning: the coach in sector A, the guardian in sector B, the counsellor in sector C and the facilitator in sector D. The European model of mentoring draws on all four of these roles, giving a rich picture of the developmental alliance he recommends for mentoring. Clutterbuck suggests that the most effective developmental mentors will be able to adopt whatever role is necessary, using coaching and counselling behaviours when needed, and alerts practitioners to the spectrum of directiveness in the guardian role and the role of broker to expand the client's network.

In addition to the dimensions described above, Clutterbuck's model presents the stages of mentoring as:

Rapport building

Direction setting

Progress making

Maturation

Close down.

The stages are shown in Figure 6.4 alongside the intensity of learning at each stage.

FIGURE 6.4 Evolution or phases of the mentoring relationship

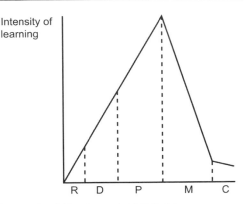

SOURCE: Clutterbuck (1998: 95) and Megginson *et al* (2005: 20)

The relationship begins with rapport building and low learning intensity, moving towards direction setting and progress making with high learning intensity. As the client becomes self-reliant the mature relationship moves towards its close, with reduced learning intensity.

David Megginson was one of the first researchers in the UK to examine mentoring in business and, together with David Clutterbuck, has championed developmental mentoring in the UK. Their definition of mentoring as 'offline help by one person to another in making significant transitions in knowledge work or thinking' (Clutterbuck and Megginson, 1999: 3) emphasized the role of mentoring in career progression. They have focused increasingly on mentoring behaviours for senior personnel in organizations as well as the mentoring process model, a combination model for developmental mentoring (Clutterbuck and Megginson, 1999) shown in Figure 6.5.

The techniques recommended by Clutterbuck and Megginson emphasize the importance of a client's ownership of goals (Megginson and Clutterbuck, 2005) and the whole person development which includes high levels of empathy (Megginson and Clutterbuck, 2009), putting their models into the developmental quadrant.

Lois Zachary

Lois Zachary (2000) offers another phase model with four stages:

- Preparing: the pair explore personal motivation and expectations.
- Negotiating: the pair agree on learning goals, the content, the process, a shared understanding of when and how as well as accountability and closure, a rather neglected area in training.
- Enabling: this is the longest phase where nurturing occurs and the mentor's job is to create an open learning climate.
- Closing: this is where the pair evaluate and celebrate.

FIGURE 6.5   A process model of executive mentoring processes

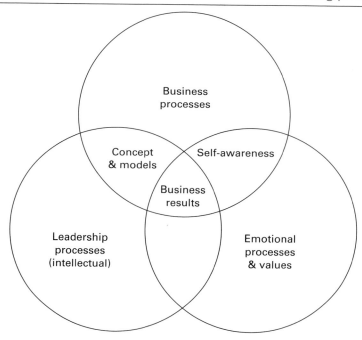

SOURCE: Clutterbuck and Megginson (1999: 22)

The model is suitable for both engagement and developmental purposes. She offers the phases as signposts to help mentors to keep on course, although time is a concern in each phase and she recommends that in the preparing phase time expectations are discussed. Modern mentoring relationships span a shorter period than traditional ones as they are usually tied to accomplishment of specific goals. This echoes the 'contract' mentoring relationship identified by Morton-Cooper and Palmer in Chapter 4.

Zachary emphasizes the nurturing nature of mentoring in the engagement quadrant and maintains that 'tending to the learning' is key because 'When learning is not tended to the mentoring process is reduced to a transaction' (Zachary, 2000: 2). This seems to differentiate between performance mentoring and engagement work. However, Zachary clearly recommends that mentoring is for development, as she analyses a mentor story in terms of developmental stages. In *Tuesdays with Morrie* (Albom, 1997) the mentoring relationship follows the four stages as Morrie and his client (Albom) journey from their initial meeting as teacher and student (preparation); agreeing how they will work together (negotiating); Albom becoming a reflective learner (enabling); and the last months of his life as Morrie moves towards his death (closing). The model includes high levels of mentor disclosure and a focus on values in Western culture, and a description of Morrie as a charismatic learner-centred teacher. The Morrie mentoring fits our description of developmental mentoring, based on the author's own account of his radical change to transformation.

Julie Hay

Julie Hay's mentoring model of seven stages emphasizes the quality of a relationship which recognizes and values the clients' world, adopts humanistic principles and, because of its person-centred approach, promotes radical change (Hay, 1995). The relationship is defined as a developmental alliance, and the model is in seven 'A' stages:

Alliance – getting to know you and establishing a contract, the all-important building of a relationship within agreed boundaries.

Assessment – a reminder of Dickens' character Fagin who 'assessed the situation'.

Analysis – a chance to see things differently and become aware of potential opportunities and problems.

Alternatives – exploring options, even silly ones, and challenging/confronting.

Action planning – what each option means and selecting.

Application – how to proceed.

Appraisal – review the actions from last session.

We would want to include a closing for each session as well as an ending for the relationship itself.

The developmental mentoring relationship has been described as intense and powerful, as befits a connection which leads to radical change and transformation. There is evidence that unconscious elements are at work when mentors choose or are chosen by protégés. We summarize the literature about this below in a brief diversion.

The unconscious in developmental mentoring

The parallel in developmental mentoring with biological phases of development and mating behaviour has been noted as well as the status and dependency implicit in the mentoring relationship (Bushardt *et al*, 1991; Auster, 1984). All relationships carry an unconscious element, the deep energy in each partner which can fuel creativity and radical change, as well as potential problems. The unconscious fantasies which each partner brings to the mentoring relationship can feed hopes and dreams as well as collusion and defensiveness.

Researchers have shown that the anxieties and defences in such situations are powerful echoes of early life experiences (Lapierre, 1989; Clarkson and Shaw, 1992). The nature of unconscious defences is discussed in full in Appendix 5. Clients in mentoring relationships may relive emotional experiences that they had with their parents as young children, and if these are painful they can lead to behaviours known as 'projective identification'. Here both parties in the relationship may defend against inner pain by projecting troublesome aspects of themselves onto the other. A typical consequence of such projection is the taking on of these aspects by the receiver, who feels and enacts them as if they were their own. Hence the projector is able to disapprove of their troublesome quality when portrayed so exactly by another (Krantz, 1989).

The parent/child analogy, noted by Levinson *et al* (1978) and others (Kates, 1985; Kahn, 1981), and psychoanalytic analyses of mentoring have concentrated on the early life stages, with all the anger and aggression this implies (Baum, 1992). The power of unconscious expectations within mentoring pairs has been explored, and findings reveal that effective mentor relationships incorporate an intensity of emotion not unlike parenting or falling in love (Phillips-Jones, 1982). Indeed, this deep version of mentoring has been described as 'a kind of love relationship' (Levinson *et al*, 1978: 100).

Rooke and Torbert: leadership

William Torbert and David Rooke developed their seven developmental stages based on research spanning 25 years with executives who were undergoing leadership transitions. They found that what differentiates leaders is not so much their personality or their style of management but their internal 'action logic', ie how they interpret their surroundings and react when their power or safety is challenged. Relatively few leaders, however, try to understand their own action logic, or have explored the possibility of changing it. Leaders who make an effort to understand their own action logic can improve their ability to lead effectively (Rooke and Torbert, 2005).

They discovered that leaders who do undertake a voyage of personal understanding and development can transform not only their own capabilities but also those of their companies. This research confirms our contention in Chapter 1 that development activity leads to systemic transformation as well as individual transformation.

The seven action logics

Their research was based on a survey tool called the Leadership Development Profile, designed to identify how they interpret their own actions and the world around them; these suggest which one of seven developmental action logics – Opportunist, Diplomat, Expert, Achiever, Individualist, Strategist or Alchemist – will characterize a leader's dominant way of thinking. Rooke and Torbert claim that leaders can move through these categories as their abilities grow, so taking the Leadership Development Profile again several years later can reveal whether a leader's action logic has evolved. However, no such results are reported.

Torbert and his colleagues have administered the survey to thousands of managers and professionals, most between the ages of 25 and 55, at hundreds

TABLE 6.1 Leaders in transition: a road map

Core challenge	Diagnostic question	Action
1. Promote yourself	Are you adopting the right mindset for your job and letting go of the past?	
2. Accelerate your learning	Are you working out what you need to learn, from whom to learn it and how to speed up your learning process?	
3. Match strategy to situation	Are you diagnosing the type of transition you are facing and the implications for what to do and what not to do?	
4. Secure early wins	Are you focusing on the vital priorities that advance long-term goals and build short-term momentum?	
5. Negotiate success	Are you building your relationship with your boss, managing expectations and marshalling the resources you need?	
6. Achieve alignment	Are you identifying and fixing frustrating misalignments of strategy, structure, systems and skills?	
7. Build your team	Are you assessing, restructuring and aligning your team to leverage what you are trying to accomplish?	
8. Create coalitions	Are you building a base of internal and external support for your initiatives so you are not pushing rocks uphill?	

SOURCE: Watkins (2003)

of US and European companies (as well as non-profits and governmental agencies) in diverse industries. What they found is that the levels of corporate and individual performance vary according to action logic. Three types of leaders associated with below-average corporate performance (Opportunists, Diplomats and Experts) accounted for 55 per cent of their sample. They were significantly less effective at implementing organizational strategies than the 30 per cent of the sample who measured as Achievers. Moreover, only the final 15 per cent of managers in the sample (Individualists, Strategists and Alchemists) showed the consistent capacity to innovate and to successfully transform their organizations (Rooke and Torbert, 2005). Mentoring which takes leaders to the higher levels of action logic can support organizational development to transformation.

Michael Watkins: The First 90 Days – transition mentoring

This ground-breaking book by Michael Watkins, *The First 90 Days* (Watkins STaRs model, 2003), offers a guide for transition mentors who are supporting leaders-in-transition. New leaders take time to be able to contribute in their role. To begin with they are taking in more value than they are giving out. The break-even point is that point where leaders give as much value as they take from their organization. Thereafter they become net contributors. The Watkins road map model is shown in Table 6.1.

We turn now to models which are primarily appropriate for engagement mentoring.

Norman Cohen

For induction mentoring the functions described by Norman Cohen have provided a useful framework for new mentors who may be senior but are unsure what the role of mentor entails. Cohen identified six functions in mentoring, reported in the context of business and government (Cohen, 1995). The six functions of mentoring are described below, together with some ideas of what to do.

The six mentoring functions and what to do

Relationship – Relationship is the key to reflective learning and essential for adult learning and development. Mentors need to use their emotional intelligence to enable rapport to be established rapidly with their protégés.

Information – Mentors need to judge how and when to offer information. Sharing expertise can be valuable but can overwhelm the protégé, so sensitivity is needed. A good rule is '**if in doubt – don't**'.

Facilitation function – Using this function the mentor enables the protégé to draw on their own resources to enable progress to be made. This function mirrors coaching.

Challenge – This includes confrontation, so that negative and positive factors can be highlighted. Any challenge is best accompanied by support in the relationship.

Mentor role – The clear definition of what the mentor role does and does not include. The mentor needs to be assertive about boundaries.

Vision – Enabling protégés to articulate their hopes and realize their ambitions by expressing their desires and intentions. We describe the functions and what to do in Table 6.2.

TABLE 6.2   The six functions and what to do

Function	Description	What to do
Relationship	Understanding and acceptance of the protégé's world, feelings and experience without judgement	Practise responsive listening Restate and summarize Ask open questions Offer empathy
Information	Fact finding about the protégé's abilities, potential, goals, opportunities and dreams. Giving information when appropriate	Ask probing questions Make restatements to ensure clarity Ask factual questions to identify current issues. Offer guidance and advice but be wary of overload
Facilitation	Support the protégé's examination of their intentions, their actions and outcomes	Ask hypothetical questions Offer support in disappointment Explore available options from *TINA to *TAANA
Challenge	Confront with care and respect inconsistencies or avoidance of commitment or responsibility	Use careful probing to ensure protégé's readiness to benefit from challenge Affirm belief in protégé's positive qualities
Mentor role	Defining the boundaries of the role Clarify with protégé your understanding of what is, and is not, mentoring, coaching and counselling Agree which activities will be part of your role	Agree boundaries with protégé, particularly time, space and confidentiality Achieve joint understanding of the difference between mentoring, coaching and counselling
Vision	Encourage protégé to pursue their dreams, to aim high and to visualize their ideal future	Ask questions about protégé's abilities and qualities Express confidence in potential for success

*TINA = There is no alternative
*TAANA = There are always numerous alternatives

This model, with its single loop emphasis, lies within the performance quadrant. However, the focus on trust and relationship edges it towards the engagement field and, while the confrontive focus leaves a door open to the developmental corner, the presence of advice leaves it indisputably as a performance perspective. The scale provides for 55 specific mentor behaviours clustered into the six categories, and Cohen provides a self-assessment questionnaire for potential mentors to rate themselves on the six principles. An adaptation of this questionnaire was used in the CILT and Intellect cases described in Chapter 9.

Brockbank and McGill

Our recommended model for engagement mentoring is the NEWW model:

NOW

EMPATHY

WHAT

WHEN

Empathy has been included in the acronym to call attention to the need for its presence in engagement work. The temptation to go straight to interrogation may place the mentoring in the performance quadrant, and we recommend that mentors make a conscious choice to offer primary empathy before questioning. The mentor first explores what is happening NOW to the protégé; offers primary EMPATHY immediately before questioning; then proceeds to WHAT the protégé desires and how it might be achieved; and finally identifies WHEN suggested actions may be carried out. We describe levels of empathy in Chapters 9 and 10.

The model may be used for one session or a series of sessions, so that early sessions work with NOW, ensuring the EMPATHY is offered, later moving on to WHAT and finally deciding on actions and WHEN they will happen. For mentoring we recommend an informal or formal agreement between mentor and protégé which establishes the nature of the relationship, the logistics of mentoring sessions and how the relationship may end. We offer a template for such an agreement in Appendix 2 and we describe how to structure a mentoring session using the NEWW model in Chapter 9.

As part of our NEWW model we recommend some Dos and Don'ts in mentoring:

DO:

- use the first meeting to establish rapport;
- define boundaries at the start;
- listen carefully and pick up key words;
- be empathic in the first meeting;

- ask open questions;
- restate and summarize;
- be caring when you confront;
- be open to off-the-wall ideas;
- record your meetings and messaging;
- be aware of equal opportunities.

DON'T:

- be afraid to assert boundaries if they are breached;
- give advice;
- tell the story of *your* life;
- ask closed questions;
- ask leading questions;
- get over-involved;
- expect your protégé to agree with you;
- put down your protégé even in fun;
- break confidentiality;
- make sexist or racist jokes;
- make promises you may not be able to keep;
- dismiss your protégé's ambitions.

We also invite new mentors to consider what difficulties might arise and recommend that they provide for them in their contracting.

Mentoring difficulties

Like all relationships, not all mentoring couples work out. Problems which might arise and possible remedies are given in Table 6.3.

For managers who have never taken on the mentoring role before, the first meeting is a hurdle and we include in our model some points to help here.

The first meeting

- Your first meeting is face-to-face, so that valuable rapport can be established, as this will facilitate the relationship thereafter.
- Your first meeting should not be rushed as your protégé will need time to talk in a relaxed way, especially if meeting you for the first time.
- During your first meeting you should try to be empathic as a basis for trust.
- During your first meeting you have the opportunity to learn about your protégé, and this can be achieved by listening, empathy and questioning.

TABLE 6.3   Problems faced by mentoring couples and possible remedies

Problem	Remedy
Not getting on	Divorce is possible – best early on
Lack of time	Reconsider the mentoring contract
Protégé rejects mentor	Mentor initiates discussion with protégé to identify relevant issues
Protégé becomes over-dependent	Mentor articulates difficulty to protégé and begins to let go
Losing sight of objectives (just chatting)	Reconsider the mentoring contract
Cloning, ie mentor wanting to develop protégé in own image	Mentor consciously focuses on protégé's agenda rather than mentor's
Breaches of confidentiality	Accept loss of trust and rebuild the relationship emphasizing trust
Mentor using protege's abilities to further own career	Protégé challenge to mentor and resolution or withdrawal
Gender issues and gossip	Careful meetings and recognition of potential problem
Inappropriate behaviour by mentor or protégé	Refer to mentoring contract.
Jealousy or competition between protégés	Mentor reassures protégé and emphasizes exclusive focus on protégé's agenda
Meeting arrangements breaking down	Mentor renegotiates with protégé
Mentor too possessive	Protégé articulates difficulty to mentor and mentor responds by backing off
Conflict of interest	Reconsider contract or divorce

- During your first meeting you will build the beginning of a good relationship if you are able to empathize and summarize what you have been told.

- The first meeting should include discussion of the protégé's development aims.

- During your first meeting you have the opportunity to talk about yourself in a way that will benefit the relationship, ie briefly.

- At your first meeting you should establish how you will contact each other, in particular whose responsibility it is to maintain contact.

- At the end of your first meeting you should have a mentoring agreement (see Appendix 2 for sample).

- At the end of your first meeting you should know when you will next meet your protégé.

Chapter summary

In this chapter we have reviewed existing mentoring models, for work in the engagement and development quadrants. Many organizations use mentoring for induction or engagement and developmental models, with their nurturing emphases, are less suitable for these purposes. Developmental models dramatically depart from the definitions of mentoring given by the ICF and the UK's CIPD, which describe mentoring as performance-related transmission. We have presented the NEWW model which may be used in the engagement quadrant, together with some guidance for new mentors.

07 Coaching models

Coaching models can be used in three quadrants: performance, engagement and developmental. A model offers practitioners a structure to work with for each session and sometimes for a cycle of sessions. Some of the models can be used in more than one quadrant, the key differences between quadrants being: ownership of objectives and degrees of empathy.

As discussed in Chapter 1, the ownership of objectives influences the type of coaching which is possible and limits the learning outcome. The use of questioning and empathy define where and in which quadrant each model is likely to be effective.

For working in the performance quadrant, questioning is the key skill and rarely, if ever, is empathy used, so for the performance quadrant we recommend GROW, OSCAR, COACH and SOS, none of which call explicitly for the use of empathy but major on questioning. Clearly a skilled coach may import empathy at any stage of the models and many do this, taking their work into the engagement or development quadrant.

For engagement coaching we recommend our own NEWW model which calls for primary-level empathy only. However, the use of empathy in engagement coaching is often limited to yet another question, 'How do you feel?', which many employees are unlikely to be able to answer (Orbach, 1994) because of the lack of emotional education in the Western world. Even if they can say how they are feeling, they might hesitate in case their feelings were going to be 'used against them'. This inhibits managers from offering empathy. For engagement coaching, questioning and empathy are equally important because of the need to connect with employees and build a trustful relationship. As the relationship is limited because of the ownership issue, the degree of empathy here is critical.

For developmental coaching we present the models which are capable of working in the emotional domain with high levels of empathy. For developmental coaching, that is, professional or executive coaching, we recommend the FLOW, JENNY ROGERS and EGAN models because they enable the client to generate their own goals as well as their own method of achieving them, using Rogerian principles throughout. Our own NEWW model may also be used for development with advanced degrees of empathy.

Performance and engagement coaching models

In this section we describe the acronym models:

- the GROW model developed by Sir John Whitmore, based on Tim Gallwey's book *The Inner Game of Tennis*;
- OSCAR, created by Karen Whittleworth and Andrew Gilbert of Worth Consulting;
- the COACH model in various forms, used for sales training and performance management as well as dedicated coaching;
- the SOS model in two modes, preview and review.

These models start with a definable goal, which may or may not be owned by the client, and proceed to methods of achieving that goal. Primacy of questioning in all performance models conforms to this focus on goals and goal setting and none of them includes an emphasis on relationship, emotion or empathy. Although trust and relationship are mentioned, there is no indication of how this is to be achieved.

The GROW model

The GROW model, developed by John Whitmore, starts from his definition of coaching as 'unlocking a person's potential to maximize their performance. It is helping them to learn rather than teaching them' (Whitmore, 1996: 8). The purpose is declared as improvement and the process as humanistic, if it includes empathy, so the model can fit into the engagement quadrant. Whitmore is clearly seeking to promote coaching using humanistic values, as he suggests that 'To use coaching successfully we have to adopt a far more optimistic view than usual of the dormant capability of people, all people', indicating a person-centred or humanistic value. To move the model into the developmental quadrant the goals would need to be generated by the client and there is access to emotional material in the coaching process.

Let us examine the method in more detail. First we unpack the acronym to reveal the meanings behind the letter GROW as follows:

G → establish the goal;
R → examine the reality;
O → consider all options;
W → confirm the will to act.

In a purely performance context the GROW model enables the coach to check out that their client agrees to the organization goals, to examine the current situation for their client, discuss possible options and finally, establish what action will be taken, when and by whom. However, Whitmore recommends that before embarking on the model proper the coach explores their client's levels of awareness and responsibility. Awareness includes self-awareness and this is described as 'recognizing when and how emotions or desires distort one's own perception' (Whitmore, 1996: 28). This definitely is not offering empathy to an employee. In addition in his exploration of responsibility, Whitmore suggests that when a client is given choice, responsibility and improved performance follow. The addition of choice moves the model at least into the engagement quadrant. To move the coaching into the developmental quadrant there would need to be total choice of objectives for the client, as is the case in executive coaching, as well as high levels of skill in the coach, particularly dealing with emotional material.

So the model can work at several levels, performance, engagement and possibly developmental, with high levels of empathy. However, the prime positioning of goal setting suggests that the subjective world of the client is less important than the organizational objectives of the coaching, making client generation of goals unlikely. In performance mode there may not even be any attempt to gain assent to the prescribed goals and this limits learning to single loop improvement. We explore how to use the model below.

Goal setting

G is for goal setting and this will differentiate performance activity from developmental. For performance or engagement coaching the client is invited or persuaded to align their personal goals with organizational objectives. For developmental coaching, clients generate their own goals. For either purpose, goal setting can be done using a choice of acronyms, SMART, MMM or RAW, and we discuss their meaning below:

SMART:

S means that the goal should be *specific* and concrete, not vague and undefined, eg 'I will have completed this 5000 word report by [a specified date]' rather than 'I must finish this report soon'.

M means that the goal should be *measurable*, even if the measure is just a presence or absence of something, eg the report is complete or it isn't.

A means that the goal is *achievable* and here the coach may help by checking out with their client how likely it is that the report can be completed by the specific date.

R means that the goal should be *realistic* and this refers to the ability of the client to achieve the goal, eg is the report within the capability of your client?

T means that the goal should be *time-bounded*, ie by the specific date given.

MMM:

M means that the goal should be *measurable*, so 'I am going to get better at using the spreadsheet' is not measurable whereas 'I will have completed a spreadsheet for the departmental budget by [specific date]' is measurable.

M means that the goal is *manageable*, so the coach checks out with their client whether the date is realistic and whether they have the skill required to complete the goal.

M means that the goal is *motivational* for the client as otherwise it is unlikely to happen. So an exploration of WIIFM? is useful here. The answer to What's In It For Me? will reveal what the client hopes to gain from achieving this particular goal. If the outcome is more unpaid overtime doing the company accounts then your client may decide that this goal is not motivational, but if the use of the spreadsheet will release their time or staff then it may well be.

RAW:

R means that the goal should be *realistic*, so the coach, after listening and restatement, uses open questions but focused to check this out with their client, eg 'You say you must complete the competency programme this year – what has to happen to do that?'

A means *achievable* and this entails further listening, restatement and questioning, eg 'How will you complete the programme in time?'

W means *worthwhile* and this may be difficult for the performance or engagement coach, as it's the client who must believe the goal to be worthwhile, not the coach. This time it's summarizing that enables the coach to check out their client's attitude, eg 'you say you *must* complete the programme – WIIFY?' (What's in it for you?) and for developmental coaches 'you don't sound too keen'.

Reality

R stands for *reality* testing and this can be done by Socratic questioning, which we discuss in detail in Chapter 10. Open questions are the key to this part of the model, so the coach uses What? Why? When? Where? Who? and, most important, How? For instance, our report-writing client above may be asked 'How will you complete a 5,000-word report in two days?' In order to be able to deploy open questions effectively the coach will need to have some knowledge about their client's situation and this means listening first, restatement for checking, and then they are in a position to offer open questions which will test the reality of the given goal. We discuss listening and restatement in Chapter 10.

Options

O stands for exploring *options* and this can be done using the key skills for performance coaching, first listen, then restate, question and summarize. For instance, with the report client above, 'You were saying that you have been given too much work: is that right?' and 'How are you going to manage the report?' and 'What other options are there?' 'Who', when and where are likely to be starters here.

Will

W stands for verifying the client's *will* to act and this is achieved by restatement and summary. In performance and engagement coaching the client may be assenting to an outcome which is outside their dispositions. For instance, a coach may summarize 'so you have agreed to do three hours overtime to deliver the 5000-word report by [date]', although the client likes to work a nine to five day. In developmental coaching the coach should ensure that the summarized outcome is within their client's dispositions and this can be ensured by the coach asking the client themselves to summarize, eg 'what have you decided to do then?' Where the coach is summarizing they might like to be aware of Clutterbuck's wonderful list of the different meanings of the answer 'yes', which we replicate below:

7	Yes	I'll dedicate myself to seeing this through
6	Yes	I'm committed to following this up
5	Yes	I'm willing to help follow that up
4	Yes	There's something in this
3	Yes	This is exciting and engaging
2	Yes	It's quite interesting
1	Yes	I'll go along with it
0	Yes	Over my dead body

SOURCE: Clutterbuck (1998: 61)

The GROW model is recommended for clients who are willing and co-operative, and is especially suited for performance or engagement coaching. The structure ensures that clients are informed about the performance purpose of the coaching programme and there is less potential for disappointment. The model may unearth a performance purpose within an engagement programme and coaches may need to deal with this outcome. However, with the addition of key factors like choice, responsibility and empathy, the model may be used for developmental purposes by executive coaches. The GROW process may be used in one session or take six months to achieve, and may be repeated for different projects.

The OSCAR model (The OSCAR Coaching Model © Worth Consulting 2002)

OSCAR is presented as a powerful mnemonic for line managers to use in performance management. It stands for Outcome, Situation, Choice and Consequences, Action and Review. The model was developed by Andrew Gilbert and Karen Whittleworth and has won wide acclaim and a National Training Award. The model builds upon and enhances the popular GROW model and is particularly useful for managers seeking to adopt a coaching style in performance management.

Here are some examples of the coaching questions they suggest for using the OSCAR model:

O – Outcome
    'What is your long-term outcome?'
    'What would success look like?'
S – Situation
    'What is the current situation?'
    'What's actually happening?'
C – Choices and Consequences
    'What choices do you have?'
    'What are the consequences of each choice?'
    'Which choice(s) will best move you towards your outcome?'
A – Actions
    'What actions will you take?'

This model is perfectly suited to the performance quadrant, with solution-focused questioning and interactions without empathy. With the addition of empathy and a skilled manager it could also be used effectively in the engagement quadrant. The upfront focus of the model on 'your outcome' implies that the objectives are owned by the coachee but the work reported by its creators suggests otherwise, so it sits in either the performance quadrant or possibly the engagement quadrant.

The COACH model

This acronym has three versions at least and probably more.

First, the opaque version from Ken Blanchard and Don Shula (Blanchard and Shula, 1995):

C = Conviction-driven (whose?)
O = Overlearning
A = Audible-ready
C = Consistency
H = Honesty-based

We can confirm that coaches trying to use this have difficulty remembering what the letters stand for, so rarely use it.

Second, the well-known sales version:

C = Commitment (whose?)
O = Observe
A = Assess
C = Communicate (at last!)
H = Help (thank goodness)

The third one of these comes from the 'How to' guide for improved performance (Webb, 2011):

C = Collaborate (good idea)
O = Own
A = Ask/knowledge
C = Communicate
H = Help

To be fair to the creators we would need to explain what each of the terms means in more detail and we refer readers to our sources.

The SOS model

We turn now to another model adapted from Parsloe and Wray (2000), designed by the authors for a corporate client, which enables the coaching pair to identify the focus of a coaching session and whether that focus lies in the past, in the future or both. The SOS model suggests that coaching should focus on:

- (S) The situation, issue, task or project.
- (O) How others feature in the situation.
- (S) How self can act to progress their issue.

Let us examine the model in more detail and explore how to use it in practice.

S stands for the situation in which the client finds themselves or the context in which the coaching is taking place, such as a client who seeks an additional qualification in her work. For the performance or engagement coach this may seem obvious as they understand the benefit of gaining the qualification. However, what they have not heard is the client's own 'take' on that situation, ie their power horizon (see Chapter 2) to which a developmental coach would attend, eg the client may be a single mother who is not able to find time to study.

O stands for others who feature or act in the client's world and these may be colleagues, staff, senior managers, family or friends. The open question starting with 'Who?' is relevant here and can be followed up by other open questions. For instance, the coach will try to focus on the client's sources of support and how colleagues and manager view her situation as well as the significance of studies in the workplace.

S stands for self and this is where the performance coach is clearly differentiated from the engagement or developmental coach. There is a temptation to identify the failings of the client, highlighting their faults or shortcomings, and this is typical performance behaviour. Engagement coaches seek to encourage their client and celebrate their attributes, while still seeking to persuade them to adopt the required dispositions. Executive coaches will seek to connect with their client, offering an empathic under-standing, thereby providing the potential for a transformational learning outcome.

In addition, the coaching may focus on the past, called REVIEW mode, or the future, called PREVIEW[1] mode. We show the options in Figure 7.1.

FIGURE 7.1   Coaching focus

Mode / Focus	S Situation	O Others	S Self
REVIEW			
PREVIEW			

Alongside the three points of focus given above, the coach will find that the discussion deals with either the past or the future, and this indicates either review coaching or preview coaching. For instance, if the client is discussing their performance in the previous week and trying to work out what went wrong, the process is review coaching, and this is important for laying the basis for the next stage, ie preview coaching. Here the process aims to prepare the client for a future event, often drawing on what has been discovered and realized in the review mode part of the coaching. Some typical questions for preview and review coaching are given below.

Review coaching questions

1 What were you trying to achieve?
2 What were the facts? What happened exactly?
3 Was the performance better than, worse than, or equal to the objective agreed?
4 What were the reasons for your level of performance?
 – clarity;
 – competence;
 – environment.
5 What is the improvement plan?

Preview coaching questions

1 What are you trying to achieve?
2 How will you know if you are successful?
3 How will you handle it?
4 What might get in the way or affect your performance?
 – clarity of objectives;
 – competences (skills knowledge behaviours);
 – environment.
5 Can we confirm your action plan now?

The SOS model is popular with managers taking on a coaching role with their staff as it is simple, easy to remember and can be used in review or preview mode. The power of the model depends (as they all do) on the skills of the coach and even SOS could be used to effect for developmental coaching.

An engagement model

The NEWW model created by Anne Brockbank and Ian McGill

This is a simplified version of Egan's skilled helper model which we describe in full below. As empathy is included explicitly the model is suitable for work in the engagement quadrant but of course may be used for development, with high levels of empathy. Empathy is included explicitly because it is absent from other models and this accounts for the disappointment and failure of so many coaching interventions. The acronym (another one!) means

NOW
EMPATHY
WHAT
WHEN

- NOW: Here listening and restatement are used to establish the current state of play for the employee. This is likely to include an exchange about objectives, and difficulties about commitment may surface here. The key skill here is resisting the desire to question and collect information. The coach will be told what they need to know.
- EMPATHY: The manager's skill in using primary empathy will assist in enabling their employee to express their negative, or indeed, positive feelings about the imposed organizational objectives. Contrary to a widespread belief in the business world, empathy does not constitute agreement but does communicate understanding and is hugely powerful in building connection and relationship in preparation for the next stage. Feelings about the coaching itself may emerge here.
- WHAT: Here questioning is used to establish what now needs to happen, who is responsible for what and then how this feels for the employee. A variety of options may be discussed and there will be an emotional charge attached to each one, which the manager's empathy will acknowledge. This stage is where agreed employee actions are distilled from a range of options or choices, each attracting an emotional reaction with a matching empathic response from the manager.
- WHEN: Questions here are focused on the actions which the employee is agreeing to take and the 'when' question is powerful in establishing a time line for performance. There may be additional 'who' or 'what' questions, but again the use of primary empathy attached to a future action will reassure the employee that they are understood, appreciated and respected.

A session using NEWW is presented in Chapter 9.

Developmental models

The Flow model

This five-stage model was developed by James Flaherty (1999) and is illustrated in Figure 7.2.

Flaherty (1999) states very clearly the criteria for coaching to occur. Coaching must allow for people to change, to become competent and to become excellent. The psychometric testing which 'fixes' people in predefined categories denies the possibility of coaching and has no place in it. We refer to this issue again below. His five stages are:

- Establish relationship.
- Recognize opening.
- Observe/assess.
- Enrol client.
- Coaching conversations.

FIGURE 7.2   The flow of coaching (Flaherty, 1999: 38)

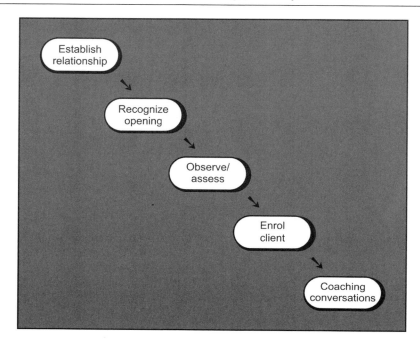

The first stage, establishing the relationship, is equivalent to a contracting stage which we discuss in Chapter 13, with the emphasis on shared commitment, mutual trust, mutual respect and freedom of expression. It has even been declared that if there is no shared commitment there can be no coaching. Where there is an existing relationship the task at this first stage is to establish how it can be used as the basis of a coaching relationship. Performance and engagement coaching may need to develop coaching relationships within historical, and not always comfortable, company relationships. Developmental coaching almost always starts from a new beginning in that the coach/client relationship can be defined by both parties from the start. Hence executive coaches discuss and agree with clients exactly how their relationship will work for the duration of the coaching project.

The second stage, recognizing openings, relates very much to performance and engagement coaching, as it is designed to find a time when the client is approachable for coaching. The idea of openings is to be ready to take advantage of a moment when the client is experiencing difficulties in performance or commitment and to offer coaching then. The temptation for managers, when their client declines coaching, is to revert to traditional management techniques of command and control. For developmental coaches the relationship supports an egalitarian connection where the idea of an 'opening' does not occur.

The third stage of observation and assessment also seems to relate very much to performance or engagement coaching and we note again here that the concepts of personality inventories and learning styles are inconsistent with coaching as they present individuals as collections of fixed properties which cannot be changed. However, the interpretation of assessment in this model aims to explore with the client their concerns, their history, their desires and their satisfactions as well as their qualities, skills and commitment to their declared goals and is clearly aimed at developmental coaching. There are three assessment models on offer, covered in detail in James Flaherty's book *Coaching: Evoking Excellence in Others*. The first, with five elements, covers the client's immediate concerns, commitments, future possibilities, history and mood. The second explores the client's domains of competence as follows: the 'I' domain or self-management; the 'we' domain or relationships with others; and the 'it' domain where the client seeks to understand technical matters, systems and mechanisms. The third assessment model identifies the necessary sources of satisfaction and effectiveness as intellect, emotion, will, context and soul. These three assessment models are coaching models in themselves, with the first taking stock and looking to the future similar to the Rogers (2004) model discussed below; the second, based on a focus on 'I', 'we' and 'them', is similar to the SOS model discussed below; and the third mirrors the Egan model, which is recommended for developmental coaching.

The fourth stage of enrolment is the moment when the client 'buys into' the coaching project, and this again has echoes of performance or engagement coaching. The necessity to 'buy in' does not arise in developmental coaching as the client generates their own objectives and the executive coaching process addresses them.

The fifth stage is coaching conversations, where Flaherty offers us three types of conversation which correspond approximately to performance, engagement and developmental coaching. An example of the trigger for the first (performance) type of conversation is 'clarifying standard for performance', which sets the scene for a dialogue aiming at improvement. The second (engagement) type of conversation takes place over time and its purpose is to address a client who is, for example 'not being open to the input of others', which suggests some overcoming of resistance, a characteristic of hidden performance objectives to which the client may not have assented. The final type of conversation is clearly developmental, being described as 'more profound, it will bring about deeper change'; and 'in most business situations there is not very much of an opening' for it (Flaherty, 1999: 107). This confirms our recommendation that developmental coaching approaches work best with external coaches.

The excellence model described above, although utilizing many valuable developmental approaches and methods, does not present itself in developmental mode, where the client holds ownership of their objectives, and seems more appropriate to performance and engagement mode, where the client is invited to align themselves with organizational or societal objectives.

Jenny Rogers' model

Jenny Rogers' model for developmental coaching, Creating Trust, Taking Stock and Choosing the Future, offers a clear process for developmental coaching and includes all the skills needed (Rogers, 2004). Her model, firmly based on the quality of the coaching relationship, draws on the Being Self and the Doing Self, and the coaching arena is where they intersect. This is shown in Figure 7.3.

FIGURE 7.3   Jenny Rogers' model of coaching

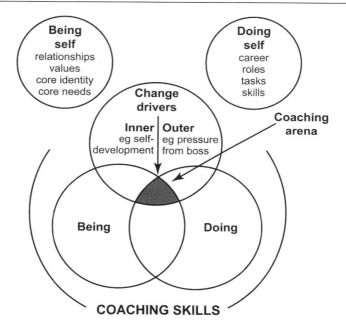

Jenny Rogers is quite clear that 'you cannot coach a client who does not want to change' (Rogers, 2004: 8), placing her approach firmly in the developmental quadrant. Her six principles are descriptive of client ownership of goals, humanistic values within a holistic approach. The principles are:

- Client is resourceful.
- Coach's role is to spring loose the client's resourcefulness.
- Coaching is holistic and addresses the whole person.
- Client sets the agenda.
- Coach and client are equals.
- Coaching is about change and action.

In addition, Rogers offers some helpful guidance on how to avoid giving advice and resisting over-disclosure by spotting the statements embedded in questions.

We move now to a well-known model for developmental coaching based on Gerard Egan's publication *The Skilled Helper.*

Egan's skilled helper model

We recommend this model for developmental coaching because it is suitable where there are generous time resources available, coach and client can take their time, and there is a clear beginning and end to the work. In particular, the model assumes that the client has freedom to choose their own objectives and work towards them in their own way, both characteristics of developmental coaching.

The model provides a structure to maintain focus and enable appropriate use of skills, including advanced empathy, challenge and confrontation. Although the structure appears linear, and tends to hold the coach in each stage until the client is ready to move to the next stage, the model can be repeated as often as necessary for emerging objectives.

The model is a three-stage one, shown in Figure 7.4.

FIGURE 7.4   The skilled helper coaching model

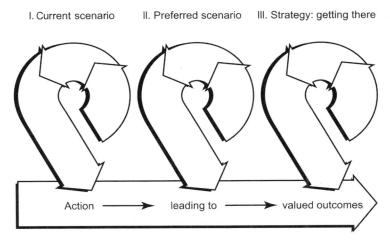

I. Current scenario   II. Preferred scenario   III. Strategy: getting there

Action ──────▶ leading to ──────▶ valued outcomes

SOURCE: Adapted from Egan (1990: 30)

The model proceeds in three stages:

1 **The Current Scenario,** where the coach helps the client to clarify the existing situation.

2 **The Preferred Scenario,** where the coach helps the client to develop goals and objectives based on an understanding of the situation.

3 Action Strategies, where the coach helps the client to develop strategies for accomplishing goals, ie getting from the current scenario to the preferred one.

Each stage has within itself three stages as follows:

1 The current scenario: Identifying and clarifying problem situations and unused opportunities

- Telling the story, as the client sees it, and this may be incoherent or told in terms of other people. The coach is challenged at once to connect with their client, offering primary and advanced empathy as described in Chapters 9 and 10, so that the client's world is unconditionally accepted and the coach is mentally noting issues that strike them as crucial.

- Recognizing unawareness, and gently easing the client, through restatement, advanced empathy and questioning, towards a more complete picture without judgement and without being directive. This process should continue throughout the model.

- The search for what will make a difference, where the coach is in Socratic questioning mode, helping their client to prioritize, and thereafter enable a focus on the chosen issue for their attention.

FIGURE 7.5   Stage 1: The current scenario

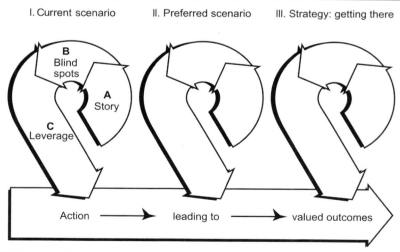

SOURCE: Adapted from Egan (1990: 36)

FIGURE 7.6   Stage 2: A preferred scenario

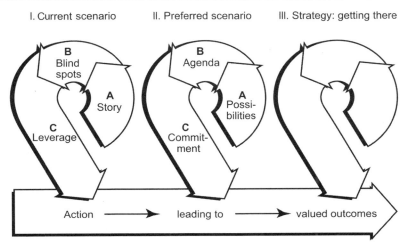

I. Current scenario   II. Preferred scenario   III. Strategy: getting there

Action ⟶ leading to ⟶ valued outcomes

SOURCE: Adapted from Egan (1990: 43)

2 Developing a preferred scenario

- Exploring a range of possibilities, and this is typically where the coach may be seduced into a linear process, following their client down one line of enquiry, without consideration of alternatives. Lateral enquiry demands that the coach stops the process, repeats the client's own words and may say 'How would having this job change your life?', possibly using 'clean language', which we describe in Chapter 10.

- Creating viable agendas, ie the coach helps their client to identify which ideas are capable of being put into action. This stage uses some of the techniques for recovering deep structures described in Chapter 10.

- Making a choice and commitment to one preferred agenda and investigating incentives, particularly if the choice is a tough one. The WIIFM? (What's in it for me?) technique is simple and useful here, as well as advanced empathy in future mode, eg 'that sounds like it could be exciting'.

3 Action strategies and plans

- Brainstorming strategies, where the coach enables their client to consider a wide range of possibilities rather than going with the first thing that comes to mind. As many strategies as possible should be considered, as even seemingly outlandish strategies, responded to with empathy, can provide clues for realistic action

FIGURE 7.7 Stage 3: Action strategies and plans

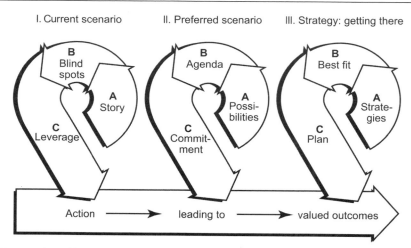

SOURCE: Adapted from Egan (1990: 48)

plans. Repeated questioning and acceptance of any ideas, however crazy, will result in a variety of strategies to choose from, and strategies are known to be more effective when chosen from a number of options.

- Choosing the best strategy, where the client finds the 'best fit' for their needs, desires and resources, with the coach using advanced empathy and challenging skills to enable their client to really find where they truly want to go.

- Turning the strategy into an action plan is the final stage of the model, where the client is enabled to formulate a plan, a step-by-step process which will achieve the desired goal. Techniques for goal setting discussed on page 121 are useful here, as an action plan includes steps and realistic timing.

Gerard Egan (1990) offers a seven-point checklist for goal setting which is right for developmental work. It addresses the client's values and the reality of their situation as well as the need for objectives to be concrete, specific, measurable etc. This seven-point checklist is replicated below with developmental examples:

Goal setting: seven points to check

1   Objectives should be stated as outcomes using the 'past participle' method. For instance, the statement 'I want to change my management style' is a description of an aim. To become a goal it needs to be phrased differently, eg 'I want to have changed my management style', the past participle being 'changed'. So goals need to be described as something that is 'acquired' or 'achieved' or 'decreased' as the case may be.

2   Objectives should be clear and specific using the verbal techniques we discuss in Chapter 8 to recover deep structures. For instance, 'I want to be a better manager' can be made more specific by unpacking what 'better' means and establishing 'better than what?' If the goal is clear and specific it will define what better means, eg 'I will have achieved above average 360° ratings from my staff'.

Objectives should be measurable and verifiable, using the clear and specific statement of the goal as above as a basis. Any defined outcome can be verified, either by counting or at least by its presence or absence, eg I will have achieved above average 360° ratings from 50 per cent of my staff.

3   Realistic goals are dependent on the necessary resources being available, external factors not militating against it, the goal being controllable by the client and the cost not being too high. If any one of these is questionable the goal may be unrealistic.

4   A substantive goal will be stretching for the client but not to breaking point. An inadequate goal will be set too low for the client concerned. The goal of an appraisal that is 'good enough' may not represent a substantive goal for a client who aspires to promotion and needs to achieve an 'excellent' appraisal.

5   Goals that are inconsistent with a client's values are unlikely to be achieved, as the client experiences dissonance and even distress. For instance, the bankers in the Sterling case study in Chapter 8 were unhappy about being asked to 'hard sell' financial services to their customers, as their value system was based on serving their customers, not taking advantage of them.

A goal to be achieved 'sometime' is unlikely to see the light of day. As a coach you are responsible for persisting in the question 'When?' so that clients can set their goals in exact terms, eg 'I will have qualified in accounting by the end of the year' or 'I will have completed my report by Monday next' or 'I will have achieved above average 360° ratings from 50 per cent of my staff by my yearly appraisal'.

The model has power in direct proportion to the skills of the coach using it. For developmental coaches, using the model ensures that the client explores their emotional world in detail before addressing their desires in the second stage. Hence when goals are agreed (having been generated by the client) they have the seven characteristics needed for success, described above. The model encourages a dialogue which is person-centred, including high levels of empathy, and the learning outcome is potentially transformational. So the ideal use of the model is developmental, and it is used extensively by professional and executive coaches.

Chapter summary

In this chapter we have reviewed the available models for coaching in the performance, engagement and developmental quadrants. Some of the models, used without empathy, will never take the coaching out of the performance quadrant. When primary empathy is included these same models may be effective in the engagement quadrant and we recommend our own NEWW model for engagement purposes. For developmental coaching we discussed and recommended more in-depth models which include advanced empathy, as well as high-level skills of challenge and confrontation.

Note

1 We acknowledge this idea as originating from our work with The Oxford Group.

PART THREE
Coaching or mentoring in each quadrant

We begin with the performance quadrant (in the right-hand lower corner of our framework in Chapter 1) where managers coach or mentor their staff to achieve the purposes of the organization. In this situation, the employee, although likely to be willing and potentially enthusiastic, is not generating their own goals, so ownership remains with the organization. The personal world of the employee is not part of the process and therefore the approach tends to be solution focused, often using a problem-solving method. The relationship is a line management one, with the manager having the power to influence the future for the employee. Questioning skills are the major component in performance work, together with the manager's ability to summarize action points. The process is instrumental as it is designed to support goals which are a measurable aspect of the employee's job. There is little choice here if they wish to retain employment so their feelings are not relevant. For this reason attention to feelings and emotions is unlikely in performance coaching.

In the engagement quadrant (Chapter 9) we discuss what happens when a more humanistic stance is employed, with persuasive elements included in the mentoring or coaching process. The process seeks to align personal ownership of goals with those of the organization, so the personal world of the employee is relevant in this quadrant. The relationship is often offline so the mentor or coach may not have the power to influence the employee's career prospects directly. In this situation feelings and emotion are directly addressed through primary empathy in order to build a relationship which supports the improvement sought. Many external practitioners are employed to carry out engagement coaching, with a performance objective, working with managers and team leaders to attain an organizational goal. The limitations of working in the engagement quadrant are the doubt that exists about ownership of goals. Where there is autonomy and ownership of goals the work moves into the developmental quadrant with the potential for individual transformation. Much of what is currently offered about coaching and mentoring urges managers to adopt developmental methods with their direct reports and expects them to achieve transformation without realizing the limitations of the line relationship.

For the developmental quadrant in Chapter 10 we find the coaching approach which appears in most coaching manuals, in its appropriate place. The client is voluntarily being coached and has ownership of their goals, the relationship does not include a power element and the learning outcome is potentially transformational for the individual. Traditional lifelong mentoring also sits within the developmental quadrant, where the activity is voluntary, goals are self-generated and the process is non-directive, leading to potential transformation. Such transformation is linked to the emotional world of the client. The approach is therefore deeply humanistic and includes high-level skills of empathy, challenge and immediacy, as well as the basic skills needed in the other two situations.

In Chapter 11 we discuss how an organization may transform itself through mentoring and coaching. Performance coaching or mentoring as described in Chapter 8 will not lead to systemic transformation for an organization and the idea of line managers triggering such change through performance management is at best fantasy and at worst an unfair expectation. The route to organizational change lies through coaching or mentoring which begins in the performance quadrant for day-to-day efficiency, uses persuasive methods to gain engagement from employees and also offers developmental opportunities to key personnel.

When there is sufficient critical mass of developmental work in an organization there is hope of organizational transformation and systemic change.

Performance

Coaching or mentoring in the performance quadrant of the situational framework requires appropriate skills. The purpose of activity in this quadrant is managing staff performance to meet the organization's objectives. The learning outcome in this quadrant (the bottom right-hand corner of the situational framework) is improved performance through developing competence in a given aspect of work.

Here we are likely to find the manager-as-coach, or manager-as-mentor, with minimal training, who is handling day-to-day performance issues with employees. Examples of such issues are included in the chapter. The skills needed in the performance quadrant – questioning, listening, restatement, feedback and summary – are explained and some examples provided, as well as reasons for the absence of empathy in this quadrant. We include here receiving skills, ie the skills that employees receiving performance coaching or mentoring might be glad to have at their disposal. Our examples in the skills section are chosen from the retail industry.

How does coaching and mentoring support performance management?

Coaching is currently used in 71 per cent of organizations as a method of day-to-day performance management and this is defined as follows:

> Performance management is about helping people to understand how they contribute to the strategic goals of organizations and ensuring that the right skills and effort are focused on the things that really matter to organizations and will make an impact on organizational performance.
>
> (CIPD, 2011b: 2)

As the line manager role is crucial in the delivery of performance management they will normally receive some coaching training and be told to 'do it' with their staff or team, acting as an internal coach. Where the organization's purpose is enhanced performance, there is an objective goal to be achieved, with little or no exploration of the employee's personal world. The model of reality is objective, with a focus on problem solving; there is no intention of stimulating individual development, the relationship is a line relationship and the process has been described as follows:

> a structured two-way process in which individuals develop skills and achieve defined competencies through assessment, guided practical experience, and regular feedback.
>
> (Parsloe, 1995: 1)

This description can also apply to performance mentoring where the manager-as-mentor is functioning as described in recent definitions of mentoring at work:

> Mentoring is a technique for allowing the transmission of knowledge, skills and experience in a challenging environment much like coaching.
>
> (CIPD, 2010b: 2)

and

> Mentoring can be described as a developmental process which may involve a transfer of skill or knowledge from a more experienced to a less experienced person through learning dialogue.
>
> (EMCC/ICF, 2011)

So the manager-as-mentor acts rather like a tutor, imparting skills, knowledge and experience to their direct reports in order to improve their performance.

Whose purpose is served by performance coaching or mentoring?

In this case the organization has funded training for managers with the express purpose of using coaching or mentoring as part of a performance management process. The purpose for the organization is enhanced, improved, indeed, **measurably** better performance from employees, declared by the CIPD as follows:

> its purpose is largely defined by its role in aligning individual effort and objectives with business outcomes... and provides a clear line of sight of priorities throughout the organization'. Indeed 'appraisal, objective-setting, review and development still top the list of activities most commonly carried out under the banner of performance management'. (CIPD, 2011b: 13, 14, 21)

Hence coaching or mentoring in the performance quadrant seeks learning outcomes which cover knowledge and actions.

Ownership of performance goals lies with the organization in the person of the manager, although employees may be happy to work within the organization's mission statement, gaining satisfaction from a job well done as well as security of income. The company ethos and value system can make a significant difference here, and coaching or mentoring approaches seek to make performance management more than a mechanistic data collection exercise to determine development strategy or pay allocation.

However, line managers, having been trained, may find themselves in a dilemma. The dilemma for line managers is expressed in this survey response from a senior manager, and trained coach, in a telecommunications company:

> The effectiveness of coaching in most large corporations is compromised by the organizations' strong focus on achievement of increasingly challenging objectives with ever-decreasing numbers of staff coupled with the strong pressure of publishing quarterly results to the markets. Managers are very time strapped, especially at the quarter's end when extra projects and initiatives are assigned to ensure favourable financial results. They therefore struggle to find the quality time needed to properly coach their staff and most interactions become more like 'mentoring' with the manager largely instructing the employee what to do as they can't afford the luxury of taking the time to help the employee to explore solutions for himself (which would yield more learning and self-fulfilment).
> In addition, due to the high-pressure environment, there is little, if any, time to explore the employee's model of the world and take this into account in their coaching sessions and discussions are largely 'matter of fact' and solutions focused. The end result is that both the managers and their staff are left feeling disappointed and stressed about most of their interactions and employee morale is dropping due to the scarce amount of individual attention, empathy and development opportunities provided by the relationship with their line manager.

What process is being used in performance management?

Peltier (2001) recommends that managers conduct a behavioural observation and analysis of their colleagues' work in order to offer them feedback. Thereafter it is believed that managers can trigger changes in behaviour through a combination of sanction and reward. This represents a behaviourist approach. Despite the negative connotations of behaviourism, the method is useful for measuring and evaluating the process. The benefits of behaviourism, in combination with a recognition of how employees might be thinking, can support performance management which is problem-solving and solution-focused. Connecting behaviour to consequence using an 'if... then...?' formula can be powerful in performance coaching and mentoring. In some performance training, managers are taught that the employee's beliefs and thinking are linked to how they feel about events and that this therefore influences their behaviour. This idea is reported as being used by neuro-linguistic programming (NLP) coaches (Neenan and Dryden, 2002). In fact, how feelings affect behaviour is rarely explored in a performance context for the reasons given below. In the engagement quadrant a humanistic approach to coaching will always attend to the emotional domain, and we discuss this in the next chapter. In performance coaching or mentoring a perceptive manager may realize that employees may have strong feelings about their situation and we discuss this in the skills section below.

A note about contracting in the performance quadrant

In a performance management situation the implicit coaching contract relates to the line relationship. The manager or team leader is responsible for the performance of his or her team, while the individuals in it are normally obliged to conform with managerial requirements as part of their contract. There is therefore no need for a separate contract for performance management but there is a need for clarity, as noted below.

Skills in the performance quadrant

Why are special skills necessary for performance coaching or mentoring? There is general agreement that coaches and mentors are not born – they are made by a combination of experience and development of people skills. For many the skills come naturally, so this chapter will put names to what you are doing already. Questioning is a key skill for coaching and mentoring, as is listening, summarizing and feedback. However, most of us are poor listeners and it is possible to make improvements in how we listen. The ability to restate what your colleague has said enables you to build rapport with them. What about advice? Obviously there is a place for advice and we make the assumption that all our readers know how to give advice and that developing that skill is not a priority.

So if it isn't giving advice, what skills are needed?

> coaching is a process that enables learning and development to occur and thus performance to improve. To be a successful coach requires a knowledge and understanding of the process as well as the variety of styles, skills and techniques that are appropriate to the context in which the coaching takes place.
>
> (Parsloe and Wray, 2000: 42)

What skills are needed in performance coaching?

- questioning;
- basic listening;
- simple restatement without empathy [as discussed on page 133, empathic response is limited in performance coaching];
- summarizing; and
- giving feedback (to include challenge).

Let us assume that the organization's mission includes aims which translate into specific objectives for your staff. For example, a mission which states 'to be the leading retailer in Europe' translates into 'achieve consistently high year-on-year results in this unit' with the accepted measures for such standards. These are likely to be financial results but may include staff turn-over and absence rates.

So your first questions will refer to what these specific objectives mean for your particular unit or department within it. Then you will be able to use your listening skills and ensure that you and your staff member have a shared understanding of what the organization wants. A good way of checking that you are both on the same page is the use of restatement. For example, who is responsible for the chill cabinet? You as manager or the team leader? When it is time to summarize you will find that your earlier restatements will help you to remember what has been agreed. We discuss restatement on page 133.

Questioning

For performance management, as noted above, the first objective is employee understanding of the organization's aims. The employee may or may not assent to these aims and the process tends to assume consent. Thereafter the manager will seek to explore how their colleague can meet these objectives in their day-to-day work. Hence for performance management, questioning is the first skill in use.

Types of questions include:

closed – questions that can be answered by yes, no or one word or phrase;

open – questions beginning with 'what', 'where', 'why', 'who', 'how' and 'when';

rhetorical – questions that contain their answer;

probing – questions that go deeper;

multiple – more than one question at once;

leading – questions that prompt agreement.

A closed question can be answered in one word, usually either 'yes' or 'no'. This is ok in some circumstances, but may not be useful in performance situations because they may close down an employee's willingness to speak or offer ideas for improvement. For monitoring and checking performance, however, closed questions like 'did you lock the cool room?' are necessary for good management. So closed questions are needed.

Open questions are likely to produce more than a one-word response, and an easy way to remember how to do them is Kipling's stanza:

I had six honest serving men
They taught me all I knew.
Their names were what and why and when
And how and where and who. (Rudyard Kipling)

So open questions always begin with one of the following: 'what', 'how', 'why', 'who', 'where', 'when'. Continual use of 'why' can be experienced as interrogation, so care is needed with this powerful open question. A typical open question for performance management in retail would be: 'What is our target this week?'

Rhetorical questions are statements in disguise and many questions are hiding their statements. A typical rhetorical question is: 'Isn't that window display effective?'

Probing questions need to be open to be effective, and may include the word 'exactly' to establish what is really meant. For example: 'What exactly does *fresh* mean for customers in the context of our chilling cabinet?'

The popular probing coaching question 'how do you feel?', when presented in a business context, expects, and is normally responded to by, **a statement of thought or opinion, not by a feeling statement**, eg 'I feel that the display could be improved', which is an opinion. When an employee does express a feeling there is no provision in performance coaching to process it, for the reasons given on page 135 below.

Rhetorical or leading questions risk agreement from your colleague that may not be genuine. We refer the reader to Clutterbuck's wonderful list of the meanings of 'yes' on page 108.

Multiple questions are likely to confuse and when presented to an employee they will answer the one they find easiest.

We give some examples of each kind of question below:

Closed – 'Have you done anything like this before?'

Open – 'What are the duties in the new post?'

Rhetorical – 'You know you can do it, don't you?'

Probing – 'What exactly did you do last time you held a similar position?'

Checking – 'You said you'd like to do x and y, is that right?'

Multiple – 'In your last position, what were the duties, how much of the job did you do, can you remember what you did?

Questions can be used for clarification, eg 'What exactly does in stock mean?'; for probing assumptions, eg 'What would happen if all the stock was in the cabinet?; for probing understanding, eg 'What do you think causes a rush at 4pm?'; checking assent to objectives, eg 'Why should we reduce this line?' and of course there are questioning techniques used for decades by sales people that coaches and mentors may like to use. For instance, the funnel technique begins with general but closed questions and gradually focuses on more detailed open questioning. It does rather resemble interrogation, so needs care. An example: Did that customer make a purchase? Why not? What happened with that customer? What did they want? What did you say?

When the question is a statement

A final point about questioning. You may find yourself, as a coach, asking a question which is really advice in disguise, and you can test this by identifying the statement which is hidden in your question. For instance, 'Have you thought of reading the job specification' is actually 'I suggest you read the job specification' and 'What about getting your sales sheets ready? is actually 'I suggest that you get your sales sheets ready'. These are hidden statements of your opinion. You may like to check your questions for hidden statements, and open questions avoid the problem. There is no reason to hide it if you think advice is called for. When you decide to give advice it is probably best to admit it and then both parties understand what is happening.

Additional questioning comes after listening to what your colleague has to say, without judgement, and restating it so that some trust and confidence have been established.

Basic listening

As part of performance management, the manager-as-coach or mentor will need to listen to their employee unless a monologue is the chosen method. When a coaching or mentoring relationship is working effectively, the coach is **really** listening. We regard this as one of the most important skills because although it is a basic skill, the remainder of the skills we address in this book depend on it. By listening we mean the ability of the coach or mentor to:

> capture and understand the messages (*communicated by the employee*), whether these messages are transmitted verbally or nonverbally, clearly or vaguely.
> (Egan, 1990: 108) (our addition in the parenthesis)

People spend much of their lives listening, unless a person has an impediment in their hearing. It is a very familiar activity. However, despite the significance of listening, people experience *not* being listened to and may react powerfully to not being heard:

> A riot is at bottom the language of the unheard. (Martin Luther King, 1968)

It seems that listening is not as easy as it sounds! The difficulty and rarity of real listening were noted by the psychologist Abraham Maslow (1969) and his comments are still relevant today:

> To be able to listen... really wholly, passively, self-effacingly listen – without presupposing, classifying, improving, controverting, evaluating, approving or disapproving, without dueling with what is being said, without rehearsing the rebuttal in advance, without free-associating to portions of what is being said so that succeeding portions are not heard at all – such listening is rare.
> (Maslow, 1969: 96)

It is easy to state the above, but there is a significant tendency for us to lose some of what a person has said, because we are human. We may lose a significant part of what is being said simply because the act of verbal communication is itself complex even though we take it for granted. We illustrate what happens when A communicates with B in five stages in Figure 8.1. When A communicates with B accuracy may be compromised, and the message reduced or distorted at every stage in the process:

FIGURE 8.1   A communicates with B in five stages

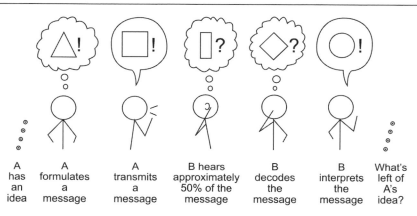

| A has an idea | A formulates a message | A transmits a message | B hears approximately 50% of the message | B decodes the message | B interprets the message | What's left of A's idea? |

SOURCE: McGill and Brockbank (2004: 166)

1 A formulates an idea. A's idea: 'I want staff to greet customers with good morning or good afternoon.'

2 A transmits a message which may or may not exactly replicate A's original idea. A's message: 'We are losing money. Customers are coming into the store in the afternoon.' You may be surprised by this but it is all too common that what we say is not quite what we mean.

3 B hears approximately 50 per cent of the message as B may be distracted and create arguments, perhaps while A is still speaking, and may miss part of the message but doesn't know which part he has missed. B may hear 'we are losing money in the afternoon' or B may hear 'customers are coming into the store' or B may hear 'they are being ignored'.

4 B decodes the message, and may decode incorrectly for all sorts of reasons, including lack of understanding as half the message is missing. B may also be confused by conflict between verbal and non-verbal information. B decodes into 'customers are coming into the store and we are losing money in the afternoon'.

5 B reconstructs the message to fit her cognitive map, ie B tries to make sense of what she has heard by linking lack of customers with losing money. B reconstructs to get 'customers are not coming into the store in the afternoon and we are losing money'.

In this 'Chinese whispers' example, after the five stages of communication not much is left of A's original idea and B has got the wrong end of the stick!

But surely listening is a 'natural' skill? Weren't we born knowing how to listen? Burley-Allen suggests that the reason for our poor showing on listening lies in its absence from our education (Table 8.1).

TABLE 8.1   Communication

Mode of communication	Years of formal training	Estimated % of time used
Writing	12	9
Reading	6–8	16
Speaking	1–2	35
Listening	0–½	40

SOURCE: Burley-Allen (1995: 39)

How can we reduce this loss of what is transmitted? The largest loss occurs at the point where B receives or 'hears' A's message and this is where restatement can improve the situation. You can use simple restatement to check your listening accuracy.

Further aspects of effective listening

There are other ways in which you may impede the effectiveness of your listening. You may:

evaluate – 'he is so old-fashioned wanting good morning';

filter – miss the point about losing money;

be distracted – 'he wants us to do more hours';

interrupt – 'but we made our target last week';

just be working out your own next response – 'I must remember to get that list from him'.

The foolproof way to check your listening accuracy is to restate what you think you have heard, and we describe how to do this now.

Simple restatement

When you are ready to respond to your colleague, what will you say? We recommend that before anything else, you restate what you have heard using their exact words, but changing the 'I' to 'you'. The re-presentation to your colleague of what he has just said is incredibly useful, laying the basis for a complete summary later. Often he may not be quite clear about what he wants to say, or indeed has just said (as above). When it is restated for him he can adjust it or agree to it and move on. This may seem a waste of time but experience shows that, time after time, what managers thought had been agreed just hadn't been clear to the employee concerned. Restatement is a sure-fire way to unpack anything which is confusing or unclear as well as those unspoken assumptions. For example, who is responsible for the staffing rota? You as manager or the team leader of the relevant team?

If your responses are critical or questioning too early, the learning may be killed off before it starts, particularly if your colleague's contributions are attacked or ignored. The skill of 'receiving' contributions without evaluation is the key to building rapport and probably the most valuable skill for coaches (and indeed managers) to learn. Restatement reflects back to your colleague the key points in what they have said. This enables you to check your understanding and also offers them an opportunity to revise what they said. The technique of 'restating' is also a useful way of discovering what you do hear and improving your accuracy, as well as enabling your colleague to reflect on what *he* has said, and critique it himself:

> one of the most useful tasks we can perform as we seek to develop
> critical thinking in other people, is to reflect back to them their attitudes,
> rationalizations, and habitual ways of thinking and acting.
> (Brookfield, 1987: 75)

For instance, a staff member says 'I just don't know where to start in this job – how are we going to be ready for the regional manager's visit?'

Once your colleague has spoken, you may respond to him in order to clarify and confirm that what you received is an accurate account of what he conveyed. Given that you will wish to restate at least some of what you think you heard, you may wish to start with phrases like:

> What I think you said was that you want to improve your understanding of the
> job and you are unsure how to start?
> OK, you want to discuss how to prepare for the regional manager's visit.

This description may appear simple, obvious or even banal as set out on this page. It is stated here because of our social tendency to assess and interpret and think what we are going to say even before the speaker has finished. The purpose here is to **accurately** restate back to your colleague what you thought he said. Using some of his exact words in 'reverse' may be helpful if it is unclear, ie changing 'I' to 'you' and changing 'my' to 'your' as above.

An inappropriate response would be to give an interpretation of what was said rather than an accurate response, eg 'You're quite insecure, aren't you?' Or to make and convey an assumption beyond what was said, eg 'You want to impress the regional manager'.

Many people find the prospect of restatement or 'reflecting back' embarrassing and are uncomfortable with it, possibly resorting to an inappropriate response because of that discomfort. Your colleague is unlikely even to notice that you are restating – the luxury of being responded to in this way is so rare and precious that they are likely to move on enthusiastically. The discomfort is in the coach or mentor and, with practice, the awkwardness dissolves as the increased potential for understanding the message becomes obvious.

One final point about coaches or mentors who are non-responsive, preferring to listen in silence. Listening in silence has its place; however, in the initial stages of a management relationship, your employee will be anxiously seeking a response from you and this is where the 'atmosphere' of the relationship is established. If the first response is silence, which may be perceived as negative or critical, then they may withdraw. If, on the other hand, a listening response is given, eg a brief restatement, then the climate of support and safety is established from the start.

What if your employee expresses, verbally or non-verbally, unwillingness or downright resistance? Where emotions are present, how does a performance coach or mentor proceed?

Emotions and empathy in the performance quadrant

For managers who are performance coaching or mentoring, to encourage their staff to express emotions or to offer them empathy is experienced by them as deeply fearful for three reasons:

- First, they are afraid that both employee and manager will be overwhelmed by emotion and find themselves unable to function. For example, managers dread a staff member who bursts into tears and may feel incompetent in dealing with 'counselling' or 'therapy' issues.
- Second, there is an implicit belief that offering empathy represents agreement in some form and therefore weakens a manager's position when attempting to impose a standard on their staff. This mistaken belief is not helped by the current practice of using the form 'I feel that' to precede what is essentially a thought or opinion. For example, 'I feel that the company is losing talent by making experienced staff redundant'. As no feeling has been clearly expressed, a restatement like 'You feel that the company is losing talent etc' may be construed as agreement with the opinion and is not empathy.
- Third, employees are wary of expressing their true feelings when their jobs may be under threat. Knowledge of how a person feels is privileged information and employees voice their fear by saying 'It may be used against me'. Alternatively, when they are asked how they feel they may not be able to express their feelings clearly, a difficulty prevalent in many business environments.

Hence the current practice in performance coaching avoids empathy; indeed, most managers are unaware of the skill. This is in spite of the EQ movement, which tends to be limited to manipulation of employees or the simulation of positive emotions like 'have a good day'. Where managers have been properly trained and are able to deploy the skill of empathy with confidence, their performance management is likely to be painless and productive. However, while the intended learning outcome is limited to adjustment of behaviour in line with organizational objectives, there is little to be gained by exploring how the employee feels about them as there will be no freedom of choice. For example, staff members may be encouraged to use a new procedure for tracking orders, whatever they think or feel about the new system. This will be achieved in the performance quadrant through clarification of objectives, questioning and summarizing to agree action, as described below. We discuss empathy in the next chapter about engagement.

Problems arise where employees have expectations of coaching which go beyond these performance issues and expect personal, even emotional support in their endeavours. The expectation that a manager can work developmentally with their staff while performance coaching is not helpful when neither has any choice in the learning outcome. It has already been established as organizational policy. We recommend that these points are clarified to employees at the start, so that there is clarity of intent, agreement about process and realistic expectations about outcomes. As noted above, in a performance management situation the coaching contract is implicit in the line relationship. Line managers coaching in the performance quadrant would not normally need a separate contract, but there is a need for clarity.

Summarizing

Restatement builds material for a competent summary which is your responsibility as a performance coach or mentor. As you have restated key points, you will be able, with or without notes, to give a résumé of your employee's issue and action points for their benefit. Summary relies on the quality of earlier restatement. Identify the key points in what has been said. You will find this easy if you have already done some restatement. Vocal or non-verbal activity suggests a key point for the employee, and remember that the key points noted by you may not be the ones that are important for them, so check. For instance:

> Ok, this is a new position for you and you will need some time to get to grips with it. We can have a session later on today. Meanwhile you are thinking about getting ready for the regional manager's visit.

Feedback

Giving your staff feedback is part of your managerial role and a key ingredient in performance management. Effective feedback on our actions and behaviours is a way of learning more about ourselves and the effect our behaviour has on others. Constructive feedback increases self-awareness, offers us more options for how we can act, relate to others and take the opportunity to change our behaviour. We describe the characteristics of effective feedback below.

Effective feedback does not only mean positive feedback. Negative feedback, given skilfully, is just as important. Destructive feedback is unskilled feedback that leaves the recipient simply feeling bad, with little to build on. However, the most commonly voiced complaint is lack of feedback, or feedback that can't be used by the recipient.

Feedback is of little value to the recipient unless: a) the recipient can understand it; b) the recipient can use it.

Should we always give feedback? The person offering feedback must make a judgement about appropriateness. When – is this the right time; where – is this a good place; who – am I the right person to give it; how – how can I do it most effectively?

What if the feedback is negative? How can I give positive feedback without sounding sloppy? We look at some of the difficulties below and identify the skills needed to give feedback properly.

Positive feedback

Often we may not give positive feedback because:

- We may forget to do so in taking a person's qualities and skills for granted when something has been done well. We may be more likely to draw attention to those aspects that have not gone well.

- We may be embarrassed to say something positive to others for fear that it may be misinterpreted or may not seem genuine or that the receiver may be embarrassed.

- We may be brought up to think of self-effacement as better than too much self-confidence.

Some or all of these reasons may inhibit the giving of positive feedback, which is an important part of learning. Staff need to know what was effective about their work so that they can repeat it, otherwise it's a guessing game.

Negative feedback

Giving negative feedback may feel uncomfortable to do, as we fear it may be distressing for the person receiving it. However, persistent failure to give negative feedback may result in:

- the tendency for negative feedback to be 'stored up' and, under pressure, explode in a destructive way;

- no change in the person's practice because they are unaware that it is causing any difficulties;

- a continued practice that is less effective.

What are the skills in **giving** feedback?

We will take a customer service example to illustrate:

1 *Clarity.* Be clear about what you want to say in advance. In order to achieve clarity, first observe carefully and record your observation (mentally or as notes) in concrete and specific terms, ie what as a coach you have seen and heard, eg details of your colleague's behaviour and reports of its likely effects. For example, 'I noticed that you were not looking at that customer when she was asking about the product and she left without purchasing.'

2 *Start with the positive.* Most people need encouragement, and staff need to know when they are doing something well. Do not take the positive aspects for granted. When offering feedback, it can really help the receiver to hear first what they have done well, for example: 'I liked the way you worked with your customer on this issue – because you listened they were prepared to accept the point. **And** I observed that they then seemed to wait for something from you.' (Note avoidance of the word 'but' when linking positive and negative feedback, as 'but' tends to devalue what has just been said.) The use of a feedback 'sandwich' has been recommended, where a negative piece of feedback is sandwiched in between two positives.

3 *Be specific not general.* General comments are not useful in feedback when commenting on a person's behaviour. For feedback to be useful (ie it can be used by the recipient) it needs to be specific. Statements like: 'That was brilliant' or 'You were awful' may be pleasant or dreadful to hear but they do not enable the person to learn what was brilliant or awful and act upon it.

4 *Select priority areas.* Highlight the most significant feedback, especially if it is negative feedback that you are giving. If possible, don't let it build up into one great bundle! Many people can only 'take' one piece of negative feedback at a time, even when sandwiched between two positives.

5 *Focus on behaviour rather than the person.* Reporting what was seen and heard ensures that the focus is on behaviour rather than the person. For example, the comment 'You dominated there' is potentially damaging and less useful to the recipient than 'I noticed that you interrupted the customer'.

6 *Refer to behaviour that can be changed.* It is not very helpful to give a person feedback about something they can do nothing about, eg a personal attribute, dialect or accent.

7 *Descriptive rather than evaluative.* Telling the person what has been seen or heard and the effect it had is more effective than saying something was merely 'good' or 'bad'. For example, 'When you received a customer query, I noticed that you looked away without speaking. She seemed rather put off by this.'

8 *Own the feedback.* Effective feedback is 'owned' beginning with
'I' or 'in my view' rather than with 'you are...', which may suggest
that a universally agreed opinion is being offered about that person.
Starting with 'I' means that in giving the feedback you are also taking
responsibility for what you are saying. For example, 'I was impressed
by your patience with that customer query – it was a tough one'
or 'I think your customer was put off when you turned away'.

9 *Give the feedback as soon as you can after the event.* Staff want
feedback as soon as possible, and immediate feedback should be
given if possible. The exceptions to this would be:
   – if the staff member is feeling very emotional about the behaviour
     or the event;
   – the feedback would not be constructive; and/or
   – if it is inappropriate, eg others do not need to hear it.

10 *Feedback should be based on observation rather than inference.*
Based on what is seen, heard or read, rather than on interpretations
or conclusions made from what is seen or heard, which may
contaminate observations and therefore affect the quality of
the feedback. For instance, 'You seemed impatient this morning –
I expect it's because you didn't get that raise' includes an
interpretation.

11 *What is said rather than why it is said.* The aspects of feedback that
relate to the what, how, when and where of what is said are
observable characteristics. Why something is said goes to the inferred
rather than the observable – motive or intent. Why questions can be
received interrogatively and lead to defensiveness.

12 *Limit negative feedback.* Limit feedback to one or two areas if you
are giving feedback on weaknesses as after two pieces of negative
information, we suggest the receiver may 'switch off' and hear no
more of the feedback being offered.

Feedback patterns

Some ideas for structuring your feedback:

1 When you
   When you .... I thought ....
   When you .... I felt ....
   When you .... I noticed ....

2 Recommending
   I would like you to do more of .... because
   I would like you to do less of .... because
   I would like you to continue .... because

3 What, what and what

Tell them what they did.

Tell them what the effects were.

Tell them what you'd like them to do.

The prospect of receiving feedback often inspires fear as most people expect negative feedback and are not in a receptive listening mode. The person giving feedback should take into account the receiver's state and check out if the feedback has really been heard and received, possibly ensuring that it is recorded, especially if it is positive. So having given feedback, can I receive it? We discuss receiving feedback below.

Receiving performance coaching or mentoring – what can help?

Disclosure

In order to convey your genuine and real issue you will need to engage in some self-disclosure. In operational terms this means that you will tend to make 'I' statements, owning your statements, rather than using 'you', 'they', 'one', 'we' or 'it', all of which have a tendency to distance you from ownership of what is being said.

Although the term self-disclosure may put people off, as it sounds exposing and like being stripped naked, in reality in all our relationships we self-disclose, and we control how much we reveal of what we are thinking and especially feeling. How much we disclose is likely to be related to differences in culture, gender, class or race. It will also relate to the nature of the relationship concerned – your likely relationship is highlighted below:

- a loving partnership;
- a working relationship as
  - colleagues;
  - manager and managed;
  - doctor and patient;
- woman to woman;
- man to man.

Any disclosure you make will be transmitted through messages between yourself and your manager, and may be subject to some loss and potential misinterpretation. We discussed this under listening, above, and the skill of restatement is valuable here. As a colleague you may also disclose intentionally or unintentionally. The messages you express that carry disclosure may be conveyed via:

- the body – face and parts of the body;
- the voice – our tone of voice, ie how we talk;
- touch – physical contact with another;
- verbal – what we say;
- actions – what we do as a contrast to or confirmation of what we say and how we say it.

Appropriateness of disclosure

Too much self-disclosure is embarrassing. Too little and we may find we do not relate to others and this may reduce our capacity to reflect upon ourselves at work. How far we disclose depends in part upon our values and the norms of the workplace. Some people value openness, others privacy. Over-disclosure occurs when the disclosure is inappropriate to the context.

The level of disclosure which is suitable to the context can be called appropriate self-disclosure. 'Appropriate' is defined by:

- amount (how much);
- depth (how deep);
- duration (how long);
- the target (to whom);
- the situation (time and place).

We all have experience of a myriad of versions of the above combinations. For example, someone who insists on talking in detail about themselves constantly and at length (duration) is deemed inappropriate, as is the over-discloser who reveals intimate details (depth) to almost anyone (target) on any occasion (situation). So we have a true sense of appropriate self-disclosure and moderately well-adjusted persons disclose appropriately for human contact and social intercourse. In addition to the above, the literature on self-disclosure reveals that women are higher disclosers than men, and that disclosure is reciprocal in effect, ie where high disclosers are present this increases disclosure by everyone (Cozby, 1973).

There may be strong cultural imperatives against self-disclosure and this may inhibit your behaviour, especially in conditions where you perceive yourself to be under test. For many people, self-disclosure implies weakness and supports the reverse halo effect (where a weakness in one area is presumed to exist in other areas), and fear of shame and rejection are strong inhibitors, especially in a relationship where no trust has been established. And here we have the conundrum. A sure way to establish trust is some self-disclosure, and on the other hand, you may fear self-disclosure until you are confident of trust in the relationship. How can this loop be breached?

Our experience of manager/employee relationships is that staff do engage in self-disclosure as the atmosphere of trust develops between them and this relates to empathy which is discussed in Chapter 9.

Receiving feedback

As an employee you will need to receive feedback in a way that will enable you to improve your performance. The concept of feedback comes from systems theory and the idea that systems which include individuals can be self-correcting, as a consequence of information from inside or outside the system. Performance coaching is an example of the latter. Effective feedback on our actions and behaviours is a way of learning more about ourselves and the effect our behaviour has on others. Research suggests that constructive feedback increases our self-awareness, offers us more options to how we can act, relate to others and take the opportunity to change our behaviour (London, 2003).

In order to maximize the benefits of feedback, we describe here how to receive it effectively.

1 The LAW rule: Listen and wait

Listening to the feedback rather than immediately rejecting or arguing with it. Feedback may be uncomfortable to hear but we may be poorer without it. People do have their opinions about us and will have perceptions of our behaviour, and it can help to be aware of these. However, having listened carefully it is important to clarify your understanding of what you have heard.

2 Clarify

Be clear that you understand what has been said without jumping to conclusions or being defensive before responding. A useful device is to restate what it is you think you have heard to check for accuracy. This also gives you time to consider how you will respond. A useful discipline is writing the feedback down and reading it slowly before responding or even opting to take it away and consider it at leisure. There is no rule which says the receiver of feedback must respond. Restatement and summary as above.

3 Consider whether you agree or disagree

If you agree you may like to accept the feedback and you may also wish to comment on its significance for you. Again there is no rule about this. You are free simply to accept the feedback and say nothing more. Alternatively, you may disagree and choose not to accept the feedback as it stands. Here you may choose to consider checking out the feedback with another, ie get a second opinion.

4 Check out with others where possible rather than relying on one source

In a workplace situation there are always others who can confirm or dispute the feedback you have received and you can always seek a second opinion, as others may give another view.

5 Ask for the feedback you want but don't receive if it does not occur naturally

Feedback is an important part of learning for you and you should ask to receive feedback from your manager when you need it.

6 Decide what you will do because of the feedback

You may wish to take time to consider the feedback you have received, check out with others, as above, and finally decide on what you will do in response to the feedback.

7 You may like to recover the deep structures within the feedback

When you receive feedback you may like to consider what is hidden beneath the surface, and this is known as recovering the deep structures in many surface structure statements. You can do this by asking what is known as recovery questions. See Table 8.2.

TABLE 8.2   Recovery questions

Surface structure	Deep structure	Recovery question
You are always late	You were late on X and Y occasions and I am annoyed	Could you say when I was late?
You are too slow at reception	I believe you are slower than I would be or the previous receptionist was	Could you say who I am too slow in comparison with?
You will have to do better	I want you to answer the phone after two rings minimum	Could you say what you mean by better?
This report is too long	This report is longer than other reports I have read and I am afraid it will bore the CEO	Could you say what the report is too long in comparison with?
You should see someone	I believe that you need to see a counsellor or therapist	Could you say who you think I should see, please?

Surface structures and deep structures are based on Chomsky (1957, 1969) and are routinely used by NLP practitioners who believe they invented the method.

Programmes in the performance quadrant

An example of performance mentoring for improvement is revealed in the organizational programme described in the case study below where mentors were volunteers from within the organization and the purpose was an increase in qualified staff, using senior managers as mentors.

CASE STUDY A professional awarding body

The awarding body is a self-funding organization dedicated to promoting higher standards of competence and integrity through the provision of relevant qualifications for employees at all levels and across all sectors of the industry concerned. With 90,000 members this organization has been at the forefront in setting professional standards for its industry for over a century. Its broad portfolio of education and qualification services is continually expanding to meet the changing requirements of its customers.

The organization set up a mentoring programme to offer educational support to staff working towards professional qualifications when government funding cuts had significantly reduced the level of local tuition for these qualifications. The organization was anxious to provide additional resources to the normal face-to-face courses. In addition, the programme was intended to offer opportunities for mature members to enhance their continuous professional development (CPD) plans.

The hoped-for benefits were that staff would have a better chance of passing exams, while at the same time gaining a network of more senior contacts via their local network. For mentors the benefits included a realization of their membership promise when elected to Fellowship of the organization, as well as fulfilling their CPD commitment and, more importantly, helping to engage young members and keep the local network alive.

Mentors opted to join the scheme and were allocated by the local scheme organizer to a member studying for a qualification. Organizers at local level were provided with materials which supported the recruitment and selection of mentors, briefing notes and performance measures, as well as ideas for mentors' meetings and how to deal with difficulties. Mentors were provided with materials describing the role and giving details of the skills (described above) needed to help a student to learn, as well as pro formas for record-keeping and reviewing. A brief document defined the role for both mentor and student.

On completion of the programme two years later, members reported feeling more attached to the organization than was the case previously, feeling part of the local industry community and feeling less isolated. Senior members who acted as mentors benefited from CPD points which preserved their membership category and, in addition, they found that their status in the local industry community was enhanced. The programme resulted in improved pass rates for those who took part, noticeable awareness of mentoring, and increased understanding of the benefits of mentoring on both sides.

Our second example is a coaching programme which attempted to use performance management techniques to promote engagement with a new policy. Without ownership of objectives, and no empathy training, the programme failed.

CASE STUDY Sterling Bank

Sterling Bank has been in business for three hundred years and operates worldwide employing 100,000 staff. For UK high street branches, the impact of online banking in recent years has affected traditional business detrimentally, and to deal with the situation the bank launched a coaching programme for senior managers. The managers, almost all home-grown, having been in the bank all their working lives, came from a tradition of service in local branches, often playing a significant role in the community. The programme aimed to introduce managers to the idea of coaching their staff in a new role.

The programme was designed to persuade, through coaching, the managers and their staff out of their traditional role and into a selling role, where they would be required to 'push' financial services products to their long-term customers. The improvement agenda was diversification of the product offer but was presented to participants as an additional service offer, together with professional development for themselves as coaches.

Most of the managers (mostly in their fifties and nearing retirement) were horrified at the prospect, believing that, having established themselves as 'pillars of the community', they were being asked to become, and to coach their staff to become, common salesmen.

The coach training was painful and difficult as trainers found themselves in engagement mode, using humanistic techniques to persuade participants to accept the hidden agenda. Participants were generally resistant and angry, especially as they realized that there was little choice if they wished to finish their career with Sterling. The programme enabled the bank to argue that managers had been offered the option and, if they didn't manage to cross over to more selling, they were vulnerable to redundancy.

Sterling was a case of performance coaching, where branch bank managers were to be coached out of their traditional role of service to their customers and into their new role as salesmen of financial services such as pensions and the like. The purpose was a massive culture change for quite legitimate corporate reasons, ie the demise of hands-on banking owing to IT products flooding the market. Also, the managers as coaches were expected to change their own dispositions, acquire saint-like qualities and present idealized role models (Beech and Brockbank, 1999).

The outcome for performance mentors or coaches

No wonder mentors using performance approaches were subsequently found to 'become more anxious and more demoralized about mentoring the longer the relationships continued' (Colley, 2003: 103). The same effects were found in business contexts. Terri Scandura reminds us that even the most comprehensive studies of mentoring of every kind fail to address evidence of 'negative and damaging experiences in mentoring' and describes the evidence as the 'dark side' of mentoring (Scandura, 1998: 463). Our recommendation is that programmes like Sterling would be well advised to 'come clean' about their purposes but recognize that in the situation described this would be far from easy.

What happens to the client in these circumstances? Because the objectives are not theirs, they are unlikely to be achieved. Because there tends to be covert surveillance where the contractor seeks to assess 'progress' by reports from mentors or coaches, clients present an acceptable face to their mentor. Typical ingratiatory behaviours include pretending to agree, flattery and false self-presentation. The result of this is an incongruent relationship. The prevalence of the assumption that managers will help their employees with emotional problems is evident. The expectations held by clients and their mentor or coach, as well as the process itself, are widely divergent (Beech and Brockbank, 1999), and this is confirmed by the authors when expectations are explored at training events.

Evaluating coaching or mentoring in the performance quadrant

As the activity is carried out mainly by line managers, evaluation refers to the coaching or mentoring element of their work. A quantitative measure is available in the results on objectives for which they are responsible and this may be presented at appraisal. In addition, descriptive evaluation would include feedback from individual members of staff who have been coached or mentored, and this may be formal or informal, anonymous or direct. For judgemental evaluation, ie a measure of the 'worth' of the activity, a combination of measurement and description, together with a senior manager's assessment, would give a composite evaluation of the coaching or mentoring element of a line manager's work.

In addition, many organizations evaluate performance management through engagement measures, because the former is seen as a clear driver of engagement and engagement surveys may include satisfaction measures about performance management (CIPD, 2011b). We discuss engagement in the next chapter.

Accreditation of coaches or mentors working in the performance quadrant

Practitioners working in the performance quadrant are likely to be accredited by the EMCC at Foundation level. Such individuals are described as:

individuals with an understanding of the practice of coaching/mentoring and having the core skills of coaching/mentoring;

likely to be working with others using coaching/mentoring conversations to support and encourage development of skills/performance;

individuals who use a coaching/mentoring approach within their own field/role and clearly understand how their coach/mentor role integrates with their vocational roles.

Practitioners in the performance quadrant may also seek credentialing from the ICF, provided that they meet the ICF core competences. The key discriminating requirement is the number of hours of coaching they claim to have completed. The terms 'practised', 'proven' and 'expert' are not defined. Managers who use coaching as part of their work may apply as follows:

Associate Certified Coach (ACC): The ICF Associate Certified Coach credential is for the practised coach with at least 100 hours of client coaching experience.

Professional Certified Coach (PCC): The Professional Certified Coach credential is for the proven coach with at least 750 hours of client coaching experience.

Master Certified Coach (MCC): The Master Certified Coach credential is for the expert coach with at least 2,500 hours of client coaching experience.

Continuing professional development for coaches and mentors

There is an expectation that all ICF-credentialed coaches will continue their education and build on their level of experience. The resulting growth in competency and professionalism will be evidenced by their journey to the MCC credential.

Practitioners who seek individual EMCC accreditation as mentors and coaches at Foundation level are required to provide evidence that they engage in 16 hours of CPD per year and one hour of supervision per quarter year. Most adults in managerial roles are likely to engage in professional development for at least 16 hours in a given year and receive one hour of supervision from their own line manager as part of their quarterly review. Because performance work is unlikely to involve the manager-as-coach or mentor in any emotional intimacy, there is no need for non-managerial supervision and this provision seems adequate to maintain a professional standard.

Chapter summary

In this chapter we have described the characteristics of coaching and mentoring in the performance quadrant in terms of the purpose, which is defined and owned by the organization and carried out by line management; the process, which is solution-focused; and the learning outcome, which is improvement. We discussed the skills needed to work in the performance quadrant (which do not include empathy) and how they differ from engagement skills. The limited learning outcome was emphasized, relating to the fact that employees are not in a position to generate their own goals, being required to work according to their contract with the organization. However, performance coaching and mentoring offers value for time-pressed managers who seek to deliver workplace activities to the standard required by the organization. Two case studies illustrate the importance of checking out whose purpose is being addressed at the start of a coaching or mentoring contract or programme.

There are controversial findings in relation to performance management which are relevant here. The CIPD survey of 2009 found that 21 per cent of respondents did not consider that performance management had a positive impact on individual performance or organizational performance (CIPD, 2009). Some suggestions have been made which cite 'values and behaviours' as needing rather more attention than the focus on objectives. This supports our contention that activity in the performance quadrant may not lead to organizational transformation. However, coaching or mentoring in the engagement quadrant is more likely to support such development and to this we now turn.

Engagement

We now explore coaching and mentoring in the engagement quadrant in a range of internal and external roles. The skills needed are described (some were also used in the performance quadrant) and the particularly important skill of empathy is described in detail, with examples of accurate primary empathy in use. The recommended degree of empathy reflects the reality of engagement, namely the need to align individual objectives with those of the organization.

The UK's CIPD has stated that 'there is no short cut to building and maintaining employee engagement' and 'levels of affective (meaning feelings and emotion) engagement are the highest in an engaged workforce' (CIPD, 2010c). However, the degree of empathy must not exceed what is practical in the engagement situation.

The skills needed here are those of persuasion and encouragement, in order to build the commitment and trust which supports engagement. Examples of engagement programmes complete the chapter.

What is engagement?

Engagement can be defined as: the commitment of staff to the organization's mission and their part in achieving it. Research carried out by Kingston Business School for the CIPD (UK) defined engagement as: 'Being positively present during the performance of work by willingly contributing intellectual effort, experiencing positive emotions and meaningful connections to others' (CIPD, 2010c: 5).

The drivers of engagement are identified as 'the way... managers behave... as they contribute significantly towards making work meaningful and engaging' (Robinson *et al*, 2004 cited in CIPD, 2010a).

The UK's CIPD has more to say about employee engagement as:

> commitment to the organization and its values and a willingness to help out colleagues (organizational citizenship). It goes beyond job satisfaction and is not simply motivation. Engagement is not something the employee has to offer. It cannot be required as part of the employment contract.
>
> (CIPD, 2010a: 1)

Here we see the recognition that ownership of objectives has to be negotiated as employees have choices and can decide what level of engagement to offer the employer (Purcell, 2003). However, there is also a belief that engaged employees deliver improved business performance, so there is a strong rationale for using coaching or mentoring to create an engaged workforce (CIPD, 2010c).

Let us assume that the organization's mission includes aims which translate into specific objectives for staff. For example, a mission which states 'to be the best provider of health care in the UK' translates into 'achieve consistently high standards of care in this unit' with the accepted measures for such standards. These may include staff/customer ratios; customer satisfaction rates; as well as unit inspection results etc.

In this quadrant you will be working with organizational objectives but your aim is to persuade your staff member to take on board these objectives as their own. The skills needed to achieve this are more than those needed in the performance quadrant. As James Flaherty says, 'coaching you see is not telling people what to do' (Flaherty, 1999: xii). Successful engagement depends on the quality of the coaching or mentoring relationship and, following Rogers' learning principles (Chapter 2), you will be offering positive regard through listening and attending as well as empathy, the most powerful extra skill you can use for engagement.

In this quadrant you may find yourself working in one or more of the following roles:

manager-as-coach or mentor;

in-house coach or mentor;

external coach or mentor.

What are the key skills needed in each of these roles?

Manager-as-coach or mentor

As mentioned above, you will use questioning to establish the objectives of this particular job. It is worth spending some time on this as mistakes cannot later be rectified. You may find this process laborious as these objectives are owned by the organization, and maybe yourself, but they are still to be accepted by your staff member. Your role as coach is to bring this acceptance about and then work with the implications of it. As manager you hold power over your staff and this will affect the coaching or mentoring relationship. For instance, they will not be inclined to tell you anything about their failures or reservations as you have the power to sack them. So how will you build trust and acceptance?

The process of acceptance is not a purely rational one. To bring your staff member to a point where they are happy to work to imposed objectives you will need to access their emotional world. These objectives are likely to be a mixture of positive, negative and personal. To work with them you will need to listen carefully and use the skill of primary empathy. When you agree on shared objectives you will then need to work on how they will be achieved and this is likely to trigger a range of feelings for your colleague. You may find empathic responses helpful then and also when you come to discuss action points. At the same time you do not want to get into too much emotional depth as this is not counselling and there is a job to be done. Hence for the engagement quadrant we recommend primary empathy (Egan, 1990), described in full on page 154.

Thereafter you will use questioning skills; listening again; restatement; your summary feedback and challenge will progress the engagement process for you as manager-as-coach or manager-as-mentor.

In-house coach or mentor

You will find that in this situation, building a trustful relationship will be easier than the line relationship above. However, depending on the size of your organization, your client may well be deeply suspicious of so-called confidentiality. There are well-known instances of mentors and coaches leaking personal information to line managers, so you may have to do a deal of reassurance if you want to promise confidentiality. Bear in mind, however, that if you have knowledge from your client about anything illegal or which puts a minor at risk your ethical code may impel you to report it. This should be clarified with your client at the start.

Listening is considered by all the experts as the key skill for good coaching – but listen to what? You will want to use the time with your staff on work-focused issues rather than what they did at the weekend. Therefore the prime skill here is questioning. By first putting questions to your staff member you can ensure that the material for coaching or mentoring is relevant to your purpose.

In this role you can afford to take time to listen to your client and restate facts and feelings using empathy, before addressing the material issues of the job. You may be able to hold off the questioning until trust and rapport have been established through empathy. You then use primary empathy, discussed below, keeping the focus on the purpose of engagement, namely the commitment of your client to achieving the agreed objectives. Using empathy speeds up the process of building rapport as it includes accurate restatement, so the client experiences being heard. However, the fear remains that offering empathy can be construed as agreement, which together with the client's own suspicion that any expressed feelings will be 'used against' them holds practitioners back from using the skill. Instead they resort to the 'how do you feel?' question. This is unlikely to be answered truthfully for the following reasons:

- The business context routinely denies emotion and stigmatizes it as weakness so employees tend to avoid it.
- Many people are not in touch with their emotions and will give a cognitive reply like 'I feel **that** the rota is favouring x', which is an opinion not a feeling.
- The coach or mentor may also be avoiding emotional material for fear of getting into therapeutic areas where they are not competent.

The 'how do you feel?' question may also invite expression of deeper feelings which you do not feel competent to deal with. In an engagement situation, using primary empathy will protect you from getting in too deep, and we explain this under empathy below.

External coach or mentor

In this role you really need to establish who your client is. You are likely to have been commissioned by the organization in the person of a senior manager to work with one of their reports. The purpose may take some teasing out and it is often related to elements of poor performance or work relationships. The prospect of succeeding where apparently competent managers have failed is somewhat seductive and external coaches or mentors need to be wary. In this case you are actually taking on some of the senior manager's line responsibilities and you may like to consider working with that person first as they are clearly not managing their staff effectively. Our recommendation is that you discuss moving the work into the developmental quadrant and work, initially, with the senior manager on their management issues.

Given that eventually you are happy to proceed on the original request, what skills are going to be effective in this situation?

The sensitivities here are legion. Assuming you are able to establish a trustful relationship, you will need to listen carefully and what you hear is likely to include a lot of complaining about individuals, systems and the organization itself. Offering primary empathy engenders trust and will encourage your client to reveal their weaknesses and worries. Do remember that empathic responses do not constitute agreement. However, this belief may need to be dealt with early in the relationship.

There is evidence that managing an engaged workforce calls for 'soft skills' to cover the three domains of learning mentioned in Chapter 2, so that your first questions will refer to what the organization's objectives mean for your client. Then you will be able to use your listening skills and ensure that you and your client have a shared understanding of what the organization wants.

As discussed in Chapter 8, a good way of checking that you have heard accurately is the use of *restatement*. Restatement enables you to summarize later what has been agreed. As part of your restatement you will need to respond to both fact and feeling, so empathy is a key skill here. The quality of your feedback will contribute to the relationship and at its best will support engagement.

We can see here that all of Rogers' requirements (see Chapter 2) are not present in engagement coaching or mentoring, as the client is not exercising personal choice, but being socialized to align their own desires with those of the organization. The skills needed to facilitate learning in the engagement quadrant are as follows:

questioning;

listening;

restatement;

empathy;

goal setting;

feedback;

summary;

challenge.

Skills in the engagement quadrant

Questioning

Questioning skills are used first in engagement work in order to establish how far the organization's objectives are understood. However, in the engagement quadrant the temptation to over-question and interrogate may compromise trust in the relationship and limit how far the employee will choose to engage. We recommend that questioning is limited to checking that the person concerned understands the organization's objectives and is allowed to express that understanding, together with their reactions to what they are being asked to do. Using open questions as described in Chapter 8 is less likely to 'lead' your colleague and allows them to have 'the freedom to voice ideas to which managers listen', one of the main drivers of engagement (Robinson *et al*, 2004).

Levels of listening

Whitworth *et al* (1998) offer an understanding of listening at three levels and we describe these below:

Level 1 refers to the state of listening as 'what does this mean to me?' as the listener is attending to himself, and this is entirely appropriate for much of the time. In fact it's essential that we attend to ourselves and listen out for what is best for us in terms of survival. So it's ok in general but not for your practice as a coach or mentor. If you find yourself figuring out what to say next or what brilliant intervention to make, this is a clue that you are listening at level 1 when you need to be at least at level 2.

Level 2 refers to focused listening where you are focused on your client. The observed behaviour associated with level 2 listening is an attentive body, not fidgeting or moving around, eye contact and silence. Level 2 listening may prepare you to make a primary empathic response based on what you have seen and heard from all three communication channels: verbal, non-verbal and vocal.

Level 3 listening picks up emotion, body language and the environment itself and we discuss level 3 listening in Chapter 10.

Restatement

In the engagement quadrant you will use restatement as described in Chapter 8, the performance quadrant, but with the addition of primary empathy.

Empathy

The purpose of this section is to suggest that as a mentor or coach you can, with care and respect for your client, restate their story in a helpful way, using primary empathy. When you offer empathic response you attempt to 'boldly swing into the life of the other' (Kohn, 1990: 112) and you are affirming the real world of the client, particularly their emotional world.

A tendency to understand empathy as 'feeling with' skates rather close to sympathy. When you as a mentor or coach start 'feeling with' your client, you exclude the reasoning and inference that are necessary to 'imagine the reality of the other' (Kohn, 1990: 131). For 'without imagining the reality of the other, empathic feeling is ultimately self-oriented and thus unworthy of the name' (Kohn, 1990: 131). On the other hand, a matter-of-fact response which excludes the affective (emotional) part of the client's message will not achieve the 'imagine-other' of empathy. For connected knowing and reflective dialogue, thinking cannot be divorced from feeling. Hence for you to 'truly experience the other as subject... something more than an intellectual apprehension is required... the connection must be felt viscerally' (Kohn, 1990: 150). 'Viscerally' here means that there is a bodily response of some kind, a sense or feeling that connects you to your client.

The Western preoccupation with thinking as superior to feeling ensures that mentors and coaches will often feel more comfortable with the cognitive aspects of a client's story, while the feeling content may be politely ignored (and therefore for them, denied). Hence we deal at some length here with the emotive element in the client's world. We make the assumption that mentors and coaches are already more than competent with the intellectual content of the client's message. To make a true connection in dialogue demands a marriage of both and we offer a way of doing this below, using primary empathy. For coaching and mentoring in the developmental quadrant advanced empathy is needed and we discuss this in Chapter 10.

What exactly is empathy? By empathy we mean an ability to project oneself into another person's experience while remaining unconditionally oneself. Carl Rogers describes empathy as follows: 'an accurate understanding of the other's own experience' (Rogers, 1957: 99).

Being empathic involves 'a choice on the part of the *mentor or coach* as to what she will pay attention to, namely the... world of the client as that individual perceives it... and it assists the client in gaining a clearer understanding of, and hence a greater control over, her own world and her own behaviour' (adapted from Rogers, 1979: 11, our italics).

Others have developed the meaning of empathy as follows:

- a 'bold swinging into the life of another' (Kohn, 1990: 1122);
- to 'make the other present' (Friedman, 1985: 4);
- 'the imaginative projection of one's own consciousness into another being' (Margulies, 1989: 58) and Noddings (1984: 30);
- 'empathy occurs when we suspend our single-minded focus of attention and instead adopt a double-minded focus of attention' (Baron-Cohen, 2011: 10).

In addition, the skill of empathy calls for action as 'there are at least two stages in empathy; recognition and response' (Baron-Cohen, 2011: 11).

Taking these ideas into consideration we define empathy as:

> an understanding of the world from the other's point of view, her feelings, experience and behaviour, and *the communication of that understanding in full*.
> (Brockbank and McGill, 1998: 195, original italics)

So understanding your client's story is fine, but this is not the operational skill in use. For true empathy there needs to be a communication of that understanding from you to your client. The tendency to believe that in order to communicate understanding you must also agree with your client's view of the world may inhibit your use of empathy. This belief holds many managers back from using the skill of empathy. To affirm and offer empathy does not mean to agree. Simon Baron-Cohen offers a scaled instrument, including both recognition and response, which provides a measure of empathy known as the Empathy Quotient (Baron-Cohen, 2011: 14). A simple approach to levels of empathy can be found in the work of Gerard Egan (Egan, 1990). There are two levels to consider: primary empathy and advanced empathy.

How to do empathy

Primary empathy is based on two pieces of information (incorporating the affective and the cognitive domains): what your client is feeling (expressed in words or non-verbal behaviour); the experience and/or behaviour which is the source of that feeling (revealed by what your client has already said). When these two pieces of information have been identified, the next step is communication of that awareness from you to your client. Primary empathy is offered directly when there is verbal or non-verbal evidence of an expressed emotion. For advanced empathy you will be guessing or 'hunching' about your client's feelings and we discuss this skill in Chapter 10. For example, your client might say 'This job seems to be taking over my life – I'm not sure I am up to it'. You may respond with empathy by saying something like 'You're feeling unsure about this job because you're afraid it might take over your life'. In starting to use empathy it may be helpful to use the form of words below.

'You feel...... because......' or

'You're feeling...... because......' or

'You feel...... when...... because......'

'You felt...... when...... because......'

'You may feel...... because......'

Using this form of words can be a useful way to get into using the skill as it reminds us that there are two elements to attend to. First you respond to the feeling and then communicate the reasoning element in what your client has said. If the feeling element is accurate (or near accurate) your client is likely to be able to work with the cognitive material in their story. We give an example below in our words and recognize that you will use your own words in your own way. The requirement for verbal or non-verbal evidence allows you to justify your response, especially when, as it often is, the feeling is denied. For example, 'I noticed that your voice went quieter when you said "I'm not sure"'.

Let us take the following statement made by your client:

I see myself as rather ordinary. I'm not sure I'm up to this kind of role. That's who I am. Ordinary.

This statement can be followed by a number of other responses, including:

- the cliché;
- questioning;
- interpretation;
- inaccurate;
- too soon/too late;
- parroting;
- incongruent;
- giving advice;
- giving an evaluation;
- making a judgement;
- challenging.

We have listed responses above which are not empathic. Each of these responses has its place but none of them is empathic. This is not to say they are not appropriate responses, but we note that they are sometimes believed to be forms of empathy and we simply clarify that *they are not empathy*.

For instance, you may respond with a *cliché* like 'I hear what you say' or 'I understand' which in itself is of no help to your client. Such statements do not convey to your client that she is understood. They are more likely to convey that she is *not* understood and that you are responding in an automatic and inauthentic manner.

A *questioning* response to your client's statement might be 'In what ways are you ordinary?' The question does not take account of the fact that she has taken a risk in disclosing how she feels. The question (which may be relevant elsewhere) does not convey empathic support about how and whether you are understanding her.

Interpreting your client's words occurs when you respond by trying to guess what is implied in her disclosure. An example might be 'This ordinary thing is the outward problem. I bet there's something else behind it that's upsetting you', eg 'You want to get to the top, don't you?'

Your response may just be plainly *inaccurate* like 'You're not very happy with the way your work is going'.

Your client may be taken off-track or stop or hesitate because accurate empathy has not happened and she may be blocked by what has been said. You may be listening to your own agenda rather than attending to your client. Giving your client a chance to express herself gives you time to sort out feelings and content.

If you merely repeat back to the speaker what has been said you are *parroting*. You need to change their 'I' to 'you'. This shows that you have got 'inside' your client in a way that conveys accurate empathy.

You may use language that is *incongruent* with your client. Using similar language in response to that used by your client encourages rapport, provided the language you use is authentic to you. You can then convey that you are in tune with your client. The use of 'clean language' is discussed on page 184.

Giving advice, eg 'Oh dear, you mustn't worry – you will do ok if you follow the merchandising diagram'.

Judging what the speaker has said, eg 'Nonsense, you'll be fine'.

Challenging the speaker, eg 'I bet you can do better if you try'.

When your client expresses a feeling in their story it is not necessary for you to treat them as a problem, go into 'rescue' mode or offer advice. Your solution may not be appropriate anyway. Understanding of their problem or issue is much more useful – provided you communicate that understanding. We know from the work of Rogers (1992) and Egan (1990) that communication of understanding stimulates the client to move on to considering solutions and to find ways of handling them.

We offer now an example of a primary empathic response to your client's statement on page 156 above about being ordinary.

'You say you feel rather ordinary. You're unsure about the work and you're wondering if you can do it well enough'.

The skill of empathy is rather rare in social interaction – few people experience it. When clients experience empathy, they recognize the power of an understanding response that builds trust, establishing the basis for a relationship within which it is safe to engage in learning.

Summarizing

Your summary will include all the factual content that you have restated as well as the emotional material to which you have responded with empathy. This allows your colleague to hear for the second time that their 'views have been heard' and that 'they are valued and involved', two of the engagement drivers identified by Robinson *et al* (2004).

Goal setting

Although goal setting is usually the first item for attention in the performance quadrant, the building of trust and agreeing on imposed objectives is the primary task in engagement work. This is why questioning and responding with empathy are first on our list. Only when there is a solid relationship in position should the coach or mentor begin the goal-setting process.

Several mnemonics for goal setting were given in Chapter 7 and these are useful for engagement too. However, a more thorough approach to objectives can be found in Egan's (1990) seven-point goal-setting checklist (also described in Chapter 7) and we replicate the list below with engagement examples of how goals should be agreed:

a) Stated as outcomes using the 'past participle' method. For instance, the statement 'I want to improve the team performance' is a description of an aim. To become a goal it needs to be phrased differently, eg 'I want improved performance from my team'. So goals need to be described as something which is 'acquired' or 'achieved' or 'decreased' as the case may be.

b) Clear and specific using the verbal techniques we discuss in Chapter 8 to recover deep structures. For instance, 'improved' can be made more specific by unpacking what 'improved' means and establishing better than what? If the goal is clear and specific it will define what better means, eg 'I want to have raised our average customer satisfaction ratings'.

c) Measurable and verifiable using the clear and specific statement of the goal as above as a basis. Any defined outcome can be verified, either by counting or at least its presence or absence, eg 'I want to have raised our average customer satisfaction ratings to good or above'.

d) Realistic goals are dependent on the necessary resources being available, the goal can be controlled by the client, and the cost not being too high, eg does your client have the authority, time and space to engage his team in this objective?

e) Substantive means that the goal is stretching for the client but not to breaking point. You will know what is challenging for your client and what they are capable of achieving. Using listening, restatement and empathy will ensure that goals are substantive.

f) Goals which are inconsistent with a client's values are unlikely to be achieved as the client experiences dissonance and even distress. For instance, the bankers in the Sterling case study in Chapter 8 were unhappy about being asked to 'hard sell' financial services to their customers, as their value system was based on serving their customers, not taking advantage of them.

g) A goal to be achieved 'sometime' is unlikely to see the light of day. Mentors and coaches are responsible for persisting in the question 'when?' so that clients can set their goals in exact terms, eg 'Within six months my team will have raised our customer satisfaction average to good or above'.

Feedback

Proceed as in Chapter 8, bearing in mind the emotional state of your colleague which you are now aware of and appreciate its significance. This may include feelings which will stimulate behavioural responses when feedback is received, so again the use of empathic responses supports the possibility of increased commitment and engagement. Providing you have established goals as above you will be able to offer specific and concrete feedback which relates to them, and this may be challenging for your client.

Challenge

Challenge is a deliberate attempt to trigger a change of some kind in your client. The skills you already have are part of challenge. For instance, you may give feedback by saying 'You say you are ordinary – last week's takings were far from ordinary' and ask a supplementary question, 'Can you give me an example of you being ordinary?' The response might surprise you and may have nothing to do with your colleague's performance on the job. For example, 'I have always felt ordinary because my GCSE results weren't great'. With the skills above you will know what to do with this response, repeating empathy, affirmation of their performance and possibly pointing out that past exams are almost irrelevant to current performance.

You may offer primary empathy based on non-verbal evidence as challenge, eg 'You look rather hesitant – as if unsure you can do the job'. Your colleague may respond by asking for training or angrily affirming that she can do the job provided she gets enough staff. Either way the conversation is in play.

Challenge is considered by Egan (1990) to be always positive, while the negative version is confrontation. For development we recommend both challenge and confrontation and we discuss this in Chapter 10.

When an external coach or mentor has developed a strong trust relationship with an internal client, they may be able to both challenge and confront. Everything depends on the quality of the relationship.

Engagement programmes

FIRST EXAMPLE engagement mentoring at CILT

The Chartered Institute of Logistics and Transport (CILT) is the professional body for those industries and organizations that are involved in, working in, or that have an interest in the logistics and transport sectors. As an international organization the Institute has 30,000 members in 28 countries. The Institute in the UK has a membership of 22,000.

'Logistics' is the process of designing, managing and improving supply chains, which might include purchasing, manufacturing, storage and, of course, transport. Transport remains a major component of most supply chains. Logistics services and other transport companies need to understand logistics and supply chain management in order to tailor their services to meet their customers' needs.

The mission statement of the Chartered Institute declares that the Institute seeks:

To be the focus for professional excellence, the development of the most relevant and effective techniques in logistics and transport, and the development of policies which respond to the challenges of a changing world.

Members are independent qualified practitioners in their own right, working in a variety of contexts, and the Institute offers a programme of continuing professional development, part of which was their mentoring scheme.

The declared purpose of the mentoring scheme, in an industry where members need to be prepared to constantly re-skill to meet the demands of the knowledge economy, was declared as follows:

To help our members to meet the challenges of a changing world of work and to provide a source of advice on professional development.

The scheme was designed to offer members an incentive to join the Institute, to remain with the Institute and advance within the Institute, because of the career and professional development, advice and support available through the scheme. Hence it was decided that the quantifiable outcome for the Institute would be enhanced membership figures.

The scheme defined the mentor as 'an experienced and trusted advisor and guide to a protégé' and the Institute launched the scheme by providing training and support for 30 senior practitioners working with 60 protégés for one year. The mentoring scheme was offered as an aid for new members, upgrading memberships, career advice or progression, and academic support as well as maintaining and enhancing performance or knowledge.

The Director of Professional Development and her team approached the scheme with care, informed by and taking into account the mentoring literature.

The selection process was thorough, using a customized questionnaire (adapted from Cohen, 1995) and both mentors and protégés had choice. This was achieved by the provision of mentor profiles (including personal pen portraits) from which potential protégés were asked to choose their best three. On the basis of these, mentors were then offered a number of protégé profiles and made their choice. The questionnaire proved to be an ideal method of selection as the only trainee mentor who had not completed it successfully alone had difficulty in accepting the training.

The chosen mentors were offered a two-day residential training workshop in three different UK locations, which aimed to:

consolidate knowledge;

recognize skills and practice;

engage in reflective learning;

peruse documentation for mentors;

discuss requirements for accreditation;

establish support structures;

agree a review process.

The outcome of the mentoring programme, which is still running, is enhanced membership and commitment to the Institute as well as a plentiful supply of mentors.

The CILT aimed to achieve an improvement objective and used a person-centred approach to achieve it. The learning outcomes were difficult to identify as each mentoring couple will have devised their own, but the tendency was to address career development issues. The programme offered clients an experience of mentoring where they benefited in a performance way and their learning was improvement in career terms.

SECOND EXAMPLE engagement mentoring at Intellect

Intellect is a trade organization which serves the IT industry and their management board sought a mentoring programme using board members who would act as mentors. This organization, seeking Investors in People recognition, wanted to introduce a more humanistic management culture and retain young, ambitious staff. The programme involved volunteer mentor training, protégé orientation and individual coaching for mentors as required. Coaching sessions were provided by an executive coach, outside the organization, with no feedback to it.

Participants at the mentor training were amazed by the process, which used the SLO method (working in triads as Speaker, Listener, Observer) to invite reflective dialogue as well as group dynamics to deal with power issues, and 90 per cent of those present offered positive anonymous evaluation. By positive we mean that they reported some gain in learning or change in understanding. At their interim evaluation, the programme was on target to achieve its objectives, in management terms. The mentors are still at the learning stage, and, in coaching sessions, report typical learning curve insecurities and discomfort. Protégés are unused to defining and declaring their ownership of objectives, being rather afraid of offending powerful figures in the organization, and this is likely to be limiting the learning outcome to engagement.

A volunteer for the live demonstration, where I would take the role of mentor, was a highly qualified financial executive with senior responsibility in the organization. She had expressed honest doubts about the whole process (having initially rated it 3 or 4 out of 10) and said she would volunteer to 'give it a try' as a 'client' in a brief demonstration in front of her colleagues. She chose to discuss a work/life issue. This kind of issue was agreed by the group as a likely topic which might arise in the mentoring relationship. She was torn between spending time with her aunt who was not in good health and having rest and recuperation from the demands of her high-powered job. In the demonstration her story was told, heard, restated and the emotional elements attended to by empathic responses. Her feelings about her aunt turned out to be mixed and included some resentment as well as affection. She also expressed her impatience with her siblings who were not helping or 'doing their share'. When questioned she realized that she was trying to make up for the resentment by taking all the responsibility for looking after her aunt. When her true feelings were expressed her view of the situation changed, she recognized her right to her own leisure time, and she resolved to negotiate with her siblings and discuss this honestly with her aunt.

At evaluation this person changed her rating to 9.5 out of 10 as she believed the process had changed her view of the situation completely, transformed her stance towards what had previously seemed an insurmountable problem and totally altered her opinion about the value of mentoring. The power of empathy to achieve this kind of change is a precious skill for you to use in the engagement quadrant.

An example of engagement coaching which used the person-centred approach to achieve a performance objective is presented in the Addaction case study below.

THIRD EXAMPLE engagement coaching at Addaction – project managers becoming coaches

---

Addaction is a drug and alcohol charity whose mission, 'Reducing both the use of and the harm caused by drugs and alcohol', includes a vision of first-class leadership, a national reputation for clinical excellence and a leading authority on the issue of drugs and alcohol, as well as a reputation in local communities as an organization equipped to meet the challenges of the future.

As part of this mission, and in response to the National Treatment Agency's quality initiatives, Addaction identified the need for a Core Competencies Framework. The framework was created, accredited and launched with the aim of enabling frontline project workers to demonstrate knowledge, skills and values, in nine key areas of service delivery considered essential for good practice.

Project workers in Addaction are managed by project managers and team leaders who would be responsible for guiding and supporting their staff through the framework. In order to facilitate such guidance and support, all project managers in Addaction were offered coach training over a period of two years.

The training, entitled *Introduction to Coaching*, for up to 18 managers at a time, consisted of two days initially, and a week later, a follow-up review day where participants would reflect on their coaching practice. The workshop was highly participative and experiential with the aim that on completion project managers would:

1 understand coaching models;

2 identify coaching skills;

3 practise coaching skills;

4 reflect on their coaching practice as managers. (A pre-questionnaire alerted participants to their existing coaching ability.)

Two coaching models were presented: GROW and SOS, a model designed especially for Addaction, described in Chapter 7. A booklet was provided which included brief and accessible notes about reflective learning and coaching skills, as well as pro formas to enhance practice.

The first two days were intensely practical, with project managers engaging in experiential exercises and live coaching sessions with their colleagues. Addaction's project managers were revealed as deeply committed individuals, with a passion for the organization's purpose. They were almost without exception working up to their limits as project meetings usually followed their own appointments with clients. While they fully supported the core competency programme they were anxious to avoid pressurizing their staff and these concerns formed the basis of several of their live coaching sessions. The experiential nature of the training was appreciated by participants, who identified the following as effective:

role-plays and practice;

discussion and feedback;

presentation of models;

reflection on third day;

differences and overlap with supervision and counselling.

The purpose of the coaching programme was to equip project managers with the skills and confidence to guide and support their staff through the core competency framework. A degree of persuasion was required, as not all project workers were enthusiastic about the core competency framework, so the project was engagement in nature. The managers needed to deploy a broad range of skills to achieve the organization's objectives and ensure that the outcome was positive for the organization. The Addaction project managers were invited to engage in their development as coaches without generating that goal for themselves and to invite their staff to engage in acquiring their core competency qualifications, again without generating that goal for themselves. The recommended approach for their coaching activities was person-centred and the learning outcome was improvement.

We present here the NEWW model for use in the engagement quadrant. NEWW is an acronym for Now; Empathy; What; When. The model explicitly calls for empathy.

How to use the NEWW model in the engagement quadrant

Session structure

NOW: Here as a mentor or coach you will establish what the material issue of the session will be through a combination of listening, questioning, restatement and summary. For example, your colleague may be finding it difficult to fit in all the tasks which are his responsibility and there are doubts about his level of engagement with the company and his role in it. At this first stage of the model you are working with facts rather than feelings.

EMPATHY: You will soon hear the emotional charge in his description of being stressed by too many responsibilities, and your empathic restatement of this, 'You seem tired and rather overwhelmed just at present', will build trust between you. Providing you can hold off too much questioning the real issue of delegation may emerge. This would happen eventually without empathy but using the skill speeds up the process dramatically.

WHAT: Here you will work in 'what if...?'mode to elicit how your colleague may feel when he does or does not delegate and what the consequences are of both options. Your empathic responses are 'You must feel burdened with all these responsibilities' and 'You feel anxious if you don't know they were done right'. Primary empathy stimulates the trust needed for more disclosure. You may also decide to engage in some disclosure yourself about your own management struggles. Astute questioning about options and preferred ways of working will lead to further statements from your client which include potential emotions, like 'They will make a mess of it, I will be blamed and I will feel awful'. Again the primary empathy of 'You feel concerned because your staff may not get it right and you will be blamed – which will make you feel awful'.

WHEN: This is the final stage and should not happen until you are satisfied that you have received all the key emotional messages that your colleague wants to express. Your observation of body language (hand or leg movements) and non-verbal cues (eg avoiding eye contact) will help you with this. You can always offer empathy based on what you can see, eg 'You still seem unsure about this'. If you move too soon to demand action, they may withdraw or just agree without commitment. The questioning here is action focused but again we recommend that you invite your client to speculate about how each action is likely to make them feel, and how the consequences will affect them. For example, in response to 'I need to give X a chance to check the stock file and report back to me', you may respond with 'You may feel anxious about that' and 'Let's look at how you might feel if he fails/succeeds'.

The use of empathy at every stage speeds up the process because of the high degree of trust engendered. Many practitioners achieve this trust by attending to their colleague, reinforcing by nodding and remaining silent, giving space for movement towards options and actions. The use of empathy makes this happen much more quickly.

Accreditation of coaches and mentors working in the engagement quadrant

Practitioners working in the engagement quadrant are likely to be accredited by the EMCC at Practitioner level. Such individuals are described as:

Coaches or mentors who may either be working as an internal coach/ mentor, use coaching/mentoring as part of their main job or starting up as an external coach/mentor.

Likely to be working with a small range of clients or contexts and possibly within own area of experience to improve performance, build confidence and stretch capability.

Method of working is typically applying a limited range of models, tools and processes.

Practitioners in the engagement quadrant may also seek credentialing from the ICF, providing they meet the ICF core competences. The key discriminating requirement at different levels is the number of hours of coaching they claim to have completed. The terms 'practised', 'proven' and 'expert' are not defined in the available documentation. Practitioners may apply as follows:

Associate Certified Coach (ACC): The ICF Associate Certified Coach credential is for the practised coach with at least 100 hours of client coaching experience.

Professional Certified Coach (PCC): The Professional Certified Coach credential is for the proven coach with at least 750 hours of client coaching experience.

Master Certified Coach (MCC): The Master Certified Coach credential is for the expert coach with at least 2,500 hours of client coaching experience.

Continuing professional development for engagement coaches and mentors

There is an expectation that all ICF-credentialed coaches will continue their education and build on their level of experience. The resulting growth in competency and professionalism will be evidenced by their journey to the MCC credential.

Practitioners who seek individual EMCC accreditation as mentors and coaches at Practitioner level are required to provide evidence that they engage in 16 hours of CPD per year and one hour of supervision per quarter year. Most adults in managerial roles are likely to engage in professional development for at least 16 hours in a given year and receive one hour of supervision from their own line manager as part of their quarterly review. Is this enough? Because engagement work is likely to involve the coach or mentor in some emotional intimacy, there is a need for non-managerial supervision in order to maintain a professional standard. We discuss how supervision supports coaches and mentors in Chapter 13.

Evaluation and return on investment

Those who purchase coaching services are likely to wish for some measure of return on investment, if only to justify the coaching budget. Many organizations use staff surveys as a measure and this descriptive method conforms to the declared purpose of engagement coaching or mentoring. Such surveys should ensure that the three key ingredients of engagement are covered, ie knowledge, action and emotional aspects. Intellect, the organization in the case study above, carried out an interim review and used staff surveys to establish the impact of their mentoring programme. We describe these in Appendix 6. In addition, judgement evaluation may be linked to measures of retention, absenteeism and the like. If there are board-level requests for 'hard' measures of performance and output then the coaching or mentoring becomes very clearly performance and every department will have their own set of performance measures.

Chapter summary

In this chapter we have clarified what engagement means in the corporate context and how coaching or mentoring can support engagement. The skills needed in the engagement quadrant have been described and their significance identified for coaches or mentors as line managers, in-house practitioners or external consultants. In addition to the skills already described in Chapter 8, a crucial addition for engagement is the skill of empathy. We recommend that practitioners limit themselves to primary empathy as they are working with objectives which may not be owned by their client, and 'how do you feel?' questions will take them to an emotional arena where they may be unable to operate safely. We have noted that because coaches or mentors in this quadrant may use primary empathy with their clients, they will be working, albeit in a limited extent, in the emotional domain, and hence there is a need for the coach or mentor to have additional support in the form of non-managerial supervision which we discuss in detail in Chapter 13.

Development

Coaching and mentoring that supports individual development to the point of transformation requires individual ownership of objectives which may or may not coincide with those of the organization. Reflective dialogue in developmental coaching or mentoring supports a learning outcome which is deep, significant and double loop, so it has the potential for transformation. The skills needed for reflective dialogue are described below, with some examples of using them in practice. We make the assumption that developmental practitioners are already using the skills described in the previous two chapters.

What is development in human learning?

Drawing on our theory in Chapters 2 and 3, development is identified as learning where the learner's view of the world is radically changed, where their feelings are considered, their thinking may be altered, and where their consequent actions are different. Developmental coaching or mentoring acknowledges and respects the client's view of reality, and works with clients to define their own goals, while offering the potential for challenge and transformation. As a developmental mentor or coach, while attending to day-to-day performance, you are seeking, through reflective dialogue, to challenge your client to look beyond their immediate horizon and transform their view of the system in which they live and work.

Developmental practitioners may work at all levels, and are able, when and where appropriate, to adopt the processes of performance and engagement coaching as part of their approach. However, the characteristic of the developmental coach is their ability to support the client through double loop learning to transformation. Carroll (2004) identifies them as third generation and he defines them as 'professional facilitators of learning at different levels'.

The developmental purpose is personal and professional development, promoting the client's own desires so the focus is decided by the client, who becomes responsible for their own learning and development. The relationship supports trust, recognizes their client's world and may lead to potential transformation. Developmental coaching has been said to last a lifetime: 'Coaching is a powerful alliance designed to forward and enhance the life-long process of human learning, effectiveness, and fulfilment' (Whitworth *et al*, 1998: 202) and this is also said of developmental mentoring.

The crucial component of developmental coaching or mentoring is the ability to conduct a reflective dialogue, as this offers the potential for double loop learning and transformation. We discuss the skills needed for reflective dialogue below.

Skills in the developmental quadrant

The characteristics of work in the developmental quadrant, based on humanistic principles and recognizing the social and constructed nature of learning, start from the assumption that your client is willing and able to grow and develop. In addition, you will affirm the subjective world of your client, whether you agree with it or not, through empathy and acceptance of their emotional experience. We list the essentials of the person-centred approach in Chapter 2 where we note the necessary and sufficient conditions for learning based on Rogers (1983) and discuss the core conditions of congruence, unconditional positive regard and empathy.

However, we note that:

> It is easy to embrace the person-centred approach intellectually. However much personal work and practice is needed to eliminate old ingrained patterns –
> such as the need to be needed, to know best, to control, to solve the problem,
> to impress – before one can shift towards being truly person-centred.
>
> (Silverstone, 1993: viii)

The skills described in this chapter are:

- presence (can be learnt);
- listening and congruence;
- restatement;
- summary;
- questioning;
- advanced empathy (primary empathy is considered in the previous chapter);
- managing emotion;
- feedback;
- challenge;
- immediacy; and
- confrontation.

Coach or mentor presence

The first thing you bring to a relationship is your presence. This has been defined in rather new-age terms as characterized by 'the felt experience of timelines, connectedness and a larger truth' (Silshee, 2010: 118). The ICF have defined presence somewhat more clearly in their competence list as: the ability to be fully conscious and create a spontaneous relationship with the client, employing a style that is open, flexible and confident:

a. is present and flexible during the coaching process, dancing in the moment;

b. accesses own intuition and trusts one's inner knowing – 'goes with the gut';

c. is open to not knowing and takes risks;

d. sees many ways to work with the client, and chooses in the moment what is most effective;

e. uses humour effectively to create lightness and energy;

f. confidently shifts perspectives and experiments with new possibilities for own action;

g. demonstrates confidence in working with strong emotions, and can self-manage and not be overpowered or enmeshed by client's emotions.

(ICF, 2011)

You are present to your client by virtue of your posture, gesture, facial expression and your position in relation to your client, even before you use your voice to communicate. Your non-verbal messages are in the room, like body language, facial expression and voice, which are thought to deliver meaning quite independently of words (Argyle, 1975; Ekman and Freisen, 1975; Pease, 1981; Morris, 1977).

In fact, non-verbal and vocal channels often carry a bigger proportion of meaning than the verbal message. For instance, communication of approval has been explored and found to favour the non-verbal channel (90 per cent), leaving the spoken words with only 10 per cent of meaning (Mehrabian, 1971). Where the non-verbal or vocal channels are inconsistent with verbal messages, ie spoken words, receivers accept the meaning carried by the non-verbal channels. A clear example of this is sarcasm, where, whatever the verbal message, the voice tone, ie the message in the vocal channel, is the message received.

Clearly, cultural factors influence how far meanings carried by non-verbal channels are universal, and this point receives a thorough treatment, as do all non-verbal communication issues, in Bull (1983). Of particular interest are the findings on dominance and status and how they are communicated by interpersonal distance and posture. Suffice to say that as coach or mentor you communicate, whether you know it or not, a host of messages through non-verbal and vocal channels and, of course, your client will communicate through the same channels, eg yawning, fidgeting, glazed eyes are all indications that they have disconnected.

Awareness of these non-verbal communication channels is likely to enable you to make sense of responses from your client. For instance, if your client keeps his head down, avoiding eye contact, and fidgets while he talks, he is clearly preoccupied with something, which may relate to his work or personal life, and you may enable him to voice those concerns.

One key aspect of non-verbal behaviour that affects your relationship with your client is your physical stance. In Figure 10.1 we draw on the work of Heron (1993) who has studied the stance and posture of facilitators and

FIGURE 10.1a Coach or mentor posture – crouched and defensive

FIGURE 10.1b Coach or mentor posture – open and potent

insists that even charisma is learnt behaviour. He suggests that a facilitator's personal presence enables her to be in 'conscious command of how she is appearing in space and time' (1993: 32), and this seems a good thing for a coach or mentor to be. He further suggests that many facilitators crouch in defensive positions, slumped in chairs with ankles crossed and head jutting forward. Heron suggests that if you are in such a position you are likely to be: 'about to talk too much, exhibits anxious control, and missing a lot of what is going on' (Heron, 1999: 222). In this case 'going with the gut' might not be the best plan for a coach or mentor.

When crouching in the way shown in Figure 10.1(a), awareness is reduced, and you are likely to be perceived as a talking head. A simple adjustment to posture, with head, neck and spine rearranged with a sense of lift, lengthening and widening the back, pelvis, thighs and legs grounded through contact with the floor, as shown in Figure 10.1(b), is suggested by Heron. You move from slouch and impotence into a commanding and potent posture. The body wakes up and is ready to receive energies in the field around it. Such posture projects presence, and the posture **can be learnt** (see SOLER below, page 175).

Coach or mentor congruence

We define congruence as a way of being genuine, being real, sharing feelings and attitudes as well as opinions and beliefs/judgements, through self-disclosure. The act of self-disclosure is a direct example of trust behaviour, where you take the risk of disclosing and thereby encourage your client to do the same.

You will also model congruence by demonstrating the crucial characteristic of 'owned' statements (which begin with 'I' or contain 'I' statements). Such statements are likely to be real disclosure while use of the distancing 'you', 'they' or 'one' serves to mask disclosure.

As a coach or mentor you are modelling appropriate self-disclosure in the relationship even though this is not designed for yourself. Because self-disclosure is reciprocal in effect, your disclosure gives permission for your client to follow suit and express some positive feelings about what they are doing and some negative feelings too. In particular, it allows your client to say 'I've never done this before', 'it feels like counselling'. These feelings, expressed openly, although fairly superficial, are the hallmark of trust-building self-disclosure.

Where your client refuses, or is unwilling, to disclose, you may judge that your client has made a conscious choice, and that choice should be respected. We would urge you to ensure that your client is enabled to speak about himself, early in the first session. Many practitioners are surprised to find that their clients are wordless when they first meet, as the relationship is at zero point. The coaching or mentoring relationship is embedded in a number of oppressive social systems, eg sexism, racism, ageism etc. If your client belongs to a minority group they may well lack confidence with a coach or mentor from the dominant group. You may like to address the issue when agreeing guidelines at the very beginning.

The significance of congruence or truth-telling in developmental relationships is revealed in the NCH case study below.

CASE STUDY   NCH orange cardigans

The children's charity, NCH (formerly known as The National Children's Home), is the leading UK provider of family and community centres, children's services in rural areas, services for disabled children and their families, and services for young people leaving care. The charity values the unique potential of all children and young people and promotes the support and opportunities they need to reach it.

A was surprised when asked to consider being a mentor to E, and flattered, while at the same time thinking 'It won't be long before she finds me out'. E sought a mentoring relationship to support her professional development as a manager of people. E was keen to progress to a management role in NCH. E chose A as her mentor because of E's 'really positive view of the way A supported colleagues and worked with people and thought it would be useful to have the opinions and input of a colleague working outside of her direct team'.

The mentoring couple (A mentoring E) described below both work for NCH. They developed a model based on their reading and research about mentoring, which included a loosely structured agenda, regular lunchtime meetings, a confidentiality clause and a commitment to explore and develop as the need arose.

As the mentoring relationship progressed over a period of one year, A was pleased to find out how much she knew that would be of benefit to E, sometimes because she is older and more experienced but also because she is a different person with a different perspective. A has observed that E has benefited by simply articulating her own assessment of a situation and sometimes A could add something, but mostly A simply offered affirmation and recognition of E's self-assessment. In this way, A's mentoring helped E to make the most of her own innate skills.

A has little experience in E's field of expertise and this was not necessary as the mentoring was not designed to support E's day-to-day work. What A brings to the mentoring relationship is her ability to see E's strengths and affirm them. E hoped to get someone else's 'take' on her management style, her behaviour and how she was dealing with situations. She hoped to learn from A's experience and approach.

Both women saw the relationship as multi-roled in that all the terms, mentor, coach, adviser, guide and friend, were relevant at various points in their relationship. They both noted that they reached a stage when they crossed from using a semi-formal agenda to just getting on with it. Both A and E have gained from the relationship, with E gaining in confidence and a promotion to a management position in NCH. E perceives the mentoring relationship as having helped her to see and analyse situations more objectively, and to value development and support so that she is now acting as a mentor herself. A found pleasure in supporting the development of a colleague outside the line manager relationship and has recognized her skill in nurturing others. She has felt refreshed by her contact with E whom she describes as positive, constructive and committed, and recognizes that they have both found security in being able to 'check out' turbulent situations in the safety of their confidential relationship.

The relationship developed from mentor/coach/adviser into a friendship which includes supporting each other in their commitments to honesty, truth-telling, taking shoes off in the office and the wearing of matching orange cardigans. Their admiration for each other is evident with A's acknowledgement of E's accomplishment and abilities and E's recognition of A's valuable contributions and continuing support.

Their final comments: A mentions that 'through my relationship with E, I have realized my yearning for a similar mentor of my own'. E remarks that 'since I've had the job it's just good to have someone there who knows all the little chips I have on my shoulder, the chinks in the armour etc, and can help me deal with them in my new role without judging!'

Here the client generated her own agenda and goals for the relationship. The person-centred approach is revealed by the evident regard and empathy between the two parties. The learning outcome was transformation and the relationship continues.

Listening

We discussed basic listening skills in Chapter 8. As a developmental coach or mentor you will need to engage in active listening and we discuss this in more detail now, using the example of your client speaking as follows: 'I'm not sure about applying for this job. I might not be up to it and I have all these other commitments...'

Attending to your client

In order to listen it is necessary that you first attend to your client. The reinforcement power of attending means that attending can alter another's behaviour (quoted in Egan, 1976: 96). Indeed, the withdrawal of attention in relationships has been described as psychological punishment (Nelson-Jones, 1986).

Attending refers to the way in which you can be **with** your client both physically and psychologically. Attending is how you are personally present, physically receptive, calm and grounded without anxiety, ready to tune in to verbal and non-verbal messages. By this is meant the quality of the attention you are giving to your client. Your body stance and orientation will influence the quality of your listening, and Egan (1990) has characterized this with the SOLER mnemonic to assist you in adopting an attentive posture in order to convey the minimum requirements for attending to your client:

S – face your client *Squarely*, that is, with a posture (usually seated) that conveys involvement, and indicates that you wish to be with them. This is in contrast to a posture which turns away from them or appears uninterested. The square posture shows that you are not distracted and ensures stereophonic reception.

O – adopting an *Open* posture to signify 'receive' mode. Crossed arms and legs may convey a closed stance towards your client. Such a posture may not necessarily mean that you are closed towards her, but it may convey it non-verbally. The key question to ask is to what extent is my physical posture conveying an openness and availability to my client?

L – at times it is possible to *Lean* towards your client in a way which suggests engagement. We can see this when viewing people in pubs and restaurants by observing how people lean forward, lean back or lean away.

E – maintain *Eye* contact with your client. This is a useful indicator of involvement which does not have to be continual to be effective. It does not mean 'eyeball to eyeball' either!

R – be relatively *Relaxed* in your stance. This means not being physically distracting or fidgety. It also means being comfortable with your client so that your body can convey non-verbal expression.

Utilizing SOLER ensures authenticity without artificially contriving a physical stance that is counter-productive for your client. Negative or uncomfortable messages might include staring, getting too squared up where it becomes threatening, looking out of a window continuously or tapping a pencil on a table! Being aware of the effect of your physical and emotional presence is the key. SOLER is useful to convey the basic features of attending. To the reader unfamiliar with the approach it may appear that to adopt the features could suggest a lack of genuineness or manipulation. It is designed merely to highlight what we all do naturally when we are authentically attending. We consider now hearing, active and passive listening.

Hearing, active and passive listening

Contrast the distinction between hearing, active listening and passive listening. If you close your eyes you can hear what is going on around you as well as sounds inside you. As you hear you are likely to be interpreting what you are hearing – we place meaning on the sounds we hear quite automatically. Alternatively, you may be passively not trying to grasp meaning from it or not really caring what you hear.

Now with eyes open listen to your client.

Listening actively is not just hearing what he is saying but is a two-way process involving both sender and receiver skills. Active or effective listening can only be assessed by the speaker. So, as your client conveys his message to you, about his problems at work, perhaps, you as coach need to convey to him that you have received what he has tried to communicate. It is possible at this point for active listening to seem passive and polite, whereas it is a procedure for connection. Anyone who has tried to learn to hear the other in the other's own terms knows how difficult it is to become 'an observer from within' (Schwaber, 1983: 274). This is why active listening is a tough-minded process. We have to really work at it and if we are really listening it shows! Your client is aware of you really listening.

Active listening also involves listening to the whole person, not just the words they may be using at the level of intellect. Our culture emphasizes listening to the words people **say**. We tend to listen at the level of words – the verbal channel. But active listening also includes listening to what a person's non-verbal messages are saying – **body** messages, and, often forgotten, the messages in the vocal channel – the tone of voice used. As senders of messages we often convey our **feelings** through the vocal channel while denying them in the verbal channel, eg when we say in a wobbly voice 'I'll be alright'. Underlying these channels is the spirit of the message, your client's real feelings and will to act.

Let us take an example of your client talking about his potential promotion. He is saying that he is considering going for the promotion because he is well qualified for the post – the verbal channel. His body is sending out messages that convey his lack of confidence about the post, as is his tone of voice. Underlying these messages is another that is transmitted about his will or spirit to go for the promotion. If you passively went by what he said you would conclude that all he needs to do is to get on with the application form. However, by actively listening you are picking up the more complex messages from the other two channels.

Listening with sympathy

A common and human response, but sympathy can get in the way for your client. For example, at a later session your client reports that he applied for the promotion but was 'pipped' to it by another candidate. You could offer your sympathy and replicate his feelings of disappointment and loss at not getting the promotion. By doing this, you could be disabling him as he is unlikely to move on from there. Being with him empathically is different, as we shall see below.

Silence (often a valuable moment – stay with it!)

At times your client may pause or not want to express words. There may be a tendency to fill the silence or space with a question or a response. There is, in fact, no silence – it is just that your client has stopped using words! That 'silence' can be precious for your client and there are non-verbal cues to observe without words. The session is for your client. It is space for him. If that space includes silence it is to be respected.

Active listening

We have noted that the message is carried through both verbal and non-verbal channels. Attending effectively to the speaker means that as coach or mentor you are in a position to listen carefully to what your client is saying verbally and non-verbally. Egan (1990) describes active or complete listening, as follows:

1 observing and reading the speaker's non-verbal behaviour – posture, facial expressions, movement, tone of voice, and the like;
2 listening to the whole person in the context of the social groupings of life;
3 Tough-minded listening;
4 listening to and understanding the speaker's verbal messages.

1 As noted above, much of the message has been shown to be carried by the non-verbal or vocal channels. Over half of the message may be communicated by facial expression or body language, while over 30 per cent travels in the tone, pitch, volume or paralanguage (ums, ahhs or grunts) of the voice (Argyle, 1975).

2 At this point you do not form responses to your client, but listen. An example would be when your client is telling you what it is like for her, working in an office environment where her manager questions her commitment because she does not work late. While your client is saying what it is like for her as a working mother, coping with her job and her family commitments, you may have some views about how you would cope in such an environment. For example, you may reflect to yourself: 'I could cope with that' or 'It would not be a problem for me'.

In this you are 'playing the doubting game' (Elbow, 1998) and falling into the trap of empathy mis-defined as 'the recognition of self in the other' (Kohut, 1978 cited by Jordan, 1991: 68). As you listen to your own thoughts on **your** way of coping you may detract from how your client is thinking, feeling and being in **her** environment. The key is for you to 'put aside' your own responses to her situation, suspend judgement, and listen from your client's standpoint – where she is coming from. Such an approach has been named 'the believing game' (Elbow, 1998). To achieve acceptance without necessarily agreeing, as coach or mentor you must also contain your approval as well as your disapproval, as one implies the other. Even when you respond, it is necessary to work with where your client is and not put your solutions forward to her. This has been described as a 'double-minded focus of attention' (Baron-Cohen 2011, page 10).

In listening to your client's story, you will, if effective, place yourself (as far as is possible) in her social context. You will endeavour to understand what it is like to be a woman in a family situation, to tackle a prevailing norm within which she feels oppressed. Rather than get trapped in your own contextual picture, what is it about **her** picture that you need to understand to enable her to deal with it? In this way you will be endeavouring to get into her personal context – how life is for her, ie in Martin Buber's words 'making the other present' or getting to 'imagine-other' (Buber, 1965 cited in Kohn, 1990: 133).

Issues relating to the social grouping of your client's life may not be part of the verbal message. However, a client who is a member of an ethnic minority may be visibly living with issues of exclusion and her message will convey something of her struggle, and may be very relevant to her learning and reflection. For example, black or Asian staff in an all-white office may be marginalized in group work and informal gatherings. Cultural factors may provide important cues for you, as you will need to be alert to the cultural context of your client and provide what is known as transcultural caring in your responses (Leininger, 1987). Cultural care has been defined as a coach or mentor using their client's notion of care, as defined by their client's culture, and accommodating to it, rather than depending on their own notion of care (Eleftheriadou, 1994). We discuss cross-cultural and diversity issues in Chapters 5 and 12.

3 Tough-minded listening requires that as coach or mentor you place yourself in the frame of your client so that you really understand where she is coming from. This means that you pick up what is perhaps being distorted or non-verbally leaked by your client. For example, she may be talking about going for a promotion in the organization and expressing how she is well qualified for the promotion. However, she is also conveying less explicitly through her voice tone, demeanour and some of her words that she may feel that she is not confident to do the job if promoted. This in turn may affect her will to apply for the post. It is for you as coach or mentor to pick up this inconsistency and hold it until it is appropriate to offer it as an observation.

4 Understanding your client's verbal message demands that you are able to translate what may be coded messages by recognizing what are known as surface structures and recovering the deep structures in what they say (McCann, 1988). When we transmit a message verbally we often do so in what linguistic experts call surface

structures (Chomsky, 1957, 1969). Surface structures are transformations of deep structures by a process of:

- deletion (missing out information);
- distortion (altering meaning);
- generalization (generalizing from the particular).

Example of deletion:

Surface structure: 'The best option is...'

Deep structure: 'The best option in comparison to the others is...'

Example of distortion:

Surface structure: 'My manager is against me'.

Deep structure: 'My manager doesn't like me and won't change her attitude to me'.

Example of generalization:

Surface structure: 'People don't understand'.

Deep structure: 'My colleagues X and Y don't understand me'.

It is possible to recover the deep structures which underlie the surface structures in most communications by identifying the deletion, distortion or generalization which has transformed them. In Table 10.1, some 'deep structures' are recovered from surface structures and the transformation identified.

How can you help your client to recover their 'lost' structures without being too intrusive? We recommend the technique of restatement described below, as when your client hears what they have just said they may immediately recognize the deletion, distortion or generalization they have used. In most cases the power of restatement is enough. Alternatively, you may choose to formulate your questions in a way that will help your client to realize their deep structure, and we discuss this below on pages 180 and 189.

In Chapter 9 we mentioned three levels of listening given by Whitworth *et al* (1998) and we summarize their characteristics again below:

Level I refers to the state of listening as 'what does this mean to me?' as the listener is attending to himself. For developmental coaching or mentoring you need to be at least at level II.

Level II refers to focused listening where you are focused on your client. The observed behaviour associated with level II listening is leaning forward and eye contact, as in SOLER above.

Level III listening is all-round listening, picking up information from everything around you. At level III your attention is wholly on your client, their words, expressions, everything they bring to the session. Level III listening is holistic, using all five senses, recognizing the value of intuition, and trusting those hunches and senses that pop up in

TABLE 10.1   Recovering deep structures

Surface structure	Deep structure	Transformation
It's just not possible	I believe it's not possible	Deletion
Nobody tells me anything	My manager has not informed me about the new rates of pay	Generalization
Obviously	It is obvious to me that...	Deletion
He never considers my ideas	He did not consider my idea on X and Y occasions	Generalization
He has an attitude problem	I am annoyed by some of his X and Y behaviours	Deletion
They always forget	X and Y forgot on W and Z occasions	Generalization
I must get on	I want to be finished by six	Deletion
No-one ever talks to me here	My colleagues X and Y didn't talk to me on W and Z occasions	Generalization
They don't like me	I believe that X and Y don't like me	Deletion
He is never here, always on courses	He was not here on days X and Y when he was away on courses	Generalization

dialogues. As a level III listener you must be receptive, softly sensitive as the messages are often infinitesimal changes in sound, or other sense. For example, if your client goes 'cold' you can feel that and 'hear' what it means for her. You are listening for signs of life within your client's agenda and also for signs of disturbance or distress. Your attention is wholly on your client and what they say but you are noting their demeanour, their tone of voice and other aspects of the vocal communication channel. For example, loud speech, almost inaudible speech, rapid gabbling or mumbling all suggest an emotional charge being expressed but not articulated. In particular, you listen for energy, the sign of their commitment to what they value and want.

Restatement of client's story

When you deem it appropriate to respond, we recommend that before anything else, you restate your client's words. We discussed how to do this in Chapters 8 and 9. You may wish to start with phrases like 'What I think you said was that you want to decide whether you really want the job or not?' or 'So you want to discuss how this job relates to your other plans?'

Because of our social tendency to assess and interpret and think what we are going to say even before the speaker has finished, restatement is an important process to ensure that you really are attending to your client and not imposing your own view of her reality. In responding, the tone of voice is important. A tone that suggests criticism or uncaring or agreeing is not helpful. The aim is to restate back to your client what they have said, their words and meaning; their emotions – feelings, will or spirit.

The restatement does not have to repeat the words your client used exactly, although use of their key words will be more accurate. It is helpful to paraphrase so that they can respond with 'yes, that's it' or 'not quite, I would put it more like this' until there is assent between your client and yourself. For instance, when your client expresses concern about a job interview, with a sense of panic in their voice, inappropriate responses might be 'you must apply – you're made for the job' or, also inappropriate 'yes, you may not be up to it'. On the other hand, an appropriate response might be 'you seem unsure about applying for the job because of other demands on you'.

The use of restatement or repetition is not a regular way of communicating in English. We mention the difference below under Socratic questioning.

Managing emotion

As coach or mentor you will need to address emotion in the relationship, because of its key role in reflective dialogue, double loop learning and connected/constructivist learning, discussed in Chapters 2 and 3. The expression of emotion is socialized on cultural and gender lines, and clients who declare that they feel nothing are likely to 'leak' their feelings in some non-verbal way, often in their body language. Non-verbal expression of emotion may include tone of voice, gesture and body language. Thus, in addition to words, your client expresses emotion through the vocal and non-verbal channels. The importance of emotion in business is emphasized by Stratford Sherman and Alyssa Freas in their paper on executive coaching, 'Candor generates emotion and emotion can be scary' (2004: 84).

Expression of emotion

Why should your client express emotions in a coaching or mentoring relationship? Our discussion in Chapter 3 about connected knowing provides part of the answer. In order to engage in connected knowing, a characteristic of reflective and double-loop learning, your client will need to access energy. We discuss in Chapter 3 the motivating power of emotion which provides the 'fuel' for the adventure of double loop learning. Emotion is an important source of energy to support your client as they swing into the double loop 'orbit' and reconsider the tfgs of their life. In addition, an ability to deal with emotional material is necessary for coaches or mentors if you wish to 'unpack' the blocks to learning which emerge in reflective dialogue. But first, what about your own feelings?

Awareness of your own emotional state

Awareness of your own emotional states is a key ability for coaches and mentors. When you are able to express clearly in words what it is you are feeling and why, you will be confident with others' expressions of emotion. You may have difficulty expressing some emotions or express them indirectly. For example, you may feel frustrated or impatient, and if not expressed, this may be leaked in your tone of voice. You may be daunted by the seniority or power of your client and expressing this is preferable to leakage. On the other hand, you may judge that the feeling should be 'parked', and we discuss this below.

We refer now to the difficult/easy continuum shown in Figure 10.2 which indicates how awkward we find emotional expression, under a variety of circumstances. An understanding of this continuum will enable you as coach or mentor to anticipate what is happening to your client.

The diagram suggests that (in the Western world) we find it easier to express negative emotion and this is borne out by our lop-sided emotional vocabulary which tends to incorporate more negative feelings than positive ones, so as a coach or mentor you will need to develop a positive emotional vocabulary. Also, the diagram shows that being able to express emotions about people in their absence more easily than to their face, you may avoid expressing feelings in the here and now. To enable reflective dialogue, you are an important model of emotional expression in the here and now, so how might you express emotions appropriately?

FIGURE 10.2   Expressing emotion: the difficult–easy continuum

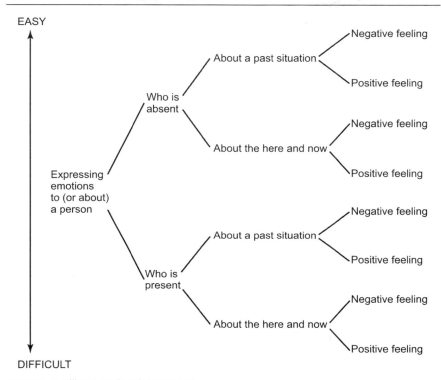

EASY

Expressing emotions to (or about) a person

- Who is absent
  - About a past situation
    - Negative feeling
    - Positive feeling
  - About the here and now
    - Negative feeling
    - Positive feeling
- Who is present
  - About a past situation
    - Negative feeling
    - Positive feeling
  - About the here and now
    - Negative feeling
    - Positive feeling

DIFFICULT

SOURCE: McGill and Brockbank (2004: 196)

Owning the feeling

Coaching or mentoring activity will generate feelings in you as well as your client. If you begin to feel impatient with your client, what can you do with that feeling of impatience? You have a choice. You can 'park' it or express it. You can express it like an accusation: 'You are really making me feel impatient' or, by owning the feeling, say: 'I feel impatient somehow – I think it's because I've lost the thread of what you're saying. Could we start again please?'

With the latter you are taking responsibility for dealing with your own feeling of impatience and trying to identify the cause. This is important. If you make the former statement, your client may feel accused, threatened and defensive, while the latter statement relates only to yourself.

Why express these feelings – can't they just be ignored?

Storing or parking

Storing up emotions is not helpful generally, for when they eventually erupt they may explode, and this is nicely stated by William Blake:

> I was angry with my friend;
> I told my wrath, my wrath did end;
> I was angry with my foe;
> I told it not, my wrath did grow.
>
> (From *The Poison Tree* by William Blake, 1756–1827)

You need to make a judgement about whether your client can cope with hearing about your feelings and indeed whether they are relevant for your client. Although it is usually better to express feelings as they arise, even if they are negative, as a skilled coach or mentor you may decide to park them and take them to a colleague outside the relationship, or your supervisor. We discuss supervision for coaches and mentors in Chapter 13.

Feelings and emotions as basic human characteristics are neither good nor bad, right nor wrong. As a learnt style of behaviour, we show some of our emotions and not others, eg hurt or anger, often depending on our gender socialization. As a consequence we may not be able to handle it in others, and this has implications for you as coach or mentor when your client expresses her feelings. For instance, if your client becomes tearful, you might feel embarrassed and deal with the situation by pretending it isn't happening or being overly sympathetic. As a skilled coach or mentor you will allow the expression to occur without intervening.

Whatever the emotional expression by your client, how should you respond? In responding to either expressed or leaked emotion in the relationship, you may use primary empathy, which we described in the previous chapter. Primary empathy responds to feelings and experience which have been expressed explicitly, while advanced empathy endeavours to 'read between the lines' or respond to feelings which may have been expressed obliquely. However, because we inhabit an environment which largely devalues feeling and emotion, some advanced empathy skills may be called for where your client is suppressing or denying what they are clearly feeling. This is particularly important when you are dealing with conflict, together with the ability to challenge or confront. We discuss below advanced empathy followed by feedback, challenge, confrontation and immediacy.

Advanced empathy

In his examination of empathy Simon Baron-Cohen suggests that empathy as a quality is 'normally' distributed in any population. (The normal distribution appears like a bell curve.) However, he also points out that when our attention lapses into single focus (for whatever reason) and we lose our focus on 'the other', we may temporarily lack empathy (Baron-Cohen, 2011). This is a common experience and good training of coaches and mentors makes them aware of this possibility. The skill of empathy has been identified at four levels (Mearns and Thorne, 1988: 42) as follows:

- level 0, where the coach or mentor has *no understanding* of their client's expressed feeling;
- level 1, where the coach or mentor has a *partial* understanding of their client's feelings;
- level 2, where the coach or mentor shows an understanding of expressed feeling, also known as *primary empathy* (see Egan, 1990);
- level 3, where the coach or mentor shows an understanding of both surface and underlying feelings, known as additive or *advanced empathy* or depth reflection (Mearns and Thorne, 1988: 42).

Advanced empathy differs from primary empathy (described in the previous chapter) in that the feelings to which we respond are not necessarily expressed explicitly. They may be revealed obliquely, through verbal or non-verbal codes. For instance, your client may be talking about his work issue in a puzzled tone of voice. You may 'sense' that the speaker is actually rather worried about the work, and not clear about what is needed for the job. The need for advanced empathy is very clear in Robert Kegan's useful method for identifying the competing commitments which build up immunity to change (Kegan and Lahey, 2009). Here the presenting objectives and behaviours are masking hidden commitments and assumptions which are loaded with emotion.

We reiterate our understanding of empathy as having both a cognitive and affective component. Our rationale for concentrating on the emotional component here is because you are likely, if Western educated, to be more than competent in the cognitive field and less so in the affective. The definition given below includes both. The process of advanced empathy is the same as for primary, except that in this case, because the feeling is not clearly displayed by your client, and, more important, **he may be unaware of the feeling himself,** care is needed in communicating what you think you understand about his world. A tentative approach using qualifiers like 'perhaps', 'it seems', 'I wonder if' and 'it sounds like' means that your client may dissent if they so wish. Offering advanced empathy needs care so that your client doesn't feel trampled on and we repeat below how you might proceed:

'Perhaps you feel...... because......' or

'I wonder if you're feeling...... because......' or

'It seems like you feel...... when...... because......'

'You must have felt...... when...... because......'

'I guess you may feel...... because......'

So for advanced empathy, the definition, as before, for primary empathy is valid, but now with the addition of some hesitancy and caution, as you may be mistaken in your 'sensing' and your response may be based on a 'hunch'. So for advanced empathy, you will, *in a tentative and careful manner*, offer,

> an understanding of the world from the other's point of view, her feelings, experience and behaviour, and **the communication of that understanding in full**
> (Brockbank and McGill, 1998: 195)

For instance, in response to your client above, who appears troubled and anxious, you might say: 'You feel unsure about the job. You seem afraid that you might not be able to do it because of your other commitments. I guess you must feel torn… and anxious about what to do.'

As an experienced coach or mentor you are well placed to 'guess' a lot of what is going on for clients. What is unusual is for clients to be offered empathy before, and possibly instead of, judgement. Clients are often their own harshest judges and offering empathic understanding may provide them with a basis for tangling with their problems.

You may also 'hunch' about your client's feelings, being prepared to be mistaken. In this case, a tentative response might have 'hunched' as follows: 'You seem very angry, John, perhaps you are angry about being overlooked at the last promotion round. I know you told me you were shocked when you got your manager's feedback.'

The client concerned may not agree with your hunch, and, if so, whatever you think is really going on, you may prefer to return to the 'safe' primary version of empathy, based on expressed feelings, giving the following response: 'You were talking about your work, John, and you looked puzzled about it.'

Your skill in summarizing also offers an opportunity for advanced empathy, as the sum of a person's statements may reveal a consistent feeling, like resentment or lack of confidence, and in your summary you may be able to draw the threads together and, tentatively, comment on the overall feeling being communicated, albeit obliquely or in code. You can also offer advanced empathy about your client's feelings of satisfaction or pleasure and celebrate them, bearing in mind that positive emotions lie at the difficult end of the continuum for both of you!

Summarizing

Restatement builds material for a competent summary, so often missing. Having restated key points, you will be able, with or without notes, to give a résumé of your client's issue for their benefit. Summarizing is a key skill for reflective dialogue and therefore for coaches and mentors. You will find it easy to identify the key points in what has been said if you have already done some restatement. Key points are recognizable by the level of energy, either vocal or non-verbal, that is attached to them. For instance, if your client has raised their voice, repeated points or gesticulated, you can guess there is an issue of importance there. The key points noted by you may not be the ones that are important to your client, so check.

Socratic questioning

Developmental practitioners will use the Socratic method to enable their clients to generate their own goals, address the prevailing discourse, their assumptions and the take-for-granteds (tfgs) in their lives. Questioning comes after contributions have been received with restatement, and, if appropriate, empathy and without judgement, so that some trust and confidence has been established.

Enabling questions are different in kind from interrogative questions, but may be equally probing. The main purpose of enabling questioning is for you as coach or mentor to enable your client to learn and develop, to reflect upon their actions, consider and reconsider their views of reality and generate their own solutions. In other words, the questioning forms part of reflective dialogue as described in Chapter 3. Using empathy coupled with open questions will enable your client to gain insights into 'forgotten' aspects of their work, such as avoiding a particular member of staff. Where the Socratic process reveals forgotten material your client may wish to consider why they have suppressed their memory of behaviour such as having a 'favourite' member of staff, without realizing it.

Questioning aims to enable your client to struggle with the issue under consideration, challenging embedded paradigms, encouraging consideration of possibilities, without restricting the range of possible solutions and without providing a ready-made solution. This mirrors a style of questioning characterized by the Socrates character in one of Plato's dialogues, *The Meno Dialogue*, where Meno challenges Socrates to demonstrate his maxim that: 'all inquiry and all learning is but recollection' (Jowett, 1953: 282). The use of repetition and restatement is natural in Greek but less acceptable in English, so for modern coach or mentors the process feels somewhat alien at first.

In addition, Socratic questioning has the potential to take your client into a place where previously held assumptions are threatened. The tfgs are being questioned and reconsidered, and this is far from comfortable. In the dialogue described above, the boy struggles with novel ideas, and Socrates' friend Meno observes that the process of learning is uncomfortable for the boy who is learning something completely new, compared to his previous comfortable state of ignorance: 'what advances he has made... he did not know at first, and he does not know now... but then he thought he knew... and felt no difficulty... now he feels a difficulty' (Jowett, 1953: 282). The discomfort may lead to a complete reappraisal of previous tfgs, the crossover point in the double loop learning diagram in Chapter 2.

When you question assumptions, eg 'why do you want the job?', it can feel like an attack and your client may withdraw. Encouraging inspection of taken-for-granted assumptions needs questions that are encouraging rather than threatening, eg 'What is it about the job that attracts you?' Also, the follow-up must affirm your client, as there is no point in asking insightful questions and then destructively critiquing the answer. Non-verbal responses to answers are notorious here and you may communicate negative views or even contempt through, for example, sighing, a tired smile, raised eyebrow, inflected voice or inappropriate laughter.

We consider now how as a coach or mentor you can work with your client's deep structures without putting them off. We described above the human tendency when speaking to cover up deep structures with surface structures, thereby making effective action difficult. (Chomsky, 1957, 1969). It is possible to recover the 'lost' structures: by calling attention to what is missing in your client's statement (recovering deletion); by analysing a distortion; and by questioning a generalization. We give some examples in Table 10.2.

TABLE 10.2   Recovery questions

Surface structure	Deep structure	Recovery Question
My manager is against me	My manager doesn't like me and won't change her attitude to me	How does she seem to be against you?
It's just not possible	I believe that it is not possible	What would make it possible?
People don't understand	It seems to me that X and Y don't understand	Who are 'people'?
Nobody tells me anything	My manager has not informed me about the new rates of pay	What is it that you want to know?
The best option is...	The best option compared to X and Y	The best option compared to what?
Obviously...	It is obvious to me	What makes it obvious?
He never considers my ideas	He did not consider my idea on X and Y occasions	When did he not consider your idea?
They always forget	My colleagues X and Y forgot on W and Z occasions	Who forgot? When?

TABLE 10.2 *continued*

Surface structure	Deep structure	Recovery Question
They don't like me	I think they don't like me	What makes you think that?
They always forget	My colleagues X and Y forgot on W and Z occasions	Always? When did they forget?
No one ever talks to me here	My colleagues X and Y didn't speak to me yesterday	No one? Who doesn't talk to you? When?

Another approach to questioning which is becoming popular with coaches or mentors is the use of clean language.

Clean language

The idea of 'clean language came from the work of David Grove (1996) when he (re)discovered that questioning a client using no presuppositions enabled them to experience and work with their own patterns, issues and changes. The rediscovery refers to early work by Rogers (1951, 1957, 1961), where he learns from his clients the core conditions that lead to change, which include staying with the feelings, thoughts and experience of the client, rather than interpreting them and rephrasing them.

David Grove built on Rogers' seminal work by developing a questioning technique for coaches or mentors called 'clean language' which validates the client's experience and brings into awareness symbolic information which is not normally available; it is claimed that transformation follows.

An example of unclean language would be:

Client: I don't know what to do.

Coach or mentor: What do you want to do?

Client: I don't know that either.

An example of clean language (with sample client responses) using the same client statement would be:

Client: I don't know what to do

Coach or mentor: And what kind of don't know is don't know?

Client: I feel stuck.

Coach or mentor: And what kind of stuck is stuck?

Client: Well, sort of confused.

Coach or mentor: And where does the confused come from?

Client: I'm all mixed up.

Coach or mentor: And that's mixed up like what?

Client: Like when I had to choose a friend to ask to tea.

The process seems peculiar and would sound odd in everyday conversation, especially as Grove recommends that the coach or mentor should:

- use slower speech time;
- use a deeper voice tonality;
- imitate the client's pronunciation and emphasis (even accent).

Grove (1996) also offers a list of nine basic questions for clean language operators and these include the following (the dotted lines refer to some of the client's words):

And is there anything else about.........?

And what kind of......... is that.........?

And where is.........?

And whereabouts?

And what happens next?

And then what happens?

And what happens just before.........?

And where does/could......... come from?

And that's......... like what?

Coaches and mentors will immediately grasp the usefulness of this tool for working with their clients, although they will want to adapt it to their own particular circumstances and might not use it in its pure (therapeutic) form.

Feedback

For feedback to be useful, your client needs to be able to:

a) accept it;

b) understand it;

c) use it.

First of all, you may need to check out who this feedback is for. Is it for the benefit of you or your client? Thereafter it is possible to give effective feedback by following some simple guidelines.

To be helpful, feedback must be delivered by someone who is aware of the emotional charge that can accompany feedback and how this impacts on the receiver. If you communicate negative emotion, usually via the vocal channel, ie tone of voice, this can have the effect of an emotional Exocet for your client. If you are angry, this should be owned and declared, using congruent words, tone and non-verbal cues so that your client can separate the feelings from the feedback itself. For example, when you are feeling irritated by avoidance, you should say so and take responsibility for the feeling, which is yours, not your client's. You may prefer to say, 'Look, I'm sorry but I am feeling so annoyed with you'. Thereafter you can elaborate by describing what exactly is irritating you, eg 'it seems to me that you are avoiding the issue by saying it's not important', and this information may be valuable feedback for your client.

Positive feedback

Positive feedback is telling your client what they have done and why it was effective. Because feedback holds an emotive element, you are in the 'difficult' part of the expressing emotion diagram on page 183, as you are trying to express a positive emotion directly to someone who is present (your client). In a Western cultural context you may be embarrassed to say something positive to others for fear that it may be misinterpreted or may not seem genuine. You may have been brought up, like millions of others, to think of self-effacement as better than too much self-confidence. Some or all of these reasons may inhibit the giving of positive feedback, which is an important part of learning, and you may be the only person who is likely to inform the client about their excellent performance.

Negative feedback

You may feel uncomfortable about giving negative feedback as you fear it may be distressing for your client. The fears associated with being the bearer of bad news, while archaic, are real. However, persistent failure to give negative feedback may result in either the tendency for negative feedback to be 'stored up' and, under pressure, explode in a destructive way, or to lead to no change in your client's practice because he is unaware that it is causing any difficulties, and hence leads to a continuation of less effective practice. Helpful and effective feedback enables the receiver to self-assess more accurately and seek feedback again (London, 1997). It is possible to develop feedback skills, by practising, focusing on clarity and simplicity, and keeping in mind the dignity and self-esteem of the receiver.

We list the principles of effective feedback below and refer readers to Chapters 8 and 9 for details and examples.

Feedback principles (adapted from Carroll, 2004)

Rationale:

- There are areas of life we cannot see.
- Feedback enables us to fulfil our potential.
- Feedback can address poor performance.

- Feedback will assist our learning.
- Feedback should be client-focused, not a discharge for the benefit of the coach.
- Giving feedback is a skill and can be learnt.

Purpose of feedback:

- Create awareness.
- Facilitate learning.
- Help change behaviour.

Points to remember:

- You cannot change the behaviour of others.
- Behaviour is difficult to change.
- Intervene as soon as possible.
- Relationships are crucial to feedback.
- Modelling is a powerful method.
- If it's working continue.
- If it's not working, stop and do something different.

Good feedback:

- Descriptive.
- Specific.
- Constructive.
- Current.
- Relevant.
- Checked.
- Emotionally aware.
- Open to discussion.
- Owned by the giver (not someone else's opinion).
- Limited (three chunks is most people's limit).

Some examples of developmental feedback formulae

1 How was it for you?
2 Would you like to know what I see from over here?
3 Positive/negative/positive sandwich.

So, to summarize the important points in giving feedback effectively:

1 Clarity: Be clear about what you want to say in advance.
2 Own the feedback.

3 Start with the positive.

4 Be specific not general.

5 One piece of feedback at a time.

6 Focus on behaviour rather than the person.

7 Refer to behaviour that can be changed.

8 Descriptive rather than evaluative.

As a reflective practitioner you may like to ask for feedback from your client. You may be surprised by what you hear about yourself.

Conflict, challenge and confrontation

Conflict is inevitable in human interaction. We experience conflict as causing pain and loss of trust. We usually receive no training in dealing with conflict in our lives, so we are left with whatever we learn at home. Many people tolerate conflict and can use it productively, but there are those of us who dread it and avoid it at all costs because our early experiences of conflict were frightening and painful. So we can fear conflict but we may also use its benefits to build trust, create intimacy and derive creative solutions. When we deal destructively with conflict we feel controlled by others, we seem to have no choice, we blame and compete with others and we hark back to the past rather than grappling with the future.

So to deal with conflict productively you need the courage and the skill to confront. We draw on Egan (1976) to place confrontation into the context of challenging skills, an absolute requirement for reflective dialogue. Egan puts three challenging skills together: advanced empathy, confrontation, and immediacy. The use of advanced empathy is 'strong medicine' and we discussed its use above. We discuss confrontation below and immediacy on page 196.

The manner of using advanced empathy as defined above, ie tentatively and with care, is also the manner needed for confrontation. In addition, Egan stressed the importance of a strong relationship in which to challenge, an established right to challenge (by being prepared to be challenged yourself), and appropriate motivation, ie who am I challenging for? Is this for me or them? The state of the receiver should also be considered; is it the right time? What else may have happened to your client today – does he look able to receive challenge today? And one challenge at a time please!

Confrontation

The word denotes 'put-in-front-of', so that when you confront you take someone by surprise, hence, again, you need to do it with care and tentatively, as you might be mistaken. Experience suggests that a great deal of work time is spent on unresolved conflict owing to people being unable to confront and deal with conflict productively (Thomas, 1976; Magnuson, 1986). Because it is a fearful behaviour, for both confronter and confrontee, we sometimes avoid it and then do it clumsily. For effective confrontation you need to speak directly, assertively and then listen with empathy to the response you get. Note here that confrontation is in the 'eye of the beholder'. Anything can seem confrontational if I'm in that mood, and what may appear low key to you can seem outrageous to others.

Because confrontation is necessarily revealing that which was previously unknown, your client will experience shock, even if they are prepared. A simple preamble is a good way of warning your client that a surprise is coming up! Confronting takes nerve to cope with the natural anxiety of causing shock, and this natural anxiety may lead you to avoid confrontation altogether. Confronting is the process whereby, as coach or mentor, you seek to raise consciousness in your client about some restriction or avoidance which blocks, distorts or restricts their learning.

There are two options traditionally available to you as coach or mentor when you want to confront: either **pussyfooting**, being so 'nice' that the issue is avoided, or **clobbering**, being so punitive that the response is aggressive and wounding (Heron, 1999: 183). We are proposing the third option, of skilled, supportive and enabling confrontation. Heron describes the process as: 'To tell the truth with love, without being the least judgmental, moralistic, oppressive or nagging' (Heron, 1999: 182), but he also warns: 'The challenge is to get it right. Too much love and you collude. Too much power and you oppress. When you get it right, you are on the razor's edge between the two' (Heron, 1999: 183). This is not an easy task and we illustrate this in Figure 10.3.

FIGURE 10.3   Mutual dependence of challenge and support

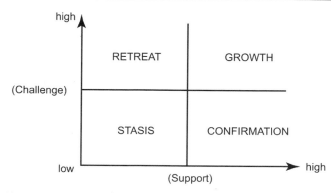

SOURCE: Reid (1994: 38)

Our earlier comments about feedback are relevant here. Who confronts and why? You may like to consider whether you have earned the right to challenge by being open to challenge yourself. Self-disclosure offers the invitation to challenge by others. What motivates my confrontation? Sometimes there are murkier motives operating than the benefits to the client and you need to be aware of possible contamination along the lines of 'it's for his own good' (Miller, 1983), where discipline is enacted for the benefit of the parent or teacher, masquerading as a concern 'for the good of' the child or, in this case, client.

Has there been sufficient listening and understanding to justify the confrontation? Will the relationship support a confrontation at this point in time? Do you have a history of accepting confrontation yourself? Is this the right time/place? Is your client in a good state to receive a confrontation? These are just some of the points to consider before launching into confrontation. And for you one good test is: 'you are not attached to what you say, you can let it go as well as hold firmly and uncompromisingly to it' (Heron, 1999: 182).

Note: Confronting here has nothing to do with the aggressive combative account of confrontation that is sometimes applied to legal, political and industrial disputes in our society.

Effective confrontation in coaching or mentoring is non-aggressive and non-combative, deeply supportive of your client, with the intended outcome of **enabling learning**. In particular, the power of confrontation for learning lies in its 'surprise' element – the fact that what was previously unknown is now known to your client. If your client can be 'held' and supported in her 'surprise' then she is free to consider how she might use the information. You may like to point out or suggest in ground rules that your client has a choice, ie to act differently or seek further information from other sources – a second opinion in effect.

So how is this difficult operation to be done, in the context of a coaching or mentoring relationship? We offer some types of confrontation based on Egan (1976) which might occur in coach or mentoring situations, with some examples:

Checking previous information, eg 'Correct me if I'm wrong but didn't you say you wanted to go for promotion?'

Observing discrepancies, eg 'You seem anxious about your interview and you have said you're not good enough; having listened to you talk about your work and appreciated the quality of it, I'm wondering what you are worried about.'

Observing distortion in what X says, eg 'X, you say that you want to go for promotion but you haven't applied.'

Articulating games (perhaps being played unconsciously by Y), eg 'Y, I'm realizing that we've been here before – at our last session you were talking about another job, weren't you?'

We note that confrontation is not always necessarily negative, so:

Observing strength, eg 'I got a sense of your ability last time we met and I suppose I wonder why it's not in evidence today. I saw then that you were clear about your plans for the job and how you would implement them.'

Observing weakness, eg 'I know you have a lot on your plate at present. How will you find space for this?'

Encouragement to act, eg 'Is there any reason why you can't go for it?'

Defence mechanisms

It is important to realize that defence mechanisms are life preserving, and therefore part of a healthy and natural human existence. However, one or more particular defence mechanisms may be counter-productive, by inhibiting learning for your client. Defence mechanisms are described in detail under group dynamics in Appendix 5.

Immediacy

Immediacy is an operational form of congruence and Egan (1976) identifies this as 'you–me' talk, reminiscent of the process of constructing our humanity through interactions of the 'I–thou' kind (Buber, 1994), where realities are forged in relationship and the interplay between you and me.

Immediacy is defined as: 'the ability to discuss with another person what is happening between the two of you in the here and now of an interpersonal transaction' (Egan, 1976: 201). This skill is crucial for resolving difficult stages which will occur in every coach or mentoring relationship. We remind readers of the difficult/easy continuum in expression of emotion given in Figure 10.2 above and note that saying a feeling to a person who is present about the here and now is the most difficult and challenging way of expressing emotion. For example, you may say to your client: 'I sense you're feeling resistant to this process, Eddie, I can feel you withdrawing and I feel disappointed.'

Immediacy is a complex skill, and in terms of reflective learning it is 'strong medicine' and may have powerful effects. As coach or mentor you need to be aware of what is happening internally and externally, and make a judgement about what is appropriate to express and what is appropriate to 'park'. The skill of immediacy takes courage, as there is no knowing how your client will react – for many it's a shock but our experience is that when your client recovers from the shock immediacy is incredibly appreciated and the relationship moves into a new plane, it is daunting and you may wait too long.

Really, immediacy is high-level self-disclosure and feedback wrapped together – what-is-happening-to-me-right-now disclosure which relates to the relationship and the purpose of the coach or mentoring relationship.

Reviewing the learning

As coach or mentor it is your responsibility to conduct a review of each session, as well as a series of sessions, making sure that sufficient time is left for it. Reviewing the learning means that your client has the opportunity to reflect on each session. This consists of your client's reflection on the session and reflection on the process of learning. As coach or mentor you may additionally need to become a recorder, ensuring that actions are noted and agreed.

The material for the review relates to what has been learnt as well as the learning process, as it has been discovered in the couple's dialogue. For example, your client may have identified, in dialogue, that she does not in fact wish to apply for promotion and would rather wait for a more challenging opportunity. When reflecting on the learning process your client may see that this realization came from the dialogue process itself, and that empathy questioning and confrontation enabled her to get there. In this way your client learns about her own learning process.

Your clarification and summary of what has been said is an opportunity for your client to take part in reflection-on-reflection. Your role includes ensuring that a record is kept (not necessarily by you) of the review, as conclusions represent evidence of reflective learning and your client may wish to record such evidence for CPD purposes and the like.

Towards the end of the learning review, as coach or mentor you will ensure psychological safety by a closing-down process, where your client may express any feelings that remain and they wish to voice. Such a closedown, which may take no more than a few minutes, is likely to be important as a time for 'healing'. Through reflective dialogue, clients may discover inadequacies in themselves or others and may be hurt, angry or disappointed. These feelings may be expressed obliquely, so you will need to have advanced empathy skills at the ready as unfinished business can block the future learning process. You should allow all the fears and worries **relating to the session or the relationship** to be expressed and received, but, at this point, stop discussion about other issues or other people.

Development of coaches and mentors and supporting them

Many managers take on the role of coach or mentor, serendipitously, in that they are asked to take part in a programme in their organization and find themselves acting as a coach or mentor. Where the programme is properly planned and structured, there may be the possibility of training, and we recommend this. The offer of training is almost always taken up by aspiring coaches or mentors. Additional ongoing support should be included, eg individual group supervision for coaches or mentors to provide support and reassurance. Such support can be tailored to organizational requirements, eg the Intellect mentors in Chapter 9 were offered private coaching. All developmental practitioners should have regular supervision and we discuss the reasons for this in Chapters 12 and 13.

Accreditation of coaches and mentors working in the developmental quadrant

Practitioners working in the developmental quadrant are likely to be accredited by the EMCC at Senior Practitioner level. Such individuals are described as:

Professional coaches and mentors who draw on a range of models and frameworks. They role model good practice.

Likely to be working with a range of clients, contexts and organizations.

The focus of work is building capacity for progression, managing complex and challenging relationships, working with ambiguity and change.

Likely to be working fluidly in the moment, with varied and often complex client issues in demanding contexts.

Practitioners in the development quadrant may also seek credentialing from the ICF, providing they meet the ICF core competences. The key discriminating requirement is the number of hours of coaching they claim to have completed. The terms 'practised', 'proven' and 'expert' are not defined in available documentation. Managers who use coaching as part of their work may apply as follows:

Associate Certified Coach (ACC): The ICF Associate Certified Coach credential is for the practised coach with at least 100 hours of client coaching experience.

Professional Certified Coach (PCC): The Professional Certified Coach credential is for the proven coach with at least 750 hours of client coaching experience.

Master Certified Coach (MCC): The Master Certified Coach credential is for the expert coach with at least 2,500 hours of client coaching experience.

Continuing Professional Development and supervision for coaches and mentors

We recommend that coaches and mentors working in the development quadrant should engage in regular supervision. Although ICF-credentialed coaches are not required to engage in supervision, there is an expectation that all ICF-credentialed coaches will continue their education and build on their level of experience. Those who seek individual EMCC accreditation as mentors and coaches at Senior Practitioner level are required to provide evidence that they engage in 32 hours of CPD per year and one hour of supervision for every 35 hours of coaching or mentoring practice.

The need for non-managerial supervision is essential when working at this level, as the coach or mentor is engaging emotionally with their clients to achieve developmental change and transformation. Because the level of emotional intimacy is advanced in this quadrant, supervision is required in order to maintain a professional standard. We discuss how supervision supports coaches and mentors in Chapter 13.

Evaluation of coaching and mentoring

Three early approaches to evaluation focused on measurement, description and judgement. These valued measures of performance, describing strengths and weaknesses in respect of objectives and, finally, the evaluator as judge of the 'worth' of objectives. Modern approaches to evaluation have moved to a fourth level of evaluation which honours the rights of all stakeholders and their concerns, without these disadvantages of earlier methods:

- The manager stood outside the evaluation taking no responsibility for outcomes.
- The method disempowers everyone except the manager and evaluator and stakeholders are at risk by such evaluation.
- Whose values are used in the judgement? The need for pluralism in societies and cultures makes such a method unidimensional.
- The method is over-committed to scientific empiricism, mistaking the certainty of quantitative data for 'truth'.
- The rich sources of data from other stakeholders are lost.
- An opportunity for growth is also missed.

Fourth generation evaluation (Guba and Lincoln, 1989) is a process which is collaborative, honouring inputs from many stakeholders and shared control of the evaluation method. The approach encapsulates elements of these earlier practices in that the method provides for recognition of initial objectives, but includes the possibility of unintended outcomes/consequences.

Fourth generation evaluation works *with* people rather than *on* them. The value system of coaching or mentoring makes the stakeholder approach a natural choice for the evaluation. The method sets out to enable participants in coaching or mentoring programmes and coaches and mentors themselves to conduct evaluations to determine some of the following:

- outcomes for organizations deriving from participation in coaching or mentoring as a development tool;

- outcomes for individuals deriving from coaching or mentoring;
- observed changes in behaviour and recognition of the coaching or mentoring process in other contexts;
- effectiveness of coaches or mentors.

The process is described in Chapter 11.

Chapter summary

In this chapter we have described the skills needed for coaches or mentors working in the developmental quadrant. These include: practitioner presence; congruence; active listening, attending, levels of listening and deep structures; restatement and summary; managing emotion and advanced empathy; Socratic questioning; feedback; challenge; confrontation; and immediacy. These skills are needed to conduct a reflective dialogue which has the potential to lead to transformational learning. Details of accreditation and evaluation complete the chapter.

The systemic quadrant

An organization may use coaching and mentoring to transform itself, changing its whole system to be more effective, efficient and successful. The situational framework in Chapter 1 showed that attempting such change through a controlling system of performance management alone is unlikely to lead to organizational transformation, largely because the desired changes are not owned by the individuals who make the organization work, but also because of the lack of empathy which exists in a performance management context. When the organization sets out, through coaching or mentoring, to create an engagement workforce, however varied this may be, this is a step towards the radical change an organization may seek. However, when developmental coaching and mentoring programmes are put in place, the transformation sought is more likely.

We discuss the social life of organizations, relationships at work and team coaching, as these are key issues in organizational development, and we include two team coaching case studies. A full treatment of organizational development is beyond the scope of this book and our discussion relates to how coaching and mentoring play their part.

The social life of organizations

The members of an organization have more influence than they realize because of the social connections they make. Anthony Giddens presents the idea of a 'double hermeneutic' where not only are people affected by the work they do and by their colleagues, they can also be seen as influencers who form the organization. As their behaviour and beliefs develop, they themselves become a force for change in the organization. They shape the very world they inhabit (Giddens, 1991, 1992) because of the continual interaction of the individuals within the workplace.

The powerful in society (and in organizations) routinely impose **their** reality on the less powerful, and this is assumed to be unchangeable. Hence as clients we enter a system where power that can influence our progress and affect our learning context is exercised. These contexts exist across the whole spectrum of organizations, from private and public companies to formal educational institutions and voluntary organizations.

In-house learning is explicitly aimed at fulfilling the purposes of the organization and is generated by leaders who are likely to influence the creation of mentoring or coaching programmes. Hence it is necessary to recognize and articulate the power relations in the client's environment, rather than treating power as a 'given' commodity, which may leave the individual feeling helpless. Where mentoring and coaching procedures recognize such power relations and the client becomes aware of practices which dominate relationships in the workplace, there is hope of personal learning and change and, ultimately, organizational transformation.

However, within the prevailing discourse, the organization will be unaware of its own culture, convinced of the 'truth' or validity of its position, and this ideological belief will be enjoyed by many of its members. Organizations that seek culture and systemic change are seeking to dislodge the prevailing discourse and generate a new 'view of the world'. The difficulty is that the very structures and procedures that maintain the prevailing discourse may work against the prospect of transformation. French and Vince describe this paradox as 'organizations espouse and want learning and change at the same time as they prevent themselves from embracing them' (1999: 18). The organization may ask for 'engagement' from its members, often through coaching or mentoring, keeping the performance purpose unseen, as learners are coached to conform using a humanistic method.

However, people construct a shared social world through their own social interactions and are rational and flexible actors. Hence there is potentiality for reflection in everyone and many are often unaware of the social relations in which they are embedded. Coaching and mentoring can be emancipatory in this regard, offering the potentiality for reflective dialogue, development and systemic change.

When the individual is considered as a reflective, acting person, with knowledge of consequences, then development makes sense. If the individual has no chance of monitoring, appreciating and understanding their social actions and environment, then it is pointless. The reflective dialogue advocated in this book seeks to explore work activities through coaching or mentoring relationships based on autonomy and trust.

Developmental coaching or mentoring allows individuals to engage in a reflective dialogue which aims to facilitate reflective learning and transformation. We seek to promote development which is wide-ranging and humanistic, encouraging a cosmopolitan attitude and enhancing 'a wide range of life values' as well as producing a 'reflexive productive citizenry' (Giddens, 1996: 266).

How organizations can transform themselves

Attempting to use coaching and mentoring for systemic change depends on the policy which underpins any coaching or mentoring programme. If the policy is one of performance improvement, then because ownership of the performance goal is primarily the organization's, this may result in improvement but not be developmental for the employee. If the organization wishes to pursue a particular organizational goal that is not owned by the employee, then engagement with that goal may be achieved but again ownership and development will not be in the hands of the employee.

If, however, the policy of the organization includes development of its employees and coaches adopt a developmental stance with employees where ownership of their development is in their hands, then systemic change may be feasible.

The risk that ownership may be taken by the employee to mean 'my' development, outside and beyond the organization providing it, may result in them leaving the organization. Although these departures may be experienced as a loss to the organization, such changes in personnel are themselves potentially transformational.

Utilizing coaching and mentoring for systemic change is an ambitious undertaking. As Megginson and Clutterbuck (2006) have shown, where this is undertaken it is a lengthy and gradual process involving, for them, four stages representing degrees of integration into a coaching culture. These four stages are: nascent, tactical, strategic and embedded.

At the *nascent* stage, an organization shows little or no commitment to creating a coaching culture. While some coaching may happen, it is highly inconsistent in both frequency and quality. If executive coaching is provided it is likely to be uncoordinated and related to performance problems with a few individuals or a status boost for senior managers incapable of (or unwilling to engage in) self-development. People tend to avoid tackling difficult behavioural or ethical issues, out of embarrassment, ineptitude, fear, or a combination of all three.

At the *tactical* stage, the organization recognizes the value of establishing a coaching culture, but there is little understanding of what that means, or what will be involved. There is minimal commitment to coaching behaviours as integral to management style. People recognize the need to tackle difficult behavioural or ethical issues, but will only do so in environments where they feel very safe.

At the *strategic* stage, considerable effort is expended to educate managers and employees in the value of coaching and to give people the competence (and therefore confidence) to coach in a variety of situations. Managers are rewarded/punished for delivery/non-delivery of coaching, typically linked to formal appraisal of direct reports. Top management have accepted the need to demonstrate good practice and most, if not all, set an example by coaching others. However, while the formal coaching process works well (in part because it is measured), the informal process creaks at the joints. Plans to integrate coaching and mentoring with the wider portfolio of HR systems work at a mechanical level. People are willing to confront difficult behavioural or ethical issues on an ad hoc basis and there are good role models for doing so with both resolution and compassion.

At the *embedded* stage, people at all levels are engaged in coaching, both formal and informal, with colleagues both within the same function and across functions and levels. Some senior executives are mentored by more junior people, and there is widespread use of 360° feedback at all levels to provide insights into areas where the individual can benefit from coaching help. Much, if not most, of this coaching and mentoring is informal, but people are sufficiently knowledgeable and skilled to avoid most of the downsides to informal mentoring. Coaching and mentoring are so seamlessly built into the structure of HR systems that they occur automatically. The skills of reflective dialogue are sufficiently widespread that people are able to raise difficult or controversial issues, knowing that their motivations will be respected and that colleagues will see it as an opportunity to improve, either personally or organizationally, or both.

Megginson and Clutterbuck (2006) have given a good account of creating this classification for the adoption of a coaching culture across organizations. They recognize that coaching is still mainly focused on individual relationships, with the connection to organizational imperatives being rather neglected.

For organizations to transform, they have to make explicit progress towards moving along these stages through systemically encouraging, supporting, managing and rewarding coaching, linking coaching to organizational drivers, training coaches and using, where appropriate, external coaches (Megginson and Clutterbuck, 2006).

Further, the need for organizations to become more reflective, as a collective, is emphasized by Reynolds and Vince (2004) in terms of its health and survival (Hammer and Stanton, 1997). How does coaching or mentoring enable an organization to become reflective?

Reflection in organizations

Reynolds and Vince (2004) highlight the need for learning and reflection to develop as a collective rather than primarily an individual process. Indeed, reflection is often paid little attention even at the individual level. In order to create development at the systemic level, utilizing coaching and mentoring, an emphasis on the collective is particularly important. Reynolds and Vince (2004: 6) assert that reflection is best understood as a 'socially situated, relational, political and collective process' for management and organizational learning. So interventions must go further than the individual; indeed:

> A successful coaching engagement goes beyond just supporting an individual's realization of specific coaching goals. A successful coaching engagement will have a cascading effect, creating positive change beyond the person receiving the coaching. (Anderson and Anderson, 2005: 17)

This is a description of how organizations capitalize on the social and emotional power of their people through the 'double hermeneutic', ie employees alter the organization itself through their own development.

Cunliffe and Easterby-Smith (2004) refer to reflection as reflecting *on* experience and organizational learning occurs when organizational members engage in 'good' conversations. These are interactions where we question not only ourselves but also each other at the level of our assumptions, our tfgs, and how these influence what we say and do and leave unsaid.

Thus reflection in organizations is both objective and subjective, as 'good' conversations include the subjective experience of people, as well as their actions and their thinking. This mode of thinking and working requires greater demands on colleagues as:

> For dialogue to 'work' both parties have to accept the need to dialogue and be able to handle the emotional consequences of receiving feedback in real time plus having to accept the frailty of individual identity. We all have to operate within institutional structures which generally hinder any radical experimentation. (Cunliffe and Easterby-Smith, 2004: 43)

In terms of the role of coaches and mentors in organizations the implication is that in challenging institutional structures and contributing to systemic change, they model good practice and nurture reflective practice. The hope here is that as coaching and mentoring become part of day-to-day life in an organization, then, through the 'double hermeneutic' mentioned above, individuals and their relationships can trigger or stimulate organizational transformation.

Relationships at work

If the double hermeneutic is real then employees have the power to change an organization through their relationships at work. Clarkson and Shaw (1992) have identified five aspects of relationships at work:

- the unfinished relationship;
- the working alliance;
- the developmental relationship;
- the personal relationship;
- the transpersonal relationship.

How do these relationships affect employees and any coaching or mentoring activity in the organization?

As its name suggests, the **unfinished** relationship is historical, left over from childhood, where unconscious material comes to the surface and enters the working environment, getting in the way of **all** the other relationships. The manager who bullies and dominates, expecting staff to read his mind, and displays uncontrollable rages is likely to have unfinished issues. The fantasies which characterize such an unfinished relationship, like a manager's belief in his god-like status, can lead to inappropriate or exaggerated behaviour and so can be dysfunctional. An understanding of the nature of unfinished relationships will enable organizations to deal with them appropriately, usually by referral. Coaches and mentors normally are not trained to deal with such unfinished material in people's lives and should not be expected to 'counsel' the situation better; in this case referral is the proper course of action. We discuss this further in Chapter 12.

The **working alliance** relates to shared tasks where workers generate the energy and will to complete the task together, without being driven or supported by the organization. Such alliances are the key to modern 'flat' structures with less bureaucratic control and, though largely self-facilitated, they may benefit from coaching or mentoring support. This relationship can be seriously interfered with by unfinished relationships and, again, colleagues at work, coaches or mentors should not be expected to deal with 'unfinished' issues.

The **developmental** relationship appears when adult (not unfinished) needs for growth are met, by methods like mentoring or coaching for the benefit of colleagues and the organization. The most likely models utilized will be developmental, as the individual identifies their own development needs, the process is humanistic/person-centred and the learning outcome is transformation. The potential for developmental activity to trigger feelings, fantasies and memories/experiences from the past may take the coaching or mentoring relationship into the realms of the 'unfinished relationship'. This is likely to obstruct the contractual work relationship as it transfers elements of past relationships into the present (Clarkson and Shaw, 1992). However, when sufficient members of an organization benefit from developmental relationships, there is hope of organizational transformation.

The **personal** relationship is based on the trust and authenticity which develop between colleagues who respect each other, and who, over time, become close and affectionate friends. The provision of company coaching or mentoring can optimize such relationships for the benefit of the organization. Engagement mentoring or coaching provided in-house will nurture these relationships and build the potential for connections across the organization.

The **transpersonal** relationship is that connection between parts of an organization which combine energy towards a corporate vision or mission. Like the working alliance, this relationship is self-facilitating but may benefit from action learning, senior mentoring or team coaching. Here the combination of working alliances across groups and departments helps to support organizational transformation.

This view of organizational life suggests that healthy work relationships hold the key to productive endeavours, confirming the link between learning, relationship and effective business. Key skills in developmental coaching and mentoring, such as empathy and confirmation/affirmation, are likely to enhance a relationship which provides the individual with the information, support and challenge they need to meet their development needs (Clarkson and Shaw, 1992). The description of such a developmental alliance suggests the ideal developmental relationship: one based on explicit, consciously chosen contractual arrangements between the parties involved (Clarkson and Shaw, 1992). Active learning and development are likely to emerge from developmental relationships, where they occur, as such relationships foster autonomy and independence rather than passivity and dependence (Deci and Ryan, 2000).

Such developmental alliances may also be nurtured by team coaching.

Team coaching

Background

Teams mean different things to different people, with some viewing a team as a powerful vehicle to support and build for performance, while others believe that teams waste time and resources, as well as interfering with managerial control. Early research showed a clear link between performance and teams, 'provided that there are specific results for which the team is collectively responsible, and provided the performance ethic of the company demands those results' (Katzenbach and Smith, 1993: 44). These same researchers offer this definition of a team:

> A team is a small number of people with complementary skills who are committed to a common purpose, performance goals, and approach for which they hold themselves mutually accountable.
>
> (Katzenbach and Smith, 1993: 45)

The pursuit of performance goals is generally believed to generate the common purpose of the team, or the team may adapt a given purpose to a new goal through their collaborative work. Another definition, given by a psychologist, is the following:

> A group of people who are interdependent with respect to information, resources and skills, and who seek to combine their efforts to achieve a common goal.　　　　　(Thompson, Aranda and Robbins, 2001)

And for a team to be a real team:

> A team has a real task, clear boundaries, defined authority and membership stability.　　　　　(Hackman, 2002)

Research by Robert Hackman (2002) with the in-flight cabin crews of two airlines discovered what is necessary for a team to be effective and identified five enabling conditions as follows:

- It must be a real team.
- The team has a compelling direction.
- There must be enabling structure.
- A supportive organizational context exists.
- There is expert coaching.

These enabling conditions include a clear authoritative direction for the team, and an enabling structure within which the team can work.

A *supportive context* includes a reward system (which may be recognition); trustworthy information streams; training and technical assistance when needed.

Expert coaching includes a sense of timing. Timing is critical for effective team performance as the team travels from the beginning of its project, through a mid-stage, towards its completion. There are three different coach leader behaviours which have been found to be important at these different stages (Hackman and Wageman, 2005). These are motivational at the beginning; consultative coaching at midpoints; and educational coaching at the end (Gersick, 1989).

The Hackman research tends to emphasize the importance of a clear task and transactional elements as well as timing and expert coaching. In addition, in a theoretical paper Hackman and Wageman suggest that the emphasis in the team performance literature on interpersonal processes in the team is 'a logical fallacy' (2005: 273). Instead they maintain that the interpersonal health of the team will follow from their performance (2005: 273–74).

Other research suggests that trust is the crucial element for success in a team and therefore relationships are important and that team coach behaviours do influence successful and competent outcomes:

> You can have all the procedures and processes in the world, but without trust, your virtual team or operation is going nowhere. (Ross, 2007)

> By assuring team members that their contribution will inform the final decision, leaders communicate the value they place on each member's effort. (Cialdini, 2007)

So what makes successful teams work?

Six factors of successful teams (Harvard, 2007)

1 A clear set of objectives, spelled out unambiguously by management.

2 Metrics allowing team members to assess their performance – and showing the connection between the team's work and key business indicators.

3 Ongoing training – not a one-shot deal – in communication, group leadership, and other team skills.

4 Decision-making authority over how to reach goals. But managers may need to start slowly and expand the team's scope of authority over time.

5 Team-based rewards and evaluation, not individual incentives.

6 An open culture, with easy access to team-specific information and to senior management.

Given the information above, there is an incentive to do what needs to be done to help teams succeed. Left to their own devices, they won't make it. This is the justification for team coaching.

What is team coaching?

The definition from Hackman and Wageman seems sensible:

> Direct intervention with a team intended to help members make co-ordinated and task-appropriate use of their collective resources in accomplishing the team's work. (Hackman and Wageman, 2005: 269)

Hackman and Wageman research

For these researchers team effectiveness is thought to be a joint function of three performance processes, with three coaching functions. The three processes and functions needed for team effectiveness are given in Table 11.1.

TABLE 11.1   The three processes and functions needed for team effectiveness

Performance process	Team coaching function
The level of effort that group members collectively expend carrying out task work	Motivational coaching addresses the degree of effort needed from team members
The appropriateness to the task of performance strategies the group uses in its work	Consultative coaching addresses the strategy deployed by the team
The amount of knowledge and skill that members bring to bear on the task	Educational coaching addresses the knowledge and skills that team members bring to the task

So any team that expends sufficient effort in its work, deploys a task-appropriate performance strategy and brings ample talent to bear on its work is likely to achieve a high standard of effectiveness. Hackman and Wageman (2005) are adamant that the team's interpersonal relationships do not affect the team's effectiveness, a conclusion at variance with many other traditions and practitioners' lived experience. It is possible that inter-personal issues are hidden in the third process shown in Table 11.1, where the personal learning and well-being of team members are declared as likely to affect how the team performs.

Judith Ross research

The Harvard report from Judith Ross (2007) suggests a very different emphasis in assessing team effectiveness and team coaching functions, citing the team's emotional intelligence (EI) as the biggest predictor of team success. This finding is based on research carried out by Druskat and Wolff (2001) with Johnson & Johnson, Xerox Canada and others, where they conclude: 'when you create a climate of trust and the sense that we are better together than we are apart, it leads to greater effectiveness' (cited in Ross, 2007).

The team coaching functions which create trust, interpersonal understanding and increase that sense of being better together are given in Ross's Harvard article, 'Make your good team great', as follows:

- Develop emotional intelligence (EI) and trust in the team.
- Invite team members to value each other.
- Surface and manage emotional issues.
- Celebrate success by inviting expression of positive emotions.

(Ross, 2007)

Developing team EQ

Like individual EI, the team emotional intelligence is their collective awareness of emotions and the ability to manage them. Research in cross-functional teams revealed that group EI was the biggest predictor of team success. Teams that demonstrate high levels of group EI tend to have strong elements of trust, group identity and group efficacy. They cooperate more fully with one another and collaborate more creatively in furthering the team's work. In our case study below, members of the Short Course Centre were encouraged to disclose appropriately to each other in carefully chosen pairs. Developing high levels of trust in the team is a big part of team coaching.

Make time for team members to appreciate each other's skills

Interpersonal understanding is critical to trust, and this enables a smooth flow of ideas and information. A team needs to be aware of each member's skills and personal characteristics, so when a team is being created the first session should include introductions and socializing. Even when a team think they know each other, a skilled team coach can stimulate a different level of sharing. For our case study below about the British Institute in Florence, even though members were known to each other, our one-to-one sessions allowed us to invite some disclosures to colleagues for the first time. Once a team is established, giving space at the beginning of regular meetings for members to share work progress and personal reflections helps to build the team's understanding of each individual and how together they each contribute to the shared goal. Teams where people know one another better are more efficient and productive.

Surface and manage emotional issues that can help or hinder

The inevitable anger, tension and frustration that arise in a team endeavour can be managed through group-sanctioned and comfortable methods to express and to positively redirect that energy. The members of the Short Course Centre were encouraged to be frank about their resentments with solid ground rules and safe conditions. Humour and playfulness can be helpful in defusing conflict and relieving tension, and group games are good for this (Brandes, 1982, 1998). Besides lightening the mood, games serve as a reminder that the group has established norms for expressing difficult emotions, thereby making them feel less threatening to individuals and to the group as a whole. Respondents in our mini-survey cited games as important ingredients of their team coaching recipe.

Celebrate success

Building the EI of a team also includes the expression of positive emotions, such as appreciation for help in a project or pride in a job well done. Recognizing and celebrating individual and group achievements not only strengthens a team's identity, but also spotlights its effectiveness and fuels its collective passion for excellence. For instance, at the British Institute the teamwork was celebrated by a wine reception with the director.

Twenty-six teams can't be wrong! This is shown in the results from Teresa Amabile, the Edsel Bryant Ford Professor of Business Administration at Harvard Business School, who completed a study based on daily electronic diaries collected from 238 professionals who worked directly with a team leader on one of 26 project teams in seven companies from three different industries. Her research found that feelings powerfully affect people's day-to-day performance, that those feelings are strongly influenced by daily events, and that the team leader's behaviour significantly shapes those events.

For instance, good team leaders clarify roles and objectives. They recognize and reward good work. They help relieve unnecessary stress, and they keep people informed about stressful issues. Finally, they address negative incidents, thoughts and feelings, rather than ignoring them (Amabile, 2002).

Our recent mini-survey of practitioners[1] who have experience of team coaching in organizations has identified relationship issues in the teams as one of the most important emerging issues for team coaching. This significant finding was confirmed by interviews with senior coaches who are commissioned as external consultants to work with team leaders and their teams. The trigger for seeking external support is almost always the state of team relationships, and the reported work focuses on these issues. For example, in one case the external team coach noted that 'they didn't know how to talk to each other' and in another case 'they were unaware of each other's work'. These very limited findings suggest that the Ross research is likely to be representative of the lived reality of team coaching in organizations.

We illustrate this with a case study by one of the authors from the tertiary education sector in the UK.

CASE STUDY Team coaching for the Short Course Centre at a British university: the double hermeneutic

The Short Courses unit is run as a separate profit centre from the university proper and provides important income for the institution. The Short Courses unit is sited within defined office accommodation, easily accessible for evening students, and the team comprises a finance officer, a records officer and four course advisers led by the office manager. The administration of the centre was overseen by a senior administrator from the Registrar's department of the university, with a dotted-line reporting route to the academic dean.

NB: The Western academic world uses a collegiate type of management with unclear reporting lines except for the support functions. In particular, the academic/administrator line is ambiguous and this often leads to opaque management practices.

The centre handles thousands of students each year, attending mostly in the evening, to study subjects from IT, accountancy and business to languages, music and film studies. The team was experiencing a huge variety of pressures, including:

- enrolment rushes three times a year;

- graduation rushes three times a year;

- student queries and complaints continuously;

- liaison with visiting lecturers who deliver the courses;

- quality assurance;

- space and resource issues for both students and staff on a daily basis;

- managerial insecurity.

When the request came to me from the office manager, who knew my coaching work, I first sought to establish the background to her request.

The senior administrator, whose role was what is termed in universities as academic related, to whom the office manager reported directly, was attempting to micro-manage the unit. She allowed office staff and visiting lecturers to approach her directly with complaints and often presented a completed and actioned solution to the office manager. The office manager felt undermined and was unable to command respect from her team.

The office atmosphere was becoming poisonous and jealousy was rife, nurtured by the favouritism of the senior administrator. The office manager felt helpless. Her appeals to the dean's office had fallen on deaf ears as the centre was peripheral to academic programmes in the university.

The request for team coaching came from the office manager and was funded from her staff development budget. The decision to seek a team coaching intervention emerged from her appraisal, where her line manager, the senior administrator, had told her that she needed to 'coach her team a bit better'.

Together we planned the team coaching intervention, which because of limited funds was a two-day event, with the first day comprising one-to-one coaching with each member of the team and the two managers. The second day was planned as an away day for the team, concluding with a facilitated plenary discussion on the way forward.

Aims of the team coaching event

To enable staff to air their views, individually and collectively, and to convey their issues with each other to each other directly in an atmosphere of safety.

Outcomes for the office

A cordial atmosphere in the office.

Staff motivated to work together.

Respectful staff relationships.

Direct communications.

The team coaching sessions

1 Individual interviews with coach in preparation for team coaching day.

2 Preparation: Each member of staff to prepare for the day.

3 Team coaching day facilitated by consultant.

---

1 *Individual interviews with coach.* Each of the six members of staff was invited to spend 30–40 minutes in private with the coach explaining the situation from their point of view. Each interview was strictly confidential and would help the coach to prepare for the team coaching day. The office manager and her manager were invited separately to spend 30–40 minutes in private with the coach explaining the situation from their point of view. Each interview was strictly confidential and would help the coach to prepare for the team coaching day.

2 *Preparation for the team coaching day.* Staff members, the office manager and the senior administrator were provided with a template, based on role negotiation, to complete in preparation for the team coaching day. The written material was guaranteed as private and would not be shown to anyone else, being designed to assist each member of staff to get the most out of the team coaching day.

3 *Team coaching day: role negotiation.* Six staff would meet separately from their managers. They were invited to work in pairs in a structured role negotiation method, with the aim of exchanging their feelings about issues arising from recent events. The group prepared a presentation for their managers and received a presentation from them.

The office manager and her manager met separately and worked to a structured role negotiation method. They prepared a presentation for their staff and received a presentation from them.

Towards the end of the day the facilitator invited staff and managers to combine in a group to identify their future intentions. These were recorded by the facilitator and circulated after the event.

Team coaching outcomes

The one-to-one coaching sessions revealed some of the managerial issues noted above, between the two managers. In particular, the senior administrator revealed a fear of failure, which limited her, as well as no training as a manager. Her background in academia was ill-suited to the managerial pressures of the unit. This strong academic discourse was one reason why the office manager had become unable to function properly, being silenced and unable to be heard. In addition, the discontent of one or two members of the team whose friends had been relocated within the university emerged. In coaching sessions these individuals resolved to seek a similar relocation. One individual in the team was hostile to the whole event, preferring the situation to remain as it was, and this was surfaced and admitted.

The structured method was role negotiation and the outcome in terms of staff relationships was evident immediately. Apart from the one individual who preferred the status quo, the entire team committed to a different way of working together and this was recorded in their individual negotiation accounts. The presentation session surfaced the insecurity engendered by the way they were being managed and the team members voiced their need for a reliable and dedicated senior academic to oversee their work.

The managerial outcome of this intervention was not immediately evident, as the office manager and the senior manager were unable to agree on any change in the way they worked together. In time the office manager was able to insist that the unit be managed properly, citing the team's own request, the senior administrator resigned, and the responsibility was transferred to the assistant dean, who had managerial experience.

The team members, ie the six working individuals who staffed the Short Course Centre, were able to influence their future working conditions, an example of how, as well as being affected by the discourse and system in which they work, the individuals in a system are able to impact upon it. This effect is known as the 'double hermeneutic', mentioned earlier, a most hopeful outcome which relies on empowering the individuals who comprise the system to trigger or bring about radical change rather than imposing a solution upon them (Giddens, 1991, 1992).

To illustrate the point we describe another team coaching intervention.

CASE STUDY Team coaching at the British Institute, Florence

We were invited by the director to conduct a three-day team coaching event for staff at the Institute. The purpose was to enhance staff engagement in general, develop a team ethos and, specifically, to improve communication between different parts of the Institute. Currently there was a silo effect, with competition for resources, which was leading to resentment and lack of communication between departments.

The British Institute of Florence was founded in 1917, and is registered as a charity in England and Wales. When the new director arrived in 1998 it remained enshrined in its original culture, and the governors recognized that the Institute needed modernizing, implementing changes of practice and culture, in order to conform with new legal requirements and the expectations of its various stakeholders. The director was given the task of bringing the Institute up to European standards in the excellence of its language provision, updating employment practice and improving the administrative and financial systems. The team was aiming for membership of EAQUALS, a pan-European association of language training providers which promotes and guarantees quality in modern language teaching institutions.

The team was cross-cultural in that staff were of both British and Italian nationality and employed under British and Italian terms, respectively. Over time employment conditions had become unequal, causing resentment, and neither did they reflect current good practice. The desired changes for the organization to function harmoniously had to start with improved communication (physically there was even the River Arno dividing the Institute's two centres of operation) and to build mutual respect and understanding. Opportunities for self-development and reflective practice had to be provided as a priority before change could be implemented.

The director invited the authors to make a start with a programme to integrate the staff team and encourage them to engage in their professional development to fulfil the wider aims of a modernized and dynamic Institute.

Working as a team to develop reflective practice

The team consisted of 20 staff from all sections of the Institute:

- library;
- administration;
- finance;
- academic;
- support.

Aim of the programme

To introduce staff to the concept of reflective practice and to enable them to work together as a team, through engaging with colleagues in a reflective dialogue related to their practice. NB: As an academic organization the Institute staff were happier with the terms 'reflective practice' and 'reflective dialogue' than the term 'team coaching'.

Objectives of the programme

On completion of the programme participants will have:

1   identified those elements of their practice which they wish to enhance or develop;

2   engaged with colleagues in a reflective dialogue related to their work;

3   implemented some of the outcomes of their dialogue in their practice;

4   reviewed their practice and identified their ambitions for the future.

Team coaching programme in three stages

Stage 1 (two days before Stage 2): Members of the team were invited to attend one-to-one coaching sessions, in order to identify their professional needs and aspirations and to begin the reflective process. These coaching sessions built on material submitted by team members in a pre-questionnaire.

Prior to Stage 1, team members were invited to complete a questionnaire that became the basis of these 1:1 coaching sessions prior to the workshop in Stage 2. The questionnaire was designed to elicit their personal stories, their feelings about the Institute and their desired self-development within the Institute as well as giving us an appreciation of their work, their needs and the likely focus of the workshop.

Stage 2: A one-day team coaching workshop for all members of the team who had completed Stage 1, where they would engage in reflective dialogue and establish a review process for their work. As part of the Stage 2 team coaching workshop, carefully chosen trios were used to elicit future roles and ambitions within the Institute. The trio process had the immediate effect of enabling staff to engage in coaching through reflective dialogue in order to review their existing work and consider potential future development. In addition, the trio process began a communication style which was mutual and respectful, using the coaching skills demonstrated in the workshop. The key here was the trio work, where one person acted as coach for a colleague acting as client. The third part of the trio, the reporter, remained a silent observer able to report back on the role of the coach and the extent to which they adopted a developmental role.

Stage 3: A review process (six to nine months after Stage 2) carried out by team members submitting written reports, a process agreed at Stage 2. These reports enabled participants to report on their progress since Stage 2 as team members and reflective practitioners.

Outcomes of the team coaching programme for the Institute

The period following Stage 2 led to a more positive and integrated staff, which felt valued. There were one or two dissenters who considered it a waste of time and money and ridiculed the idea of professional development, which had not previously been part of their experience.

Over time work was done in consultation with team members to set up employment procedures – job descriptions, appraisals, appropriate grievance procedures as well as aligning the respective contracts. These employment procedures were now conforming with UK and Italian law. Regular meetings were held despite the busy schedules of staff and the demands on the director who was concurrently overseeing building work, fundraising and forging new links to the city of Florence, the region and beyond.

As the Institute culture became more positive, a more mature and collective environment emerged. There was more flexibility within the team, as individuals felt able to develop creative new directions for the Institute. As with any change, the process was not comfortable for the director, staff or the governing body. The director, within the constraints imposed on her, was not politically astute enough to deal with some of these concerns, and on reflection feels she needed an independent personal mentor or supervision, but this was beyond the Institute's budget.

The director was able to build further on this initial team coaching event to improve financial and administrative systems with the support of her team, to introduce a budget for professional development with an annual review system and a peer observation scheme for teachers. In addition, many innovative and creative initiatives were carried out by the director with the support of team members and voluntary professional advice, transforming the Institute both physically and professionally in terms of its work culture.

The director retired at the end of her six-year contract. Many changes had been successfully achieved, much remained to be done, but the foundations were laid for subsequent directors and a smaller governing body to preserve the Institute's prestigious role while developing its financial viability.

ACKNOWLEDGEMENT: Christine Wilding, BA, Chevalier dans l'Ordre des Palmes Académiques

Evaluation of team coaching and strategic mentoring

For organizations that wish to use coaching or mentoring for development of staff, evaluation is an important issue. Sponsors of a programme and staff developers will want to assess its effectiveness or value for the organization and for the staff who take part. An early common-sense approach to evaluation suggests that it is a means of determining the degree to which a planned programme achieves the stated objectives. Modern approaches to evaluation enhance this idea and maintain that the aim of evaluation is to determine the value (or worth) of a programme, including the achievement of intended or unintended outcomes (Weiss, 1998); intended and unintended consequences (Owen and Rogers, 1999); and benefits to individuals and communities (Owen and Rogers, 1999; Guba and Lincoln, 1989; Kushner, 2000).

Evaluation methods have inherited a tendency to positivism in the search for objective truth, which often fails to appreciate the range of perspectives as well as the range of implicit and explicit stakeholder values which a broader approach is likely to capture.

Three earlier approaches focused on measurement, description and judgement. These valued measures of performance, describing strengths and weaknesses in respect of objectives and, finally, the evaluator as judge of the 'worth' of objectives. These three generations of evaluation can be summarized as 'something not worth doing is not worth doing well', but suffer from the disadvantages listed on page 199 and replicated below:

- The manager stood outside the evaluation taking no responsibility for outcomes.
- The method disempowers everyone except the manager and evaluator, and stakeholders are at risk by such evaluation.
- Whose values are used in the judgement? The need for pluralism in societies and cultures makes such a method unidimensional.
- The method is over-committed to scientific empiricism, mistaking the certainty of quantitative data for 'truth'.
- The rich sources of data from other stakeholders are lost.
- An opportunity for growth is also missed.

Our chosen evaluation method echoes what is known as fourth generation evaluation (Guba and Lincoln, 1989), a process where:

> the effort to devise joint, collaborative, or shared constructions solicits and honors the inputs from many stakeholders and affords them a measure of control over the nature of the evaluation activity. It is therefore both educative and empowering, while also fulfilling all the usual expectations for doing an evaluation, primarily value judgements.
>
> (Guba and Lincoln, 1989: 184)

Our approach encapsulates elements of these earlier practices in that the method provides for recognition of initial objectives, but includes the possibility of unintended outcomes/consequences.

Who or what are stakeholders here? Stakeholders are defined as 'groups who have something at stake in the evaluand (ie the entity being evaluated)' (Guba and Lincoln, 1989: 81). In coaching and mentoring, the stakeholders would include:

- coachees or protégés;
- line managers;
- coaches or mentors;
- the client organization.

Fourth generation evaluation works *with* people rather than *on* them. The value system of coaching or mentoring made the stakeholder approach a natural choice for the evaluation. The method sets out to enable participants in coaching or mentoring programmes and coaches and mentors themselves to conduct evaluations to determine some of the following:

- outcomes for organizations deriving from participation in coaching or mentoring as a development tool;
- outcomes for individuals deriving from coaching or mentoring;
- observed changes in behaviour and recognition of the coaching or mentoring process in other contexts;
- effectiveness of coaches or mentors.

The process is as follows:

1 Identify a full array of stakeholders and establish their grouping, eg managers, colleagues, HR, customers, service users, board members, funders etc.
2 Explore with each stakeholder group their concerns and interests which relate to the coaching and mentoring activities.
3 Provide for comparison of concerns and interests within each group.
4 Provide for comparison across the different groups.
5 Move to consensus or negotiation.
6 Provide a forum for negotiation.
7 Report to all stakeholders.
8 Recycle the evaluation.

Chapter summary

In this chapter we have discussed how the interactions and relationships between employees can contribute to a collective reflective process in organizations. We have explored how organizations may transform themselves through developmental coaching or mentoring programmes. In addition, there is a brief discussion of the research about team coaching, with two case studies to illustrate the issues raised. An outline of fourth generation evaluation completes the chapter.

Note

1 This mini-survey was carried out under the auspices of the EMCC.

PART FOUR
The reflective practitioner: accreditation, ethics, diversity and supervision

Acompetent professional in the coaching and mentoring industry is a reflective practitioner. This means that they invest in understanding themselves, developing themselves, and ensuring that their practice is ethical and meets the high standards of their chosen field.

Accreditation offers a benchmark and measure of quality for coaches and mentors as well as their clients. For a regulated profession accreditation ensures that practitioners adhere to the highest standards and are accountable for the quality of their work.

Ethical codes provide coaches and mentors with a measure against which they may rate their work, ensuring that they do no harm and do not exploit the privileged relationships they enjoy with their clients.

Diversity in coaching and mentoring calls for practitioners who are aware of the -isms which exist in any social context. There is a need for coaches and mentors to address issues of difference between themselves and their clients as well as the prevailing discourse and social systems in which they are both embedded.

Supervision is the hallmark of a reflective professional. There is plenty of evidence that even the highest positions in the land may be vulnerable to corruption, with consequences for clients in every field. Supervision serves as guardianship as well as support for coaches or mentors in an often isolating role.

Our conclusion completes this part of the book.

Accreditation, ethics and diversity

12

We now address the issues of accreditation for coaches and mentors, their ethical responsibilities and the potential in their work to value and promote diversity. The chapter includes a section about the difference between coaching or mentoring and therapy, and the referral process for coaches and mentors.

Accreditation

As an emerging profession, coaching and mentoring are beginning the process of regulation. This is necessary as, unlike a doctor or lawyer, anyone may declare that they are a coach or mentor. A brief review of internet offers reveals that a coach may be trained in five hours! The risks to the client are those of encountering an unscrupulous or manipulative practitioner and having no redress in law. Until there is regulation the market rules as 'caveat emptor' and history tells us that this does not protect clients. A parallel regulation process occurred not so long ago, with the psychotherapy/counselling profession, after a number of high-profile scandals involving practitioners whose standards of work fell below that expected of professionals. Private and corporate purchasers of coaching or mentoring services can check the credentials of potential providers through a rigorous system of accreditation.

For coaches and mentors there are many accrediting bodies. A selection are listed below:

The International Coach Federation (ICF), founded in 1995, which has more than 4,500 members in Europe and nearly 16,000 members in more than 100 countries. **www.coachfederation.org**

The European Mentoring and Coaching Council (EMCC), founded in 1997, which has more than 5,000 members in over 20 countries in Europe. **www.emccouncil.org**

The Association for Coaching (UK). **www.associationforcoaching.com**

The i-coach academy (UK). **www.icoachacademy.com**

Fielding Graduate University (United States). **www.fielding.edu**

Management Futures (UK). **www.managementfutures.co.uk**

NOBCO (The Netherlands). **www.nobco.nl**

The ICF and EMCC do not offer training but scrutinize providers and individuals for accreditation, and these will be discussed below. The remaining organizations also offer coaching programmes so they are both providers of training and accreditors. Details of their accreditation processes may be found on their websites and we summarize our current knowledge of their accreditation processes below.

EMCC mission statement

The EMCC exists to promote good practice and the expectation of good practice in coaching and mentoring across Europe. EMCC is a Europe-wide council that consists of representatives from national EMCCs plus direct members in countries where a local EMCC does not yet exist. The EMCC membership is a rich mixture of individual coaches/mentors, coaching organizations, training and education providers, buyers of coaching/mentoring and coach/mentor associations – all of whom share EMCC's vision to promote good practice in coaching/mentoring.

The ICF mission statement

The ICF defines coaching as partnering with clients in a thought-provoking and creative process that inspires them to maximize their personal and professional potential. ICF envisions a future in which coaching will be an integral part of society and ICF members will represent the highest quality in professional coaching.

The ICF is the leading global organization dedicated to advancing the coaching profession by setting high professional standards, providing independent certification and building a network of credentialed coaches. They exist to support and advance the coaching profession through programmes and standards supported by their members and to be an authoritative source on coaching information and research for the public.

Joint regulation initiative

The EMCC and the ICF have moved the profession towards self-regulation by their initiative in filing with the European Union a common code of conduct as the benchmark standard for the coaching and mentoring industry (EMCC/ICF, 2011).

The EMCC accreditation process (based on the authors' current knowledge)

www.emccouncil.org

Accreditation is offered in two modes (the EQA for providers and the EIA for individuals), both available at the four levels described below.

EQA = The European Quality Award

The EMCC EQA is an independent quality award for providers of coaching/mentoring training to make their qualifications and training widely and immediately recognizable. This is through linking them to recognized professional standards. It is an integral and essential step on the path to establishing the professional credibility and status of coaching/mentoring.

The EQA offers the marketplace the much-needed framework to enable purchasers of coaching or mentoring services to understand the quality of what they are buying and to make appropriate choices for their respective needs. The EQA also enables HR and learning development specialists to develop their own programmes to industry-equivalent standards and to get these programmes accredited. Training providers can design programmes which gain recognition for the quality of their provision.

In addition, individuals who wish to train as coaches/mentors are able to select programmes which have the EQA, with confidence that the content is of high quality and relevant to, and recognized by, the market they wish to enter.

There are four award categories – Foundation, Practitioner, Senior Practitioner, Master Practitioner:

Foundation, aimed at those who wish to gain an understanding of coaching/mentoring practice and to have the core skills; who are likely to be working with others using coaching/mentoring conversations to support and encourage development of skills/performance; who wish to use a coaching/mentoring approach within their own field/role and clearly understand how their coach/mentor role integrates with their vocational roles. This level of the award is appropriate for managers working in the performance quadrant.

Practitioner, appropriate for individuals who will be working as an internal coach/mentor, using coaching/mentoring as part of their main job or starting up as an external coach/mentor; who are likely to be working with a small range of clients and contexts and within their own area of experience to improve performance, build confidence and stretch capability; who will typically be able to apply a limited range of models, tools and processes. This level of the award is appropriate for practitioners or managers working in the engagement quadrant.

Senior Practitioner, appropriate for individuals who will practise as professional coaches/mentors and can draw on a range of models and frameworks; who are working or wish to work with a range of clients, contexts and organizations; whose focus of work will be building capacity for progression, managing complex and challenging relationships, working with ambiguity and change. This level of the award is appropriate for practitioners working in the developmental quadrant.

Master Practitioner, appropriate for individuals who will practise as professional coaches/mentors and will create their own coherent approach, drawing on a wide range of models and frameworks; who are working or wish to work with a range of clients, contexts and organizations, particularly towards systemic organizational transformation. This level of the award is appropriate for practitioners working in the development and/or systemic quadrant.

EIA: The European Individual Accreditation

The EIA is a Europe-wide recognized award that demonstrates that an individual is practising as a professional coach/mentor and they have the appropriate level of knowledge and the ability to apply it effectively in their coaching/mentoring practice.

The EIA sets very high standards and is recognized as a quality coach/mentor accreditation in the marketplace. It will raise standards and professionalism in coaching/mentoring by:

- setting high standards in assessment criteria;
- measuring ability against the EMCC evidence-based competence framework;
- using reliable and rigorous assessment processes;
- demanding a professional, reflective approach; and
- ensuring a commitment to continuing development.

Who is it for? The EIA is relevant for anyone involved in coaching/mentoring, whether it's just one part of your role or it's your main function. You can apply for accreditation at the level appropriate to you, from Foundation to Master Practitioner, the four levels described above. The advantage of the EMCC's accreditation process is that you can join and get accredited early on in your experience as a coach/mentor. As you develop you can gain accreditation at higher levels, reflecting your growing ability and experience.

In this regard the EMCC differs from the ICF as the competence framework is carefully graded according to the level of practice being sought. For example, neither empathy nor supervision appears as a requirement for coaches and mentors at Foundation level (50 hours), who are likely to be working in the performance quadrant. However, at Practitioner level (100 hours), where they are working in the engagement quadrant, applicants are required to demonstrate empathy with clients and engage in regular supervision. For higher-level work, at Practitioner level (250 hours) applicants will be asked to provide evidence of robust reflective practice which includes self-development, ethics and emotional expertise with clients. When Master's-level accreditation is sought (500 hours) applicants are asked to provide evidence of a contribution to the field through debate, evaluation and critique as well as even higher levels of empathy and systemic awareness.

We recommend that applicants for accreditation should refer to the EMCC website for up-to-date information.

The ICF accreditation process (based on the authors' current knowledge)

www.coachfederation.org

The ICF global credential is held by more than 7,200 coaches worldwide. Accreditation is offered at three levels in combined mode so that the individual may cite their training credential as part of their portfolio application. The training credential can be gained through one of two certified ICF Accreditation Coach Training Programmes:

ACTP = Accredited Coach Training Programme

ACSTH = Accredited Coach Specific Training Hours

ACTP and ACSTH programmes have been approved by the ICF because they align with the ICF Core Competencies and ICF Code of Ethics. ACTP and ACSTH programmes will count towards the coach training requirements of an ICF portfolio application for credentialing status.

ICF Credentialing

Associate Certified Coach (ACC): The ICF Associate Certified Coach credential is for the practised coach with at least 100 hours of client coaching experience. There are two ways to apply for the ACC: an ACTP application and a Portfolio application. The ACTP application is **only** for those who have **completed an entire** Accredited Coach Training Programme (ACTP). The Portfolio application is for all other applicants.

Professional Certified Coach (PCC): The Professional Certified Coach credential is for the proven coach with at least 750 hours of client coaching experience. There are two ways to apply for the PCC: an ACTP application and a Portfolio application. The ACTP application is **only** for those who have **completed an entire** Accredited Coach Training Programme (ACTP). The Portfolio application is for all other applicants.

Master Certified Coach (MCC): The Master Certified Coach credential is for the expert coach with at least 2,500 hours of client coaching experience. There is a single Portfolio application type for the MCC. There is an expectation that all ICF-credentialed coaches will continue their education and build on their level of experience. The resulting growth in competency and professionalism will be evidenced by their journey to the MCC credential.

As the ICF core competences, though detailed and thorough, are not graded by level, the meanings of 'practised', 'proven' and 'expert' are unclear.

A recent 'matching' exercise established that the two sets of core competences are approximately equivalent, covering much of the same ground, the major difference being the focus on self-development and reflection in the EMCC framework, which includes the requirement for supervision for those operating in or above the engagement quadrant, ie Practioner or higher.

We recommend that applicants for credentialing should refer to the ICF website for up-to-date information.

Ethics

The EMCC Code of Ethics requires that the coach/mentor is committed to functioning from a position of dignity, autonomy and personal responsibility and will conduct themselves in a way which respects diversity and promotes equal opportunities. It is their responsibility to provide the best possible service to the client and to act in such a way as to cause no harm to any client or sponsor.

The ICF Standards of Ethical Conduct require that ICF Professional Coaches aspire to conduct themselves in a manner that reflects positively upon the coaching profession; are respectful of different approaches to coaching; and recognize that they are also bound by applicable laws and regulations.

The ICF Pledge of Ethics, signed by credentialed coaches, states that:

> As an ICF Professional Coach, I acknowledge and agree to honor my ethical and legal obligations to my coaching clients and sponsors, colleagues, and to the public at large. I pledge to comply with the ICF Code of Ethics, and to practice these standards with those whom I coach.

The EMCC Code of Ethics covers the following:

- competence;
- context;
- boundary management;
- integrity;
- professionalism. (EMCC, 2008)

Details may be found at:
www.emccouncil.org/fileadmin/documents/EMCC_Code_of_Ethics.pdf
The ICF Code of Ethics covers:

- professional conduct at large;
- conflicts of interest;
- professional conduct with clients;
- confidentiality/privacy. (ICF 2008)

Details may be found at: **www.coachfederation.org/icfcredentia.**

The EMCC/ICF joint statement of a common code of conduct covers:

- professional competence;
- training;
- continuous professional development;
- ethical standards.

Details may be found at:
www.emccouncil.org/src/ultimo/models/Download/104.pdf.

How might these codes be breached?

- As a coach or mentor you should ensure that your experience, knowledge and skills are enough for the client or clients you are undertaking, and you can do this by engaging in continuous development activities, such as conferences, courses, workshops and, of course, supervision.
- Where you are working for a sponsor, you will need to be clear about expectations and especially about confidentiality. For instance, when team coaching, circulating agreed actions may not be appropriate.
- As a coach or mentor you may encounter troubled individuals and you will need to have a referral list to hand so that you can refer them to suitable mental health professionals or psychotherapists.
- You will need to be aware of any business or personal relationships which may compromise your work.
- Make sure you have agreed the level of confidentiality which is appropriate so that you don't inadvertently reveal private material. This may be limited by legal constraints, eg where you have knowledge of illegal activity or there is any issue relating to child protection you will be duty bound to refer to the appropriate authority – this should be made clear at the start.
- Be careful to disclose information only when you believe that there is convincing evidence of serious danger to the client or others if the information is withheld.
- Act within applicable law and do not encourage, assist or collude with others engaged in conduct which is dishonest, unlawful, unprofessional or discriminatory.
- Be careful not to exploit your client in any manner, including, but not limited to, financial, sexual or those matters within the professional relationship, and remember that all the above professional responsibilities continue beyond the termination of any coach/mentoring relationship.

Breaches of the codes

Where a client or sponsor believes that a member of the EMCC or credentialed ICF practitioner has acted in a way which is in breach of this Code of Ethics, they should first raise the matter and seek resolution with the member concerned. Either party can ask the EMCC to assist in the process of achieving resolution. If the client or sponsor remains unsatisfied they are entitled to make a formal complaint. Complaints will be dealt with according to the EMCC's 'Complaints and Disciplinary Procedure' and EMCC Members can provide a copy of this document upon request.

EMCC members will confront a colleague when they have reasonable cause to believe they are acting in an unethical manner and, failing resolution, will report that colleague to the EMCC.

Where ICF members are found to have breached their code, the ICF may hold that practitioner accountable and this may include sanctions, such as loss of credential and membership status.

Many coaches and mentors are afraid that straying into a therapeutic mode of work will breach their ethical code, and they are right. However, it is necessary to be practical about what is coaching, what is mentoring, what is therapy and the boundary between them.

Boundary between coaching or mentoring and therapy

Most mentors and coaches are anxious not to stray into a therapeutic situation without professional support and training in the field. We have noted in the preceding chapters that the terms mentoring and coaching are used to describe a wide variety of helping interventions. We have suggested that the key to understanding what is being offered is to identify the purpose of the intervention, whose it is, the process adopted to promote the intervention, and the ultimate learning outcome. This 'map' gave us three main categories, performance, engagement and developmental mentoring or coaching, as well as the systemic quadrant based on organizational programmes for transformation.

Performance mentoring and coaching are unlikely to come up against the boundary, discussed below, as their purpose is prescribed and therefore limited, the learning outcome being improvement without radical change so as to maintain the existing equilibrium. The relationship is less intense and the mentor or coach is using basic skills without empathy, in order to achieve the agreed objectives.

Engagement mentoring or coaching is likely to engender a stronger relationship but is still working to prescribed objectives, so the client's personal goals are unlikely to be part of the process. Where performance and engagement mentors or coaches find themselves straying into therapy it is usually triggered by mentors or coaches asking clients how they feel. This is a training issue as practitioners may be attempting to offer primary empathy without having learnt how to do it in this context, ie responding with empathy only to what is being expressed.

When more advanced skills are used, as in developmental mentoring and executive coaching, the relationship is likely to be more powerful and emotional material becomes part of the process, taking it into the developmental quadrant, and this is where the boundary with therapy may be encountered by mentors or coaches.

The developmental role has been described as psychologically risky, as 'clinical work with leaders shows that a considerable percentage of them have become what they are for negative reasons' (Kets de Vries, 1995: 221). This, together with the fearful belief in business circles that 'only sick, weak or crazy people get therapy' (Peltier, 2001: xix), makes it tough for executives to admit to visiting a therapist. Hence executive coaching or developmental mentoring becomes an acceptable form of therapy for isolated leaders with hubristic tendencies.

Where does mentoring or coaching end and therapy begin?

David Clutterbuck includes counselling in his collection of learning alliances (1998) which make up the mentoring role and he maintains that 'in the role of helping a learner, counselling is an essential part of the helper's toolkit'. We take this to mean 'using counselling skills', and he also warns that 'the most dangerous person in the organization is the one who is unaware of his or her limitations' (Clutterbuck, 1998: 53). Further to this, he lists as the most crucial behaviour for a workplace coach or mentor 'acting as a gateway to other forms of professional help... where the learner has specific needs beyond the counsellor's competence' (Clutterbuck, 1998: 53). We concur with these observations and would recommend including 'how to refer your mentoring or coaching client for counselling or therapy' in a training course for mentors or coaches. In addition, we have designated the term 'using counselling skills' for the activity often described as workplace counselling as this indicates a set of behaviours rather than a likely-to-be-misunderstood role.

Medical terminology is used by Weafer (2001: 77) who describes **contra-indications** to coaching, where the client should be referred to a therapist, as 'addictive or dependency issues, marital issues, financial issues, family or personal issues'. These do rather appear to comprise the human condition! But the serious point is the necessity for referral where clients present with 'signs of depression, anxiety attacks, alcohol or drug addiction, personality disorders, and paranoia... persistent anger or aggression, expressing suicidal ideas, self-destructive impulses or behaviours and extreme dependency' (Hart *et al*, 2001: 233).

Jenny Rogers (2004) suggests that coaching owes a debt to the therapeutic profession which is largely unacknowledged. Some general advice can be given to coaches concerning signs that a client may need referral, and she lists these as follows:

- Client cries frequently, intensely and uncontrollably.
- Client returns over and over to one relationship in their lives.
- Client appears dominated by one major fear.
- Client has experienced a major trauma in their life.
- Client is unable to move on.
- Client says 'if only...' a lot.
- Client has experienced a bereavement which has not been processed.
- Client has low self-esteem.
- Client adopts the victim role.
- Client describes themselves as depressed, having anxiety attacks, having obsessive–compulsive disorder, agoraphobia, self-harm or eating disorders.
- Client denies reality.
- Client uses drugs or alcohol to addiction.
- Client behaves inappropriately, eg flirting.

(Adapted from Rogers, 2004: 22)

Rogers describes the boundary between coaching and therapy as 'the coach needs to know about earlier life and the impact of these important relationships but does not need to dwell on them. If they need to be dwelt on, then you will refer the client to a trusted psychotherapist' (Rogers, 2004: 14). When mentors or coaches wish to refer their clients for therapy they may like to keep the details of the **British Association for Counselling & Psychotherapy** to hand. This organization holds a data bank of their members and registered practitioners and they will send enquirers a list of therapists in their local area on request (**http://www.bacp.co.uk/**). Another professional organization which offers a similar service is the **United Kingdom Council for Psychotherapy** (**www.ukcp.org.uk/**). In addition, clients may choose to seek help from their GP.

Many mentors and coaches would find some of the behaviours above disturbing to deal with, and this feeling is a good guide to referral. When you as coach or mentor feel out of your depth, trust that feeling and refer. We recommend that coaches and mentors in the performance and engagement quadrants address only feelings **which have been expressed either verbally or non-verbally by their client**. We discuss empathy in Chapters 9 and 10 and warn against making enquiries about your client's feelings. Asking a client how they feel invites a move into therapeutic areas. Any self-respecting coach or mentor should be aware of how their client is feeling or at least be able to make a guess, as in advanced empathy (see Chapter 10).

How to identify the appropriate emotional level to work with clients

The purpose of the work should indicate the emotional level required. Performance mentoring or coaching will normally keep its focus on that improvement purpose, using the models in Chapters 6 and 7 to structure the process. For engagement mentoring or coaching, expressed feelings are likely to be at a level of intensity which is typical of day-to-day life, such as frustration, satisfaction, annoyance, contentment, resentment and disappointment. Feelings at this level are relevant to the work in hand, and can be affirmed by offering your client empathy **at that level** which keeps the mentoring or coaching activity within the professional boundary. Developmental mentoring and executive coaching may move into areas which are close to the boundary with therapy and this is why training and supervision are so important. When clients generate their own objectives they are likely to come with feelings attached. Developmental mentors and coaches need to be comfortable with deeper feelings, such as hurt, happiness, anger, determination, self-doubt and the intense pleasure which comes from success. They will need **advanced empathy** and immediacy skills to handle where their clients may take them.

Criteria for the appropriate level were proposed over 30 years ago and we adapt them here as follows:

- To intervene at a level no deeper than that required to produce enduring solutions to the problems at hand. This fits performance mentoring and basic coaching as it stays with the prescribed objective or problem.

- To intervene at a level no deeper than that indicated by the client's expressed feeling. This fits engagement mentoring or coaching.

- To intervene at a level no deeper than that at which the energy and resources of the client can be committed to transformational change. This takes us into developmental mentoring and executive coaching.

(Adapted from Harrison, 1978: 555)

The fear that inhibits coaches and mentors from dealing with emotional matters is likely to come from their feeling of incompetence in this area, a predictable and cultural outcome in the Western world (Orbach, 1994). We would encourage coaches and mentors to be bolder in their work with clients, as emotions are the key to their learning and development, while at the same time taking note of discomfort in themselves, as that feeling is likely to indicate the presence of one of the 'contra-indications' described above.

We relate an instance of a colleague working on the boundary in the case study below.

CASE STUDY On the boundary

Helene Donnelly, an award-winning Forensic Paper Conservation expert, is the founder/ director of Data & Archive Disaster Control Centre (DADCC). The company specializes in worldwide emergency rescue and restoration of fire-, flood- and bomb-damaged documents. It also provides disaster management training for organizations wishing to produce or improve their disaster plans.

With experience of disaster sites all over the world, including oilrigs and major floods, Helene offers her clients advice and guidance before, during and after disaster incidents, which has become essential in today's world. Helene completed a Certificate in Mentoring Coaching and Supervision at City University, London, where her tutor was one of the authors, and as a trained coach/mentor she works in the developmental quadrant.

Recently Helene has found herself in a helping role, after a high-value residence fire, where she has been concerned to find that insurance companies are not always attending to the emotional and physical well-being of the house owner, Rachel (their client), who may be ignored for the sake of the value of the contents insured. Rachel makes the point that a support team of insurance specialists, police, fire and security experts all appear out of the blue but no one is present to actually assist the victim and deal with their post-event state of mind. Rachel is an international high-profile businesswoman, with a busy schedule, used to dealing with tough business operational situations, and more importantly, clients who expect the very best service.

This particular case followed a horrific fire which destroyed much of Rachel's home and left her traumatized and functioning on automatic pilot. She was advised to speak to Helene who agreed to meet Rachel in her (Helene's) office. From the beginning Helene made it clear that she did not offer counselling or therapy.

In the first 90-minute session, Helene allowed Rachel to recall the details of the event and the ensuing weeks, while she noted key points on a flip chart and note book. Helene responded with empathy to the details of Rachel's behaviour, as it is her experience that people put themselves down for erratic behaviour when, in fact, screaming, fainting and being angry are normal reactions to an event which is not under their control or within their experience. The validation this gave to Rachel was confirmed by her as follows: 'It made me feel that all the emotions that I was experiencing were entirely normal.'

When Helene had summarized what Rachel had been through, she constructed a diagram of Rachel's experience in the aftermath of the incident, and, from this, put to Rachel a perceptive question: 'You do not have to answer this question out loud to me but you need to recount what was going on in your life at the time of the incident.' She was more than willing to answer this question. However, this is where Helene explained she was only interested in the incident and not some past Freudian episode from Rachel's past. Both were able to laugh at this point.

Rachel found the question and discussion which followed soul-searching, intriguing and really inspirational. Helene believes that after a disastrous event which involves the near-destruction of a person's home, there is serious loss of their schema, which can have negative chemical and physical effects. So Helene recommended that Rachel should take high-strength vitamins to support her recovery and do physical training. The vitamins were named and so were the types of exercise recommended.

Rachel told Helene that it was the first time she had been able to talk about the incident without crying and has nothing but praise for the relationship, saying 'I needed to talk to someone who understood where I was at that time.'

Helene has struggled to define the nature of this type of relationship, which includes aspects of mentoring and coaching, particularly the use of counselling skills such as listening, restatement, high-level empathy and summary. Helene is clear that she is not counselling – these are ordinary people in extraordinary circumstances. Helene believes a service of this kind is essential in residential/organizational disaster contexts, and she recommends that individuals are debriefed properly during the recovery period, which may last up to three months. The individuals may also just want to speak on the phone, by e-mail or over coffee.

Most people never experience the loss of a home or their place of work. However, friends, family and loved ones may want to help by saying things like 'at least you did not lose your life'. These words actually do not help but only confuse the person more, because they do not understand what is happening to their world. Helene recognizes that it is not the 'things' they miss but the daily schema and emotional values connected to their homes and workplaces. Once gone, it takes time to rebuild and someone has to help them with the new building materials for their body and mind.

SOURCE: Helene Donnelly, DADCC

Here the activity entails working with ordinary feelings triggered by an extraordinary event. The boundary is attended to by Helene's disclaimer and she ensures that the relationship remains focused on its original purpose and doesn't wander into areas of Rachel's life which are not relevant.

What can mentors or coaches learn from therapy?

Developmental mentors and coaches are so busy making sure that people understand that they are not therapists that they fail to realize that they could usefully borrow from this related profession. For instance, an understanding of some issues which arise in coaching could be enriched by close examination of similar issues in the counselling field (Bachkirova and Cox, 2004).

An understanding of the relationships which characterize therapy is an ethical requirement for developmental mentors or coaches, and their training should reflect this requirement. In addition, mentoring and coaching lack some of the underpinning theory which supports therapists in their work and enables them to work productively and safely. This book is an attempt to remedy this lack.

It is likely that mentors and coaches are operating with their own implicit theory and they owe it to their clients to articulate it so that clients may choose to accept or reject such mentoring or coaching. Practitioners may like to consult related disciplines such as learning theory, neuroscience and human development in order to develop a body of theory to support their practice. We refer readers to our theory chapters which offer a basis in learning theory and reflective practice.

In addition, when coaches offer their services to clients they have a duty to identify their own personal issues through professional supervision, some of which may intrude on the coaching relationship, with potential damage to their client. For instance, we have seen coaching which has ignored a client's obvious account of racism and sexism, leaving them without support. When coaches find themselves experiencing strong emotions about a client or their behaviour, it behoves them to check out the connections within their own life and history, internally or with a supervisor. The process of self-questioning can be established at initial training which should include an understanding of boundaries and diversity issues; we discuss these below.

Geoffrey Ahern has stipulated two 'commandments' for executive coaches: first, follow the individual client's agenda, and second, maintain absolute confidentiality from the company (Ahern, 2001). Specific guideline provisions which emerge from these two commandments include principles which protect a client from breaches of confidentiality as a result of sponsoring and contracting arrangements. In addition, coaches are exhorted to engage in continuing professional development to maintain minimum psychological competence, and take up regular supervision. We would add to these the requirement for professional liability insurance, which the CIPD guidance recommends, along with supervision, for all coaches (CIPD, 2008: 10).

Diversity

Situations of power imbalance which may occur in coaching or mentoring situations can affect the relationship. In particular, where the coach or mentor has hierarchical authority over the staff member or protégé, the psychosocial functions which support a developmental relationship may be inhibited by the power inherent in the relationship and the coaching or mentoring remains in the performance quadrant.

Diversity issues in coaching and mentoring

By diversity in mentoring or coaching we are referring to relationships with clients who differ in gender, race, ethnicity, sexual orientation, class, religion or disability from any other groups associated with power in organizations. For example, a mentor or coach may be a white male and the client may be a black man or woman or vice versa. Similarly, a white female coach may be working with a black male client. In referring to power in organizations we are recognizing the varying degrees of power and influence that groups may have in organizations, deriving from access to resources and roles that exist over time. Moreover, when mentor or coach relationships are created, the group memberships to which each belongs will be brought into the relationship. Indeed, group membership may well influence the creation of the mentor relationship as well as what they bring to the relationship, for example senior women acting as mentors to junior women managers and mentors chosen from the same ethnic group as their clients.

Thus coaching and mentoring relationships have a political dimension, in that they represent interpersonally the sense of power and powerlessness that is found in any group or organization. This power can be described as innocent in the sense that an individual may not be aware of their position or role but nevertheless live it. Issues of power can be implicit in the relationship, so mentors and coaches will need to work explicitly with these politics to promote learning. Where the relationship denies or avoids these politics it will discourage learning, and we discuss this in Chapter 2.

Let us examine briefly the term 'innocence' used above. There is still a tendency to make assumptions in organizations about 'the way things are done around here'. Managers and staff fit into implicit norms of behaviour that actually represent and reflect the power dynamics within the organization. Our society is still in transition in this respect – some organizations are endeavouring to acknowledge and work with difference to the benefit of the previously disadvantaged, while other organizations are still living innocently with the assumptions of the past. This has been referred to as 'the power of innocence' (James and Baddeley, 1991: 115):

> People's personal positions are arrived at and sustained by being in a group of people whose understanding of the world is similar to their own... Innocence derives its power through being comfortably and unreflectively surrounded by others of like mind. From this stance individuals cannot see themselves colluding with the larger flow of institutional direction and its consequences.
>
> (parentheses in original)

The institutional nature of 'the way things are done around here' is being replaced by the acknowledgement that those who created the world in which such a condition could prevail are beginning to reflect upon those norms and share power with those who previously did not share power with them. An obvious example is where women are increasingly finding but challenging the 'glass ceiling' above them and white men are discovering the 'innocent' power they have held as being untenable.

Developmental mentoring and coaching offers the opportunity to overcome the discriminatory practices without resorting to scapegoating or blame of those who have held power traditionally as well as enabling opportunity for those who have not shared power. For both groups the result can be empowering and create a necessary pluralism:

> As the cloak of hegemony is discarded the individual can re-centre,... rediscover themselves and build their own connections, relationships and identity. This may involve a personal crisis but losing one's innocence need not entail an enduring loss of personal power.
>
> (James and Baddeley, 1991: 117)

This re-centring is further enhanced by the explicit recognition of the emotional and political aspects of learning and development in organizations. Where mentoring and coaching relationships recognize such power relations, through recognition of the discursive context, this may enable clients to transform the dominant paradigm, the tfgs (taken-for-granteds) in which they are embedded. Clients may set a political agenda for change if that is what they desire. We note here our use of the term political, often perceived as negative, and consciously wish to draw attention to the way that discourse itself promotes particular power relations by naming and then silencing unwelcome voices as 'political'. Where the client becomes aware of the reality of such discourse and identifies practices which dominate relationships in the workplace, through mentoring or coaching, there is hope of personal and organizational transformation. The importance of a learning context which addresses the power of an embedded discourse has been recognized by others (Reynolds, 1997), and developmental mentoring and coaching is one way of enabling the critical approach needed to realize its existence.

The evidence persists in suggesting that in company headquarters and executive suites the people will be 'overwhelmingly white, male, able-bodied and of a certain age' (Arkin, 2005: 26). Although there is increasing awareness of the business advantage of recruiting from a wider base which reflects the ultimate customer or end user, the fact is that 'in reality we are terrible at it' (Arkin, 2005: 26). Now that there are more women and ethnic minorities in senior positions they are often recruited as traditional mentors for the next generation, and if such role models can't be found, forward-looking businesses will seek external coaches or mentors to 'give high-flying potential managers from outside the traditional talent pool the confidence to reach for the very top'. Programmes which seek to encourage greater racial diversity are typically performance in that the objective is explicit and, while benefiting the client, aim to bring business benefits to the organizations concerned. Examples of engagement mentoring to improve the school performance of particular racial groups have some of the negative characteristics identified by Colley (2003), including payment of student mentors and the disenchantment of participants.

Whether your race or gender affects your chances of being a client was explored by a wide range of researchers and the results suggest that your gender does not mean you are less likely to get a mentor but your ethnic background may do (Clutterbuck and Ragins, 2002). So much for getting a mentor. What happens within the diverse mentoring relationship?

How diversity impacts on mentoring functions

Research has provided inconsistent results in finding out about how diversity influences the type of mentoring received, and the reason for this may be the typical use of protégés' reports which are considered unreliable (Clutterbuck and Ragins, 2002). Some gender studies show that women favour psychosocial help while men prefer instrumental, and this affects them as mentors as well. Other studies have shown equal amounts of both, and this inconsistency is replicated in race studies. When mentoring outcomes or benefits (such as income) are examined, the gender or race of the protégé has little effect but mentors who are non-white or female do not generate significant benefits. There is evidence that in mentoring pairs of the same gender and race, protégés receive more instrumental help but not more psychosocial help, and these differences are thought to relate to differences in rank (McGuire, 1999). Andy Roberts of the Birmingham College of Food Technology & Catering Science has explored mentoring in terms of two psychological dimensions, instrumentality and expressiveness. These two traits have been stereotypically associated with the male and female genders, respectively; however, experienced and successful mentors were found to demonstrate both traits, and were dubbed androgynous mentors (Roberts, 1998). The research findings alert us to possible barriers which may exist in diverse coaching or mentoring and suggest a careful examination of the factors which might influence working in diverse couples, such as stereotyping.

Stereotyping

Stereotyping is a basic human tendency to which we resort in order to help us to process information, by fitting people into easily defined groups. The process is an over-simplified mental image of some category of person, based on the perceiver's knowledge, beliefs and expectations. Stereotypes often lead to distortions in our assessment of others and this is a serious matter for coaches, mentors and their clients who may hold gendered or racially biased views about each other's competence. Mentors and coaches who belong to the in-group are advised to test their responding to clients in an out-group in terms of three levels:

- category-based responding, where the out-group are viewed as different from the in-group but similar to each other;
- differentiated responding, where the out-group are still viewed as different from the in-group but are perceived as different from each other;
- personalized responding, where each member of the out-group is perceived as distinct and the interaction is with the individual rather than with the group. (Clutterbuck and Ragins, 2002)

Coaches and mentors in the Western world may need to bear in mind that they live in a society with a range of mechanisms that exist, consciously or unconsciously, to perpetuate systems of disadvantage for persons whose race, gender, sexual orientation and capability are not white, able-bodied, heterosexual male. Many of the latter group find themselves unable to cope with black people's pain and anger, with a realization that gender equality means giving up their power, and that ability/disability and sexual orientation are individual characteristics of a human being. Because of the emotional content of stereotyping, diversity training should form part of coach or mentor training and we offer three tests which can be taken and submitted online:

The Ambivalent Sexism Inventory
(**http://www.understandingprejudice.org/index.php?section= asi&action=takeSurvey**);

The Cultural Orientation Inventory (COI)
(**www.philrosinski.com/cof/**); and

The Implicit Association Test (IAT)
(**www.understandingprejudice.org.iat/**).

We complete this chapter with a case study of diverse mentoring from Canada.

CASE STUDY   First Nation mentoring in Canada

The term First Nation came into common use in the 1970s to replace Indian, which some people found offensive. The term First Nations collectively describes all the indigenous people of Canada who are not Inuit or Metis. Aboriginal peoples is the collective term for all the original peoples of Canada and their descendants, who consist of the three groups mentioned, namely First Nations, Inuit and Metis. First Nations have unique heritages, languages, cultural practices and spiritual beliefs. The Indian Act of 1876, revised in 1985, sets out the obligations of federal government, and regulates the management of Indian reserve lands. The Indian Act describes a reserve as lands which have been set apart for the use and benefit of a particular group of Indians. The legal title of reserves rests with the Crown in right of Canada, and the federal government has primary jurisdiction over those lands and the people living in them.

Our mentor is a mature white Canadian woman, J, who is well educated, with a thriving business of her own, and lots of experience of setting up and running small and medium enterprises. Her client is an Indian man, Les, an Ojibway, from the Rainy River First Nation, one of the 633 First Nation communities in Canada, within which 700,000 citizens live on reserves. Les was adopted and brought up in a white family with four of his siblings, who had been found without their parents in their reserve home. He was 10 years old when his white parents adopted him.

J had become interested in aboriginal people and decided that she would start an aboriginal business group, hoping that through changing their status to a business person from an unemployed person on the margins of society it would increase their self-esteem and allow them to try things they normally wouldn't feel they could do. A social worker offered her space in his drop-in centre and selected four aboriginal people he thought might benefit from the group. Les was the only one of the four who attended all the meetings and did whatever was required to get the Indian products developed and marketed.

When it became apparent that the business would provide only a summer income, Les decided that he wanted to go to university. Since there was no provision for someone on Social Assistance to be able to take a correspondence course at a university, most of the profit from the sales of products went to pay for three distance education courses at Laurentian University, Sudbury, Ontario.

J, a former teacher, helped Les to set up a learning programme where he would study at a set time every day. When he passed three courses with the appropriate marks, Les was able to attend full time on a student loan. J believes that part of the reason that she and Les got along so well is that he was adopted by white people and they shared many white values. However, she believed that the only way he could proceed was to find out about his Ojibway culture. At first he was very uncomfortable with his people because he didn't know how to talk to them. Eventually, he became familiar with them and felt quite comfortable, and is now quite proud of his culture.

When Les met J, he was planning to make a change in his life, and it seemed like 'perfect timing'. Les was feeling frustrated about his lack of a home and meaningful work. In addition, Les did not know how to interact with a female in a mature way. He was never taught how to do this and rarely had female friends as he was growing up, preferring his own company. Sometimes he would say the wrong thing, like making a comment about a woman in a movie or TV show that they happened to be watching. J would correct Les and he reports that he 'would get upset and go somewhere and pout for a while. J has taught me much about life and myself'. In the 12 years since Les met J he considers he has opportunities he never had, a university degree, a home and the choice to be alone or not as he pleases. He says he is 'happy and comfortable with what these changes have provided me'.

The relationship is described by both mentor and client as a warm and respectful friendship, and Les comments that 'I consider her above all other people and will drop whatever I am doing for her'. Les was aware of her experience and expertise, and knew that 'she had quite a bit of knowledge and knew what she was doing. I trusted her in her decisions and direction'. In addition, J helped Les by offering him accommodation in her home – not a usual mentoring arrangement but deemed necessary for this homeless and low-income client. They would go out for meals and each pay their own way. Les says that J has taught him the value of money and today their friendship 'rivals no other... we have a meaningful and mature, long-lasting friendship'.

J considered that Les, having been brought up as a white person, needed to find out who he was, and this was achieved by Les setting up, with J's help, an Indian business, selling Indian-specific products at Indian functions which were held on Indian reserves. In addition, the business supplied gift stores at the National Art Gallery of Canada, Toronto Art Gallery, London and Hamilton Art Galleries. In doing this Les found his place in life, as an Indian man, working with his own people as well as white people, and he also discovered what he wanted to do with his life. Les has graduated with a degree in social work and plans to continue his studies to Master's level.

The diversity of their mentoring relationship did present some difficulties, not when they were alone, they reported, but when they were in public. Initially they had experience of disapproval from Native people who did not like them being together, although after 12 years their association has become accepted. Some people just do not like interracial couples and said so; however, they were never in danger of being hurt as Les describes himself as '280 lbs and solid'. Their colleagues and J's family and friends accepted Les fully, with J's father attending his graduation. Les describes his situation in this way:

> As a First Nation person I feel quite ordinary... even though I am a Native person I have been raised within the white world. Today I know much about the Native traditional ways but do not interact with Native people. I neither feel Native nor do I feel not Native.

The First Nation mentoring relationship appears traditional, with an experienced, powerful and older mentor guiding a younger, less experienced protégé. The duration of the relationship, 12 years, and its continuation identify it as true classical mentoring as described in Chapter 4. There is warmth and affection between J and Les as well as respect and recognition of each other. The mentoring was productive because Les was focused on what he wanted to do and J offered him the core conditions we described in Chapter 5. Les's ownership of his goals, the nature of this relationship and the transformational outcome of the mentoring place it in the developmental quadrant. If such mentoring was commonplace and offered to all First Nations the result could be developmental, with far-reaching systemic consequences for Canadian aboriginal life.

ACKNOWLEDGEMENT: Les MacDonald Ojibwe and J.

Chapter summary

In this chapter we have described the accreditation process offered by the two leading organizations: the EMCC and the ICF. We have also summarized their separate and joint codes of ethics and conduct, considered the impact of breaches of these codes and discussed the boundary between coaching or mentoring and therapy, with a case study to illustrate the issue. The impact of diversity on coaching and mentoring practice was also explored and a case study example provided.

Why supervision? Theory, sources and models

13

W e examine the historical sources of supervision, outline the basic principles of supervision and identify the main functions and tasks of supervision, before progressing to outline the main existing models of supervision. The double matrix model of supervision, introduced by Hawkins and Shohet (1996, 2007), offers analysis of the supervision process, and a cyclical model of supervision by Page and Wosket (1994) is suitable for coaches and mentors. The FIT model developed by Harris and Brockbank offers a much simpler approach for the supervision of coaches and mentors while maintaining a theoretical grounding. The option of group supervision is included and we provide a brief summary of group issues, with detailed treatment available, in Appendix 5. A description of how the FIT model may also be used for group supervision completes the chapter.

What is supervision?

The supervision requirement for those engaged in the helping professions has been variously described as:

- support for helpers (Hawkins and Shohet, 1996, 2007);
- a series of tasks (Inskipp and Proctor, 1993, 1995);
- a developmental process (Holloway 1987; Bachkirova and Cox, 2004);
- a reflective process (Mattinson, 1975);
- an impossible profession (Zinkin, 1989).

What is supervision for?

The purpose of supervision is the learning and development of the coach or mentor and this is confirmed by Hawkins and Smith as follows:

> Being a supervisor provides an opportunity to develop one's educative skills in helping other practitioners to learn and develop within their work.
>
> (2006: 145)

Supervision was defined, and largely based on understanding, by these same authors as:

> The process by which a coach (*or mentor*) with the help of a supervisor, can attend to understanding better both the client system and themselves as part of the client/coach system, and by doing so transform their work and develop their craft.
>
> (Hawkins and Smith, 2006, our italics added)

This definition has been clarified by this addition:

> Supervision does this by also attending to transforming the relationship between the supervisor and coach (*or mentor*) and to the wider contexts in which the work is happening. (Hawkins, 2011: 286, our italics added)

This welcome addition provides for a reflective dialogue which includes work in the emotional domain, and has the potential for transformation for the coach or mentor.

Other definitions of coaching supervision include:

> provides a safe and disciplined creative space for reflective enquiry into all dimensions of a supervisee's work;
>
> is learning through dialogue;
>
> is a relationship. (Patterson, 2011: 122)

Supervision appears as a requirement for accreditation with the twin purposes of accountability and development, and these purposes are acknowledged in the ethical codes of leading coaching and mentoring organizations (ICF, 2008; EMCC, 2008).

The EMCC Code of Ethics requires that coaches and mentors:

> Maintain a relationship with a suitably-qualified supervisor, who will regularly assess their competence and support their development. The supervisor will be bound by the requirements of confidentiality referred to in this Code. What constitutes a 'suitably-qualified' supervisor is defined in the EMCC's standards document.
>
> (EMCC, 2008)

The ICF Code of Ethics for coaches states that:

> Whenever facts and circumstances necessitate, they will promptly seek professional assistance and determine the action to be taken.
>
> (ICF, 2008)

We note that the EMCC/ICF joint code of conduct filed with the European Union does not include a requirement for regular supervision as such, but suggests that practitioners should:

> Maintain ready access to a more senior and/or more experienced coach or mentor, whom they should consult on a regular basis whilst active on coaching or mentoring programmes.
>
> (EMCC/ICF, 2011)

The element of support for coaches and mentors in what can be an emotionally demanding profession is beginning to be recognized in this definition from the Association of Coaching publication (Passmore, 2011):

> Coaching supervision is a relationship of rapport and trust in which the supervisor assists coaches to reflect upon their practice in order, on the one hand, to develop their capability and enhance their effectiveness as a coach, and, on the other, to process their emotional responses to their work with clients.
>
> (Thomson, 2011: 102)

Based on these and other definitions, supervision for coaches and mentors is accepted as developmental as well as acting in the role of guardianship of professional standards. Thus supervision for coaches and mentors is very different from the judgemental and inspectorial type of supervision carried out in business by line managers, proper to that role.

Researchers have confirmed the above definitions and identified the nature of 'good' supervision as having the following components:

- the quality of the supervisory relationship;
- a non-judgemental stance;
- empathy;
- affirmation;
- validation;
- encourage exploration and experimentation by supervisees.

(Worthen and McNeill, 1996)

The historical sources of supervision

Below we review the three sources of supervision and note their inheritance in modern supervision. The variety of declared purposes for supervision is a natural consequence of its historical roots. These sources of supervision impact on the rationale and therefore the process of supervision in terms of their history, namely:

1 counselling and psychotherapy – focusing primarily on exploration of the therapist's own emotional responses to their case work;

2 industry – focusing on control and monitoring the quality of process and action outcomes;

3 academia – focusing on education and learning – usually with a cognitive or thinking bias.

1 Counselling and psychotherapy

The historical roots of counselling supervision lie in Freudian analysis and the training of analysts. In order to complete a training in psychoanalysis, trainees were obliged to engage in their own personal analysis, very much along the lines first found in the original Freudian circle. The rationale for this requirement was based on an understanding of how analysis is likely to trigger emotional material in the analyst as a consequence of transference and countertransference in the relationship.

Following the Freudian model, supervision has traditionally taken the theory and practice of counselling or psychotherapy being used by the practitioner and simply applied them to the supervision process. This continues in the coaching and mentoring world with the ICF requirement that their coaches had a mentor and some suggestions that a coach should have a coach (O'Neill, 2000).

2 Industry

Another source for modern supervision lies in its history in the workplace. The earliest use of the term predates the birth of therapy as it was devised to facilitate the factory system of production, where, with the industrial revolution of the 19th century, for the first time, workers were gathered together under one roof. The factory owner/managers perceived the need for:

- controlling activities;
- assigning tasks;
- measuring output;
- checking times of attendance.

The need to control workers led to the appointment of a special group to oversee the labour process, ie the supervisors. They became powerful figures in the factory community and were known as 'labour masters', later evolving into supervisors, and key figures in labour management. In modern times, industrial supervisors have lost the power to hire, fire and fix wages, as the role has been absorbed by middle management. Within the tradition of supervision in industry – controlling activities, assigning tasks, measuring output, checking times of attendance – we can identify here the origin of how behaviour or the action domain is recognized in modern supervisory learning.

3 Academic supervision

Academic supervision has its roots even earlier in the Greek academy where pupil philosophers learnt by attending upon the masters. The first universities in the Middle Ages formed an academic community where students learnt by contact with experts. The term supervisor did not exist then, students being attached to the 'master' or 'doctor', who was expert in the subject concerned; these titles are enshrined in higher degrees today. The modern university offers supervision for research, with students being free to take part in academic discussions with senior academics, respected in their field, in order to learn from the master. The tradition remains as coaches and mentors seek supervisors who are respected and experienced in the field.

Functions and tasks of supervision

The sources of supervision are reflected in the developmental and support functions of supervision, which together with that of accountability were first expressed as *restorative, normative and formative* by Inskipp and Proctor (1993, 1995):

- restorative (meeting the support needs of a supervisee);
- normative (meeting the administrative requirements for control and guardianship);
- formative (meeting the educative or information needs of the supervisee).

These functions of supervision are linked to the conditions for reflective learning for the coach or mentor, as the three functions relate to the three domains of learning, namely:

- affect (emotion or feeling in self and in relation to others);
- conative (acting or interacting with the world);
- cognitive (knowing or leading to knowledge).

The functions, needs and domains of learning can be seen in Table 13.1.

TABLE 13.1 The functions, needs and domains of learning

Function	Needs of coach or mentor	Domain of learning
Restorative	Supportive	Affective/feeling
Normative	Administrative	Conative/doing
Formative	Educative	Cognitive/knowing

TABLE 13.2   The seven tasks of supervision

Function	Needs of supervisee	Tasks
Restorative	Supportive	Relating
		Counselling (using counselling skills)
Normative	Administrative	Monitoring professional or ethical issues
		Administrating, structure and organization
		Consulting
Formative	Educative	Teaching
		Evaluating

In order to cover the three learning domains and their related functions in supervision, we suggest that the supervisor will need to attend to the seven tasks of supervision arising out of the three functions, and these are shown in Table 13.2.

The supervision tasks

1 Relating.
2 Using counselling skills.
3 Monitoring professional/ethical issues.
4 Administrating, structure and organization.
5 Consulting.
6 Teaching and learning.
7 Evaluating.

The first two, namely relating to the coach or mentor and *using counselling skills*, fulfils the restorative function by giving emotional support to them, as appropriate. These supportive tasks are likely to address the restorative function and promote the personal development of the supervisee.

Monitoring, administration and consulting address the normative function so that supervisors model good organization and ensure that coaches and mentors adhere to professional standards.

The last two, namely *teaching and evaluating*, provide for the formative or educative function in supervision, addressing the needs of coaches and mentors for continuous professional development.

Michael Carroll's research (1996) provides some insights into how the supervision tasks could be addressed in a coaching or mentoring context. A description of the seven tasks is presented on the basis of his findings. The emphasis on tasks may vary enormously for coaches and mentors and there is no agreement about, for example, what 'teaching' or 'evaluation' means in practice.

The supervision tasks

1 Relating

The supervision relationship is considered by most practitioners as a key element in satisfactory supervision and this task suggests that supervisors may need to address and work within the emotive domain. Coaches and mentors are likely to experience developmental learning within a robust supervisory relationship which involves mutual trust and respect.

2 Using counselling skills

Supervisors are very clear about what the supervisor's relationship with their supervisee is **not**. It is not therapy. However, in order to address the emotional material triggered by their supervisee's case work, the supervisor will need to be competent and confident in the emotional domain and counselling skills, primarily, empathy, meet this need.

3 Monitoring professional/ethical issues

Supervisors are likely to consult with colleagues on ethical issues, and be directive with their coach or mentor if necessary to fulfil this supervision task. They may need to be professionally protective if necessary, and check out with coach or mentor before breaching confidentiality. Thereafter they will normally be required to act professionally to protect their supervisee and the ultimate client.

4 Administrating, structure and organization

This task may be underrated in importance, and here managerial contexts are a source of learning, where traditional administrative processes provide a 'trail' so that external auditors or accreditors may trace professional practice. The task includes record-keeping, learning logs or journals and case notes, and focuses on the practitioner's responsibility to the agency or organization concerned, all actions required to fulfil this supervision task.

The key skill here is assertion and transmitting a clear message to coach or mentor. Supervisors who avoid the early contracting stage simply confuse their supervisees. Boundaries are a necessary condition for reflective dialogue, providing clear rules about what is to be discussed, by whom, and when. They don't exist psychologically until they are articulated, so a clear statement of availability, responsibility and limits of access and so on (possibly in writing) will confirm boundaries for both parties.

5 Consulting

Here the most frequently used task in supervision is cited as the most productive, using systems theory to identify the potential 'parallel process' involved. The six systems identified in the matrix model (Hawkins and Shohet, 1996, 2007), described below, provide a rich source of material for the consultation task. Consulting also refers to the supervisor's awareness of the systems within which his coach or mentor is working, ie the institution as well as their membership of social systems, eg family and friends.

6 Teaching

Supervisors confirm that the teaching role is not a formal one, is dependent on the stage of development of the trainee, favours experiential methods and tends to use modelling as a teaching method. This echoes the use of different facilitation modes as in Heron (1993), depending on the experience, confidence and maturity of the coach or mentor.

To fulfil the teaching task in supervision we recommend the skills of reflective dialogue, particularly that of Socratic questioning described in Chapter 10.

We recommend that supervisors begin by using the basic skills of facilitation, namely listening, responding and offering empathy, which are again described in Chapter 10. We do recognize that there will be a time and place for transmission when the relationship is healthy and mutuality is established, but suggest that this comes later, otherwise a hierarchical boundary is immediately created, which may limit the potential for dialogue and, therefore, reflective learning.

7 Evaluating

Supervisors may be less comfortable with this task, as evaluation may cut across their chosen philosophy (Thomson, 2011). To address the normative function supervisors must be prepared to assess the work of their supervisee. Supervisors will find this easier by analysis of a recording (audio usually) presented by their supervisee for discussion. This allows the coach or mentor to pre-analyse the session and lead the evaluation process themselves. The tension between creating a safe place for development and carrying out assessment is dealt with by self-evaluation and the adoption of jointly agreed criteria. Here the skills of challenging are integral to the task, with confrontation, feedback and sometimes advanced empathy as relevant for successful evaluation and reflective dialogue. Recognition, by a trusted supervisor, of feelings of resistance may enable a coach or mentor to release a block.

In summary, then, a supervisor who seeks to cover all three functions and learning domains is likely to:

- be willing to receive and respond to emotional material (restorative function – supportive need);
- self-disclose where appropriate (restorative function – supportive need);
- make a firm arrangement for contact and keep clear records, including a contract stating boundaries and commitment on both parts (normative function – administrative need);
- be willing to share expertise relating to their work (formative function – educative need).

Their supervisee will:

- be willing to receive and respond to emotional material (restorative function – supportive need);
- self-disclose where appropriate (restorative function – supportive need);
- agree a firm arrangement for contact and keep clear records, including a contract stating boundaries and commitment on both parts (normative function – administrative need);
- be willing to share thoughts, ideas and opinions which relate to their work (formative function – educative need).

Supervision as reflective practice

Like any other professionals, coaches and mentors should reflect on their work in order to meet the high standards required in the industry. The reflective coach or mentor is more likely to be professional if they are continuously checking the standard of their offer. This can be achieved through self-reflection with learning logs, learning journals and the like, but the presence of a reflective dialogue offers the opportunity for coaches and mentors to reflect with the potential for transformation. We discuss the reasons for this in Chapters 2 and 3. Supervision offers a quintessential reflective dialogue whose purpose is to scrutinize and reflect on the activities of the coach or mentor concerned, bearing in mind the full range of functions as above. Supervisors who have been trained for other helping professions, like social work, health practitioners and community workers, are likely to have some of the skills needed for coaching and mentoring supervision. Purchasers of coaching or mentoring services are increasingly demanding that coaches or mentors must have supervision, just as many coaches and mentors are finding that supervisors offer them much-needed support in what can be an isolating field of work.

Models of supervision

We discuss three models of supervision which can be used for supervision with coaches and mentors: the double matrix model, the cyclical model and the FIT model.

Double matrix model of supervision

The double matrix model, based on Hawkins and Shohet's (1996, 2007) *Supervision in the Helping Professions*, is sometimes called the 'seven-eyed model'.

Rationale for the model

Many models of supervision emphasize the developmental process at the expense of the supervision process itself, while a consultancy model like this, referred to as *horizontal* rather than *vertical*, is free to explore the processes which occur in supervision. The double matrix model, a horizontal model, seeks to 'turn the focus away from the context and the wider organizational issues to look more closely at the process of the supervisory relationship' (Hawkins and Shohet, 1989: 55). The seven-eyed matrix model reminds supervisors to attend to all seven systems in which their coach or mentor is working, and analyses the supervision process in terms of the relationships between supervisor, supervisee, client and context shown in Figure 13.1.

At any time in supervision there are four elements to consider:

- the supervisor;
- the supervisee;
- the client or clients;
- the work context.

These four elements form two interlocking systems: the client–supervisee matrix and the supervisee–supervisor matrix. The two systems are shown in Figure 13.1:

1 The client–supervisee matrix is where the relationship between coach or mentor and client is reported and *reflected upon* in the supervision. Here the supervisory pair pay direct attention to the client–supervisee matrix, by reflecting together on the reported accounts given by the supervisee, analyse recordings or scrutinize evaluations. This is represented in Figure 13.1 in the vertically lined area.

2 The supervision matrix is where the client–supervisee matrix is *reflected in* the supervision process itself. Here the supervisory pair pay attention to the client–supervisee matrix through how that system is reflected in the here-and-now experience of both. This is represented in Figure 13.1 in the horizontally lined area.

FIGURE 13.1   A matrix model of coach/mentor supervision

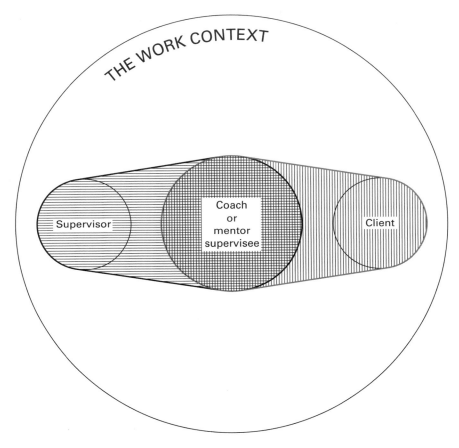

SOURCE: After Hawkins and Shohet (1989)

Each interlocking system can be subdivided into three categories, giving *six domains of supervision* described below. The seventh 'eye' is the work context, plus any other systems within which the supervisor, supervisee or client operates. The meaning of technical terms like 'projection' and 'transference' can be found in Appendix 5.

The six domains of supervision

The grey area:

1.1 The supervisory pair will attend to reports of the supervisee's interaction with clients, how the activity came about, its aims, sponsors and intended outcomes. An example of this would be a description of the client and their situation supported by a drawing of the situation or client in their context.

1.2 The supervisory pair will explore strategies and interventions, reviewing and evaluating previous actions and considering future developments. An example of this is the analysis of a session, where strategies and interactions were (un)successful, so that plans can be made for a future re-run. Detailed analysis of recordings can reveal how the coach or mentor uses empathy, questioning, summary and challenge, and how these impact on their client.

1.3 Here the supervisor (mainly) will attend to what seems to be happening between the supervisee and her clients, either consciously or unconsciously, including patterns and images which have emerged from 1 and 2. The purpose here is to understand better the dynamics of the supervisee's relationships within the vertically lined matrix. An example here would be a discussion about the consistent difficulty with late arrival or missed sessions which emerges with a particular client.

The horizontally lined area:

2.1 The supervisor works in the supervisee–supervision matrix by attending to what their supervisee is experiencing within the client–supervisee matrix, particularly countertransference, the response to unconscious material from clients being projected 'onto' the coach or mentor. An example of this is the annoyance felt by a coach or mentor who experiences a fussy client who is just like her 'fussy' mother.

2.2 The focus on the here-and-now process within the supervisory pair can hold up a mirror to the parallel process occurring between the supervisee and their client. The supervisor is a potentially powerful source of information about hidden dynamics between their supervisee and his clients. The supervisor may note a change in attitude or behaviour in their supervisee, like faster speech, uncharacteristic terms or style, perhaps more typical of the client concerned, and the articulation of this may reflect the behaviour of clients, unconsciously 'picked up' by the supervisee. (In 2.2 the supervisee 'becomes' their client, a phenomenon known as 'parallel process'.)

2.3 The supervisor focuses on their own current experience in the session. They may experience countertransference as a consequence of unconscious projection from their supervisee and this is a valuable source of information for both. For example, the supervisor may detect in herself perhaps a feeling of impatience with her supervisee, which may be a clue to the supervisee's own impatience with their client (say) being unconsciously conveyed to the supervisor.

The work context

The six domains include all the processes that occur within both the client–supervisee and supervisee–supervisor matrices, but supervisory relationships must take account of the wider context in which the supervisor, supervisee, client and organization exist, where professional, ethical and social factors will all play a part. An example of this is the situation where a coach or mentor is commissioned by the organization to use a directive approach when working with their staff, but prefers a non-directive, even developmental approach.

For many supervisors the model is just too complicated and they find themselves unable to attend to six or seven modes in one supervision session. Many experienced supervisors follow the model unconsciously but for new supervisors and some experienced ones (!) the complicated structure distracts. In addition, for many practitioners the psychodynamic language is unacceptable, so that transference and countertransference are not understood terms in their approach. We recommend the simpler FIT model which we describe on page 259.

The cyclical model

The cyclical model, based on *Supervising the Counsellor* by Page and Wosket (1994, 2001), is actually a structure within which any model can sit and allows for using a variety of different coaching or mentoring approaches. Many coaches or mentors are developing their own working models and this cyclical structure provides a supervisor with a firm framework into which any coaching or mentoring model can nest, and this is why we recommend it. The cyclical structure is holographic, so that it may represent the shape of an individual supervision session, and it may also represent the shape of the entire supervision cycle, over a year or more.

The rationale for the cyclical structure echoes the argument for using reflective learning principles in supervision. The assumptions which underpin the cyclical model are humanistic in kind and professional in effect. For example, supervision is for the benefit of the supervisee; the relationship should be characterized by warmth, understanding and empathy; addressing emotion will enable learning in the supervisee. In addition, the model recognizes that supervision may be exploratory, open-ended, reflective and also action-oriented, as well as acknowledging that learning in this way is exposing and challenging for the supervisee. The humanity of the supervisor is the most valuable contribution to the process for both.

We look briefly at how a supervisor might work in the five stages of the cycle, contract, focus, space, bridge and review, as outlined above, and refer readers to a more detailed treatment in Page and Wosket (1994, 2001).

FIGURE 13.2 Overview of cyclical model

SOURCE: Page and Wosket (1994)

The model

There are five stages, as shown in Figure 13.2:

1 contract – and possibly re-contracting;

2 focus – the subject or material under consideration;

3 space – holding the coach or mentor – support and challenge;

4 bridge – the way back to the work;

5 review – evaluation and assessment.

We review each stage now in more detail, bearing in mind that each stage can be visited in each and every session, so that the contract may be checked for suitability if things have changed, the focus may alter from session to session etc.

1 The first stage, *contract*, includes:

– ground rules, eg who contacts whom, the ethics code, timekeeping etc;

– boundaries, eg confidentiality, agreement regarding referral for therapy;

– accountability, eg professional code of conduct with implications;

– expectations, eg who is responsible for what;

– the nature of the relationship, eg not therapy.

Contracting or re-contracting, where relevant, may occur in later sessions, but will normally feature in the first. Transparency about process is a valuable element in the reflective dialogue you will seek in supervision. Boundaries should be discussed and agreed at the beginning of the relationship and any slippage addressed without delay. Both parties should agree to refer when issues arise that are on the verge of therapeutic material. The safety provided by firm boundaries enables your supervisee to deal with similar issues relating to their work, eg clients' DNA; ethical issues; boundary issues.

2 The second stage, *focus*, includes:

- supervisee's material, eg personal response to client, fees, ethics, organizational concerns;
- objectives, ie the supervisee's objective stated using the 'past participle' method, eg 'achieved professional registration in one year';
- presentation, eg tape, video, drama, narrative;
- approach, eg the balance of questioning and listening used by the supervisee with their client and awareness of potential over-involvement;
- priorities, ie what the coach or mentor considers most urgent and important except where there are ethical or professional matters which take precedence.

Your supervisee has the right to decide the *focus* of the session, unless there is a serious problem which justifies you overriding the autonomy of your supervisee. The reflective dialogue skills you need here are patience while your supervisee sorts out her desired focus, listening and responding, offering empathy where appropriate, and particularly summarizing what may have been presented in a spontaneous but possibly disordered fashion. Objectives should emerge from the discussion about the issue and agreeing objectives gives both you and your supervisee a structure for review and evaluation later.

3 The third stage, *space*, includes:

- collaboration, ie the reflective alliance formed between you and your supervisee;
- investigation, eg recognition of parallel process where the supervisor may experience in parallel some of the feelings occurring in their supervisee's own work with their client;
- challenge, eg an interaction where the supervisee may not feel comfortable but does always feel safe, described by Heron (1991: 43) as follows: 'A confronting intervention unequivocally tells an uncomfortable truth, but does so with love, in order that the one concerned may see it and fully acknowledge it';
- containment, eg when the supervision session may have generated disturbance or disorientation for your supervisee, you will ensure that emotive material is contained, by acknowledging it and articulating its effects;

- affirmation, eg the celebration of your supervisee's learning and/or struggle, a pleasant duty for supervisors which is often forgotten.

As noted above, in early sessions you will need to attend to the relationship, using the material presented to establish rapport, and deal with feelings that are getting in the way of progress for your supervisee. Here the importance of emotional facilitation is evident and empathy will be a key skill for you as a supervisor. As the relationship develops and your supervisee is enabled to get to grips with their work, other tasks of supervision can be fulfilled. The space provided at this stage of the cycle will allow for containment, challenge and encouragement of your supervisee to be creative and innovative, utilizing the dialogue skills of questioning and confrontation.

4 The fourth stage, *bridge*, includes:

- Consolidation using questions and summaries which link back to the work of the session. This is the gathering together of what has gone before. Here your restatement skills will pay off as you will find that you are able to summarize accurately what has been discussed in the session.

- Information giving, and the preferred method for supervisors is to direct their supervisee to an appropriate source or reference.

- Goal setting, eg checking out ownership of learning objectives. In addition, you are likely to encourage your supervisee to articulate learning goals, which can be addressed at the review stage.

- Action planning, eg examining all potential ways of achieving objectives.

- Your supervisee's perspective. This is the moment to create the bridge back to your supervisee's own work environment by checking out with them how they foresee the effect of the actions that have been agreed. For example, how will their client react to their intention to challenge him/her?

The bridge stage of the cycle is named to indicate the link from supervision back to the actual work. You will need to question and summarize and instigate action in this stage, ie action relating to their work. The need to record here is paramount so that you can review at a later session.

5 The fifth stage, *review*, includes:

- Feedback. The focus of this feedback is the supervision relationship itself and the exchange aims to improve the quality of the supervision relationship. The two-way mutual interaction may include dynamics in the relationship, eg dependency, skills used by both parties, as well as styles and approaches, eg questioning and empathy.

- Grounding, eg a moment of pause before moving on to evaluation and may be silent or comprise general comments about the session, eg 'Have we covered everything you wanted to talk about?' Or, 'We seem to be spending a lot of our time on the difficulties with x – have we forgotten anything important?'
- Evaluation. The purpose here is to consider the value of the session(s) and note any changes that need to be made to the process, eg allocating a minimum length of time to particular issues.
- Assessment. An activity for supervisors who have already agreed at the outset, with their supervisees, to breach confidentiality for the purpose of conveying information to relevant parties in the organization, eg the supervisee's tutor or manager.
- Re-contracting should follow evaluation. Both parties review their contract with each other, check whether it is still appropriate, revisit and renew their initial agreement. If re-contracting is part of the original contract this can be done at any session, as the relationship develops, taking account of some of the changes discussed above.

A review of the session completes the cycle and leaves both you and your supervisee ready to renew the process in the next session. As stated previously, we make the assumption that the purpose of supervision is professional learning and development, primarily for the supervisee. Some evaluation is important in this stage, and the opportunity for reviewing the process of supervision generally, but the most important part of review is the winding down of the session. As supervisor your summary will effect this, as well as your supervisee's impressions of the session. This stage is often neglected because of avoidance by both parties of endings, reluctance to discuss any deficiency in the process, or basic time management. It is the supervisor's responsibility to manage session timings so as to leave sufficient time for review.

A simple supervision model which addresses some of the unconscious material described in the double matrix model is the FIT model created by Mary Harris and Anne Brockbank (Harris and Brockbank, 2011).

The FIT model

The model is founded upon the three domains of learning. 'FIT' is an acronym for Feeling, Initiating and Thinking, which encompasses and describes the three domains of human functioning. The model for an individual is shown in Figure 13.3.

FIGURE 13.3 The single FIT

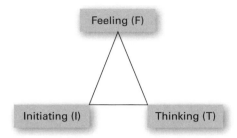

Explanation of the diagram

    'F' denotes emotions, affect and feelings – material expressed in this
    domain of the model may be accessed using restatement and
    empathy.

    'I' denotes initiating, ie behaviours and actions initiated by the
    individual – this domain of the model may be accessed through
    questioning, restatement and summary.

    'T' denotes cognition, thoughts and beliefs – this domain of the model
    may be accessed through questioning, restatement, summary and
    feedback.

The model applies to each of the three roles under consideration in supervision, namely the supervisor, the supervisee and the client whose FIT elements may be individually addressed as shown in Figure 13.5 below.

    Each triangle represents the FIT diagram for each of the following:

- client;
- supervisee;
- supervisor.

This allows the model to function both interactively and introspectively. First
it can be applied to the client. In addition, both the supervisor and supervisee
bring awareness of and apply their own FIT triangle to the supervision process. The client's triangle is described by the supervisee and then explored by
the supervisor and supervisee. These insights are then used to inform further
sessions with the client. Hence, the sessions include three working examples
of the model (even though the client is not present), which can be used in
supervision.

    The diagram places the client foremost as the focus of the supervision
session, while establishing clear boundaries between all three participants
in the process. The diagram is a map of what needs to be considered in
supervision and by whom. The focus for the session is agreed between

the supervisor and the supervisee. In particular, the area of functioning, ie feelings, action or thinking, is negotiated in the session between the supervisor and supervisee.

For example, if it appears that the supervisee's feelings towards the client are affecting their work, then the session will focus on the supervisee's F domain. This may lead to an exploration of the supervisee's emotional issues with the client, which are then explored using the 'T' or thinking domain. Alternatively, if the supervisee realizes that they tend to give advice to the client, then the session may focus on the supervisee's actions, ie the 'I' domain, as well as their possible need to rescue clients (F). This may be useful in identifying the client's role as a victim and the behaviours (I) which elicit this response from the supervisee as well as others. Furthermore, if the supervisee and the supervisor realize that they are colluding in the session by judging or criticizing the client, then the session needs to focus on their shared assumptions, ie their joint 'T'.

The model developed out of a perceived need for an easy-to-use and memorable model of supervision which attends to all three domains of learning, and ensures that each one is given its place in the supervision process of reflective learning. The model encourages the supervisee to make explicit choices about which domain they wish to focus on. The FIT supervisor holds a sense of the balance in each domain and will alert their supervisee accordingly. For example, when a supervisee chooses to focus on their client's behaviour and discusses their beliefs and thoughts, the FIT supervisor will also call attention to potential feelings which may be present for the coaching client. Alternatively, when a mentor supervisee wishes to focus on their protégé's feelings, the FIT supervisor will also check out what the protégé may be thinking and doing. The process can be applied to client, supervisee and supervisor in the three FIT versions below.

The single FIT: understanding the individual

The domains addressed when using the FIT model are described as Feeling (F), Initiating (I) and Thinking (T) and are illustrated in Figure 13.3, which depicts the three domains as they occur within an individual, ie the single FIT. The single FIT diagram shown in Figure 13.3 can be used by the supervisee to understand and explain how an individual client functions and views the world, and this can have valuable developmental implications.

The double FIT: understanding the client–supervisee relationship

The diagram in Figure 13.4 expands the FIT model and depicts the relationship which exists between the individual client and their coach or mentor, who is the supervisee in this example.

The diagram in Figure 13.4 suggests that the client's functioning in each of the three domains is seen individually as well as in relation to their coach

FIGURE 13.4 The double FIT

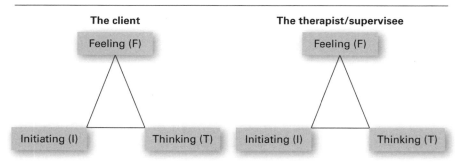

or mentor. The double FIT can give focus to an understanding of the client's issues and, additionally, the interplay between the issues occurring between them. This view provides an extra dimension to the work. The client's feelings, thoughts and behaviours towards their coach or mentor are important elements in the coaching or mentoring process and will often include aspects of which the client is unaware.

The coach or mentor (now the supervisee) uses supervision to examine the 'single FIT', which represents the client's functioning in the three domains, as well as the 'double FIT', which represents his awareness of his own feelings, behaviours and thoughts towards the client and the interplay between the two. In particular, if the supervisee's feelings (F) have been triggered by material brought by his client, supervision using this model can provide a clear framework for identifying and resolving the overlap between the supervisee's and the client's issues.

Both the 'single FIT' and 'double' FIT are then explored in supervision sessions. While continuing to hold the information regarding the client's functioning as in the single FIT above, the supervisee is asked to consider his own functioning in each of the three domains, and to consider the interplay between him and his client. The diagram can be used to explore how the supervisee's own feelings (F), behaviours (I) and beliefs (T) impact on his client work. By attending to his own feelings, behaviours and thoughts regarding the client, the supervisee is able to gain deeper insights into both the client's as well as his own functioning, which then informs and expands their work together. The insight gained by viewing the two people in relation to each other in this diagram provides useful material to be explored in supervision and also has valuable reflective learning implications.

For example, when a supervisee recounts their client session with barely concealed impatience, the double fit version of the model is appropriate as the supervision session processes their feelings of impatience with their client and articulates the reasons for it.

The supervision process may also include input from the supervisor's perspective, which constitutes the third or 'triple FIT'.

The triple FIT: understanding the client–supervisee–supervisor relationship

In order for the supervisor to foster the effective use of the FIT model, they need to be aware of their own functioning in each of the three domains, in order to hold and understand the interactions which occur between the supervisee and themselves as well as between the supervisee and their client. Figure 13.5 illustrates this relationship.

Supervision sessions using this model will sometimes consider the relationship between the supervisor and supervisee as it impacts on the work being done with the client. The diagram in Figure 13.5 suggests that supervision needs to include awareness of the supervisee's functioning as well as the client's functioning in order for the work to be effective. In addition, in Figure 13.5 the supervisor, in order to facilitate this process in supervision, must be aware of their own feelings, behaviours and thoughts towards the client as presented in supervision, as well as towards the supervisee.

When the supervisee has unacknowledged and unresolved feelings towards his client, he will react to the client's feelings, behaviours and thoughts influenced by this bias. The challenge in using this model is that the supervisee is offered an opportunity to become aware of his own process and to explore his own unresolved issues, while at the same time considering the potential impact his issues can have on his clients.

FIGURE 13.5   The triple FIT

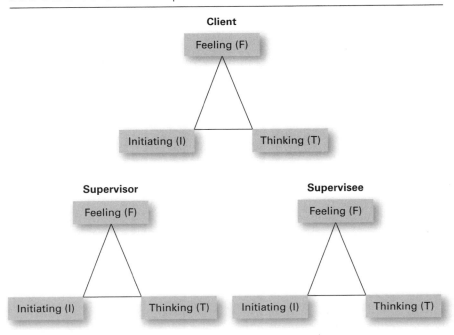

This awareness may be in the background throughout the session or may become more in the foreground when the interactions between the supervisor and supervisee identify dynamics occurring between them which may reflect the work being done with the client.

Both the supervisor and the supervisee need to be able to process the multiple interactions at the same time, ie to 'parallel process' the work occurring in the supervision and in the client sessions.

For example, when as supervisor you notice that you have an urge to rescue your supervisee who is tending to go into 'victim' mode (quite unlike them), you may use this to surface what could be happening unconsciously in the double FIT, ie between your supervisee and their client.

A mental map of the various diagrams provides an awareness of the interplay taking place within each of the three individuals involved in the process and allows awareness of the supervisor's and supervisee's functioning, as well as the client's functioning, as reported by the supervisee. Working with the FIT model, both supervisor and supervisee become increasingly adept at moving back and forth among the various domains to work with the emerging dynamics and issues. The benefit of the FIT supervision model is its simplicity while maintaining the complexity of the three relationships involved. Throughout this process, the emphasis remains on facilitating the work with the client. Even when personal material is explored by the supervisee or expressed by the supervisor, the focus remains on deepening the supervisee's understanding of their client's needs and process.

An example of supervision using the FIT model in double FIT mode

The supervisee is a trainee coach who comes to supervision feeling a bit overwhelmed by the issues being presented by their client.

The client sought coaching voluntarily, relating that he is having problems with his boss and may, as a result, lose his job. As he describes the situation, he says that he has lost two jobs in the past because his 'bosses were impossible to get along with'. He states that, because of the increased stress at work, he is having headaches, has been 'drinking more' and is having 'frequent arguments' with his wife. He is frustrated because, from his perspective, she fails to understand the nature of his 'problem', and she isn't supporting him. The client reports that he is willing to have coaching but doesn't see that he has issues to work on in the sessions.

Before looking at how the supervisee might work with their client, the supervisor invites the supervisee to consider and explore their own triangle, their feelings (F), actions (I) and thoughts (T) in relation to the client. For example, the first question put to the supervisee is as follows: 'What are you aware of right now in terms of your feelings, actions and thoughts?' The supervisee responds with a congruent awareness of strong negative feelings towards the client; she is annoyed with him and feels impatient. The FIT model assumes that the supervisor then responds in person-centred mode, responding with empathy to the supervisee's feelings. For example, 'You seem annoyed with this client – you sound short and impatient with him'.

The second question assumes the supervisee's understanding of the model: 'Which of the three domains would you like to focus on in this session?' The supervisee states that she experiences feelings (F) of dislike for the client, and finds herself thinking and judging the client (T) and wanting to change the behaviours or actions of the client (I). 'So where would you like to focus, the feeling, the judgement or the desire to change the client?'

The supervisee says: 'I think what's getting in the way of my work with this client is my dislike of him. I believe it is keeping me from working effectively with him.'

The supervisor says: 'So you are concerned that your feelings of dislike for your client may be getting in the way of your work with him. Are you saying that you would like to focus on your feelings in relation to this client?'

Supervisee says: 'Yes, that sounds helpful. There's something about him, about the way he speaks or maybe it's the tone of his voice, that sounds whiny or moany. He also blames everybody else for his problems. I get annoyed with him and have trouble focusing on what he's saying'.

Supervisor says: 'Tell me more.'

Thereafter the session proceeds along the direction which is chosen by the supervisee and may include her experience of a friend who moans and blames others:

Supervisee:	'You know, this client reminds me of that friend of mine who was always blaming others and then complaining about the outcome. He really annoyed me and we fell out over it.'
Supervisor:	'You are feeling annoyed with your client who reminds you of a friend you fell out with. That was sad.'
Supervisee:	'Yes, it was a shame.'
Supervisor:	'What would you like to say to your friend now?'
Supervisee:	'Look, stop moaning – we don't need to fall out over this.'
Supervisor:	'What else?'
Supervisee:	'Can we discuss what's getting to you?'
Supervisor:	'That sounds like you would have liked to uncover the reasons for your friend's moaning.'
Supervisee:	'Yes, now I would but it's too late.'
Supervisor:	'How is this affecting you with this client?'
Supervisee:	'I want to tell him some home truths.'
Supervisor:	'Like?'
Supervisee:	'Grow up. I don't blame your wife for wanting to leave you. She is living with a 6-year-old child. That feels better but of course I can't say that.'

Supervisor: 'What else might you do with your client?'

Supervisee: 'Well, he's frightened, isn't he, that he's going to lose another job.'

Supervisor: 'How can you let him know that you understand his fear?'

Supervisee: 'That's easy – its empathy and I know how to do that.'

Supervisor: 'So what will you say to your client?'

Supervisee: 'You must be afraid of losing your job.'

This process continues until there is a shift in the dialogue which is noticed by both the supervisee and the supervisor and the supervisee comes to a point where they feel they have choices now about how they perceive their client. So the dialogue moves into the 'T' for thinking domain and eventually into the 'I' for acting domain, where the supervisee decides on specific new behaviours with their client.

The assumption up to this point is that the supervisor–supervisee relationship is one-to-one, and coaches, mentors and supervisors may like to consider the advantages of group supervision. What do we mean by group supervision?

Group supervision

Coaches and mentors may choose to engage in group supervision for several reasons. It is usually cheaper and may be more convenient. There is the added benefit from interactions and contact with fellow professionals in a business which can be isolating. Group supervision enables sharing and comparing of professional work which supports practitioners and ensures that standards are maintained.

If you choose to run a supervision group you will need to adopt a different approach to the one-to-one supervision process as there is a need to attend to group dynamics. The need for focusing on and agreeing boundaries is part of this, for the reasons given below. An effective group supervisor defines a contract, articulates boundaries clearly for group members and teaches them to respect the supervisor's personal boundaries without damaging the relationships between supervisor and supervisees.

In addition, you may wish to draw on a range of theory about group dynamics and this is available in Appendix 5. This may be of interest to supervisors who would like to adopt a group method, and are curious about the way their group behaves, as well as possibly being worthwhile for supervisees as potential group members who would like to explore what is happening in terms of group dynamics. Meanwhile we summarize the main points below.

Dynamics in group supervision

Group working has inherent characteristics which differ markedly from traditional ways of learning such as lecturing or directive training. When, as a supervisor, you convene a group and facilitate communication within it, group effects, known as group dynamics, affect the individuals in the group and the group as a whole. A group behaves in two modes, the work group addressing the task, and the hidden group, based on emotions in the group, which has been called the secret life of groups by Jenny Rogers (Bion, 1961; Rogers, 2010).

The idea of this secret life, a holding environment, containment and defence mechanisms, ideas borrowed from psychodynamic psychology, informs group working by the need for trust, safety and boundaries. This means that the supervision group is a confidential place where client work may be freely discussed, as well as any concerns which arise for coach or mentor practice.

The secret life of the group

The most dramatic effect experienced by individuals in groups is feelings of fear and lack of safety, and we recognize that the degree of these feelings will vary with membership of the group, and between individuals. This effect exists in everyday social groups, though not articulated, and accounts for some of the discomfort experienced in some social situations, committee meetings and work groups.

Taking account of this knowledge in order to facilitate learning using a group format, the supervisor may need to accommodate the fears of group members, by establishing, very early, an atmosphere of trust and safety, so that learners can contribute and all can benefit. The boundaries and norms in a supervision group go a long way towards providing safety for group members. At an early stage, in order to establish boundaries and norms, the group should be invited to agree on ground rules for working in a group.

Typical ground rules for supervision group meetings are:

Confidentiality, as agreed by group members.

One person at a time.

Listen to others when they speak.

Be honest and open.

Don't attack others.

Challenge constructively.

No compulsion to speak.

Feelings may be expressed.

Feelings not dismissed.

Awareness/acceptance of diversity.

Observe time boundaries.

A number of these items will require discussion to agree their meaning in any particular group and understandings may differ depending on participants and context. A recent group run by one of the authors refused to turn off mobile phones. Taking a humanistic stance, there is no right or wrong meaning. Providing persons are respected, difference is recognized and context is articulated, then whatever the group decide is the meaning to be observed and this conforms to the person-centred model we recommend.

The group may need to get used to a different style of working to the fast-paced wordy interactions of the typical workplace or meeting. Facilitative methods seem slower at first and the group may wonder if anything is happening at all. Whatever they are, the ground rules provide what has been called a 'good enough' holding environment for the group, and will become a 'secure base' from which they can develop. The supervisor's role is to hold the boundaries agreed by the group in their ground rules even when the group is pushing against them, thereby ensuring the psychological safety of the group.

Defence mechanisms and the container

The supervisor needs to be aware of the effects of defences in the supervision group, described in detail in Appendix 5. There is no need for the supervisor to 'work with' any of the psychodynamic issues raised by defences; her awareness of them is sufficient. In our humanistic approach, when appropriate she may use non-technical language to gently point to what is occurring in the group. For example, the supervisor may observe that the group is in flight from the task by means of distraction, as they are moving away from the speaker's agenda, or projection, avoiding an uncomfortable feeling of anger or weakness by perceiving it in others. She may note that there is conflict between certain individuals in the group, and open up the issue in the process review. Alternatively, the supervisor may simply live with the unconscious projections in the group, observing that members are demonstrating dependency by waiting for a lead from the supervisor, or transference behaviours by offering the supervisor over-deference or hostility. The supervisor may deal with her own countertransference feelings of anger or irritation, internally, without commenting on it. This is described as the supervisor acting as a 'container' for difficult or unacceptable feelings and therefore making them safe (Bion, 1961).

The group dynamic is dominated by feeling, and group behaviour is ruled according to 'habeas emotum' (Luft, 1984: 154) which is a version of the legal term 'habeas corpus'. 'Habeas emotum' refers not to physical freedom but the psychological freedom to have emotions and express them. The supervisor needs to be aware of emotion in the group as potential energy for learning or potential blocks to learning if unexpressed. As an effective supervisor you will be able to observe, identify and, if appropriate, describe such dynamics in a group, through process comments, in simple terms, where appropriate, enabling reflection on that process by articulating it. For instance, calling attention to the group's over-reliance on the supervisor, noting where group members rather than the speaker feel angry, and mentioning the tendency to 'rescue' in the group. Process comments, if accepted by participants, are the trigger for reflection, and may be the first time the process has been highlighted for them.

The supervisor can help group members to unlock these defences, usually by making possible projections implicit, eg by noting that the speaker is being badly treated by their client's sponsor but it's another group member who is angry about it. The group can be invited to explore why this is occurring and what might change for the speaker if **she** were to be angry for herself. Where the supervisor is part of the defence, ie transference, where group members may project feelings of resentment or anger from the hurt child within, the supervisor needs to resist the temptation to offer a punitive response. Similarly, the supervisor may need to resist being carried away by the undiluted admiration given by some group members and alternatively, perhaps, dare to reveal the cracks!

In the light of the above, group supervision can offer important opportunities for reflective dialogue, challenge and learning, but the all-important element of emotional support through empathy is crucial.

We offer here a story which emphasizes support and empathy from one of the authors. It is included here as an example of using process for learning.

I recently had an experience in a supervision group of coaches that challenged the way in which I was running the group. The group had been working together for some time and had established ground rules as a framework for agreed working together. When exploring the ground rules we had devoted quite a bit of time to unpicking principles such as trust and confidentiality. We had spent less time unravelling the complex concept of support and what this really meant to people in the group.

At a group meeting one of the group presented her case that she was anxious about. She wanted to think about ways in which she could plan the way she would work with her client. The group asked many questions and some were aimed at challenging her to consider possible consequences of particular actions. At the end of the session when I asked the group to consider process issues, the coach in question commented that she felt quite angry that she had not felt supported by the group during her case presentation.

I felt challenged as the supervisor as these comments had implications for me. I decided not to ask her more questions about why she felt unsupported but to allow her to carry on talking about the way she felt and allow there to be silences as she was doing this. When she had finished describing the way she felt, I, as supervisor, acknowledged her feelings by saying 'you're feeling angry because you haven't felt supported by us' and thanked her for telling us that she felt this way. I then asked the group if they would like to say anything to the speaker. No comments were given, although there was a silence that conveyed how sorry people felt and I tentatively voiced this by saying 'I feel rather sad about this'. I then asked the group to consider what this notion of support looks like and how we might give support in a group. The group came up with the following points:

- Support is not necessarily about saying you understand or giving loads of positive feedback to make the person feel good.

- Support is about owning up to how you are feeling when a group member is telling their story. So, for example, if you feel sad or anxious or frustrated it can be supportive to share these feelings you have.

- Support is about checking out with the group member during the course of the discussion how they are feeling and what they would like from us as a group.

- Support is about paying attention to non-verbal cues and the pace of the case presentation.

Everyone engaged in this discussion and came up with a clear idea of what support looks like to them. They felt positive that they could work with this and try to put it into action. The annual review of the group occurred a few months after this event. All of the group spoke about how much they had learnt from this experience. The coach concerned commented on how she felt she had really been listened to and it would give her courage to challenge the process in the future.

I learnt that as an experienced supervisor there is still much learning to do, in particular the skill of reflection in action. I had to think and make decisions quite quickly in this instance. The decision I made was not to ask the individual concerned more in-depth questions about feeling unsupported as she had been asked enough questions over the past hour and had already felt in the 'hot seat'. Instead I chose to acknowledge her feelings, share how I and the rest of the group were feeling and move to using the skills within the group to learn from the experience and plan how we might look at the issue of support in the future.

The story illustrates the supervisor's use of empathy in verbally acknowledging the feelings of the speaker; unconditional positive regard is shown by the supervisor allowing space and silence for the speaker; and congruence is present in the supervisor's expression of his own sadness in response to what the speaker has said.

Group supervision provides training and learning opportunities not available in individual supervision, primarily because other group members may participate in role-plays, exercises and group process discussions. Feedback from more than one person, ie other group members, is an additional benefit arising in the group setting.

The group may include demonstrations of initial sessions with clients using humanistic listening skills and, at the same time, beginning to identify the client's functioning within the three domains. Supervision groups lend themselves especially well to this process as members can be asked to work in triads, acting as clients, coaches and observers to facilitate the learning. Supervision also includes case presentations based on client material brought by group members. Group members may be asked to role-play the client or the coach. The practical experience is combined with group discussions, as well as experiential activities, derived from the case material.

A further advantage of group supervision is provided by using the group itself exploring its own dynamics as a training and learning resource. Members may be asked to explore the dynamics occurring between them. Participation in these activities increases group members' self-awareness and awareness of their impact on others, particularly awareness of the effect of their interactions with clients.

Chapter summary

In this chapter we have visited the historical sources of supervision, and the three functions and seven tasks of supervision. The chapter includes a review of existing models of supervision and how they can address all the tasks of supervision as well as the FIT supervision model created by Harris and Brockbank (2011). A brief review of group supervision completes the chapter.

14 Conclusion

In this edition we have introduced a revised framework of situational coaching and mentoring. The framework yields four quadrants which represent four different situations or contexts in which coaching or mentoring can take place:

- the performance quadrant, where coaching and mentoring support performance management;
- the engagement quadrant, where coaching and mentoring nurture employee engagement;
- the development quadrant, where coaching and mentoring facilitate individuals in their desire for transformation;
- the systemic quadrant, where coaching and mentoring programmes form part of the organization's drive towards its own transformation.

We emphasize the importance of identifying which quadrant the coach or mentor is working in, in order to minimize confusion, tension and disappointment. A distinct set of skills is presented, emphasizing questioning in performance situations and recommending empathy in engagement and developmental situations. The text highlights the role of empathy in coaching or mentoring, which facilitates deep reflective learning. A truly reflective dialogue includes empathy. The level of empathy offered depends on which quadrant the practitioner is working in. Hence, line managers in the performance quadrant are unlikely to offer empathy; managers or practitioners in the engagement quadrant should offer primary empathy; and practitioners in the developmental quadrant will offer advanced empathy. In addition, further skills in the development quadrant support deep, double loop learning which triggers radical change and potential transformation for individuals. We have proposed that where organizations sponsor developmental programmes, those who have transformed themselves may trigger a similar effect in their organization.

Three-quarters of organizations use coaching or mentoring with these stated main purposes:

- tackling poor performance;
- improving employee engagement;
- lifting capability in good performers. (CIPD, 2011c)

However, these purposes cannot be achieved by the same approach, and they must be addressed in different ways. Tackling poor performance calls for performance coaching. Employee engagement calls for engagement coaching or mentoring, and lifting capability in good performers requires developmental coaching or mentoring.

To transform a business, the route includes performance management, through engagement to developmental coaching or mentoring, and hence to systemic change.

Demands on performance management systems are described by Brown and Hirsch (2011) as 'too tall an order' which are 'often seen to fail', because organizations are impatient to improve performance which they believe will rapidly revolutionize the business rather than staying with a slower, more considered evolution.

Brown and Hirsch (2011: 37) maintain that: 'You can't change a mature organizational culture overnight – it has to be an evolutionary approach to positively resonate with everyone it affects. There are no shortcuts.'

Transformational effects can be achieved through such a considered route, beginning with basic performance management, and then through engagement and developmental initiatives, to support employees to achieve their individual objectives. This evolutionary route has faith in the idea that members of an organization, by their own development, will bring it to its own transformation.

APPENDIX 1
The coaching contract, records and review

No coaching should begin without an agreed contract. The nature of this contract will vary depending on the quadrant in which you are working:

Performance: If you are also the line manager then coaching will form part of the working relationship between yourself and the staff member concerned. In this case you already have an implicit contract.

Engagement: Where the coaching is aiming at engagement there are two possibilities: you are an external coach and you must contract with your client; or you may be asked to coach a staff member whom you do not line manage and convey their progress to their manager. This breach in confidentiality should be clear in a contract from the start, otherwise the coaching partnership is doomed. Issues of confidentiality within organizations tend to affect coaching outcomes.

Development: You are an external coach and you must contract with your client and this must include total confidentiality to be most effective.

Systemic: You are an external team coach and you must contract with your clients and this must include total confidentiality to be most effective.

A sample contract is given below, based on an original idea by Michael Carroll (2004).

Developmental Coaching Contract

This is a coaching contract between .... and .... from .... until its review (or ending) on ....

What is coaching?

We are agreed that coaching is a contracted forum used by clients (those being coached) to reflect on aspects of their life and work, where they receive formal and informal feedback on that work and where they learn from their reflection how to maximize their potential.

Practicalities

We will meet for .... hours every .... at .... at a time to be arranged at the end of each coaching session. Ours is a non-smoking environment and we have agreed that each of us will ensure that there are no unnecessary interruptions (mobiles, phone, people). (Add here anything about team, if team coaching, or fees, if necessary, or equipment, eg flip charts, overhead projectors, video, audio etc.)

Procedures

We have agreed that the following arrangements will take place in the following situations:

1 Cancellation of session ....

2 Non-attendance at coaching session ....

3 Where there are disagreements, disputes, conflict areas between coach and client (coachee)

4 If there is need for extra coaching sessions ....

5 Contracts with others, eg an organization or a training course ....

6 For appeals ....

7 Keeping of notes ....

8 Emergencies (you are free to phone me if there is an emergency on the following number ....). What will you (client) do if I (the coach) am not available?

For many coaches including item 8 is unacceptable.

Guidelines

The following guidelines/ground rules will guide our time together:

1 Confidentiality (what we mean by confidentiality is ....).

2 Openness/honesty (about work done, the relationship, reports etc).

3 Line management issues that may pertain (especially if the coach is asked to report to line manager).

4 Gossip (any leakage of information in the systems).

5 Using feedback to learn.

Roles and responsibilities

We have agreed that as coach I will take responsibility for:

- timekeeping;
- managing the overall agenda of sessions;
- giving feedback;
- monitoring the coaching relationship;
- creating a safe place;
- monitoring ethical and professional issues;
- keeping notes of sessions;
- drawing up the final reports (if needed).

We have agreed that as client you will responsible for:

- preparing for the coaching session;
- presenting in coaching;
- your learning (objectives);
- applying learning from coaching;
- feedback to self and to me;
- keeping notes of sessions.

Evaluation and review

We have agreed that informal evaluation of:

- client
- coach
- coaching

will take place every sixth session. Formal evaluations will take place every year or as requested by either of us. The criteria against which evaluation of clients will take place may be arranged with an organization or solely with the client and will include criteria or competencies against which the client wishes to be appraised, or competencies given by their organization. Formal reports will be sent to .... and can be viewed by .... They will be kept at ....

The process for formal evaluation of clients (written) will be:

1 self-evaluation;

2 evaluation by coach;

3 initial report by coach to be seen and commented on by client;

4 final report written by coach with space for comments by client;

5 report sent to agreed personnel (above).

Renegotiation of contract

At any time either party (coach and/or client) can initiate discussion around renegotiation of the contract or any part of it. This will be done in advance so that there is preparatory time available.

Signed: .... (Coach)

Signed: .... (Client/s)

Signed: .... (Others, eg organization or training institute)

Development plan for coaching client

Many CPD programmes include a personal and professional development planner, and we recommend that this is used to record the objectives, achievements, career details and development reviews generated in coaching sessions. The planner includes a personal log section, which can be used to record achievement. A sample development plan is given below.

Development plan (sample)

Name:

Address for correspondence:

Telephone: Fax:

E-mail:

Overall development

Goal_____

_____

_____

Objectives	Action steps	Target date	Resources	Status comments

Coaching review

The programme will be reviewed and evaluated after 12 months, and an interim review will be carried out after six months. In addition to the formal review we would value individual views on the coaching programme in practice. On completion of the programme, please take a few minutes to complete the questionnaire and return it to xxxx by yyyyy.

Coach review of work with client A

Name:

Address for correspondence:

Telephone:

E-mail:

How many coaching sessions have you conducted with client A?

How would you describe your coaching relationship with A?

How helpful was the training you received?

On reflection, what additional training or support would you have liked?

At the start of this coaching relationship, did you agree any contract, terms of reference or ground rules?

What review process have you used with client A?

Thank you for completing this questionnaire.

Client review of coaching

The coaching programme will be reviewed and evaluated after 12 months, and an interim review will be carried out after six months. In addition to the formal group review we would value individual views on the coaching programme in practice.

Name:

How many coaching session have you had?

How would you describe your coaching relationship?

What were you hoping to gain from the coaching?

What benefits have you gained from the coaching?

At the start of the relationship, did you agree any terms of reference or ground rules?

What review of the coaching was carried out?

Are you willing for this information to be written up for future programmes?

Personal action plan for clients

Name ....

Position/Project ....

Date ....

Personal objective	Action	Timescale

Coaching record

Name..

Position/Project ....

Start date..

Date	Goal agreed	Action	Date completed

APPENDIX 2
Mentoring contract and review

Mentoring contracts (additional documents for mentoring programmes can be found in an excellent text by Lois Zachary (2000)).

Issue for discussion	Agreed
What kind of role will I take in the mentoring relationship?	
How will we deal with issues of confidentiality?	
Who will make contact?	
How often will we meet or make contact?	
How much time is to be allocated?	
How will mentoring sessions be recorded?	
What is the agreed duration of the relationship?	
How can the mentoring agreement be concluded if other than the specified time?	
Any others?	

Sample mentoring agreement

Mentor and client agreement: between Martin (mentor) and Peter (client)

We are voluntarily entering into a mentoring relationship which we expect to benefit both of us. We want this relationship to be a rewarding experience with most of our time together focusing on client development. We have noted these features of our relationship:

- Confidentiality _____

  _____

  _____

- Duration of the relationship _____

  _____

  _____

- Frequency of meetings _____

  _____

  _____

- Time to be invested by Martin (mentor) _____

  _____

  _____

- Time to be invested by Peter (client) _____

  _____

  _____

- Role to be taken by Martin (mentor) _____

  _____

  _____

- An individual development plan will be maintained by Peter (client) ☐

- Records of mentoring sessions will be maintained by Martin (mentor) ☐

- Records of mentoring sessions will be copied to Peter (client) ☐
- We agree to a no-fault conclusion of this relationship,
  for whatever reason ☐

Signed _____ and _____
　　　　　　　　(mentor)　　　　　　　　　　　　(client)

Date _____　　Date _____

Arrange the date and time of next meeting and reiterate action points.

Mentoring review

The programme will be reviewed and evaluated after 12 months, and an interim review will be carried out after six months. In addition to the formal group review, we would value individual views on the mentoring programme in practice. On completion of the programme, please take a few minutes to complete the questionnaire and return it to xxxx by yyyyy.

Mentor's review

Name:

Address for correspondence:

Telephone:

E-mail:

How long have you been a mentor?

How many people have you mentored?

Why did you choose to become a mentor?

How would you describe your mentoring relationship(s)?

How helpful was the training you received?

On reflection, what additional training or support would you have liked?

What benefits do you feel you have gained from mentoring?

At the start of this mentoring relationship, did you agree any terms of reference or ground rules?

What review process have you used with your client(s)?

Are you willing for this information to be written up for future mentors?

Thank you for completing this questionnaire.

Protégé's review

The mentoring programme will be reviewed and evaluated after 12 months, and an interim review will be carried out after six months. In addition to the formal group review, we would value individual views on the mentoring programme in practice.

Name:

How long have you had a mentor?

Why did you choose your mentor?

How would you describe your mentoring relationship?

What were you hoping to gain from the mentoring relationship?

What benefits have you gained from mentoring?

At the start of the relationship, did you agree any terms of reference or ground rules?

What review was carried out of your mentoring relationship?

Are you willing for this information to be written up for future mentors?

APPENDIX 3
Examples of ground rules

These examples are suitable for mentors, coaches, team coaches, supervisors and group supervisors.

Example 1

1 Confidentiality.
2 Safe environment.
3 Respecting each other's cultures.
4 Non-judgemental.
5 Respecting each other's opinions.
6 Acceptance.
7 Supportive in sharing experiences and ideas with each other.
8 Commitment.
9 Accessibility.
10 Enjoyment and fun.
11 Mobile phones off.
12 Telephone or e-mail contact arrangements.
13 Flexible approach.
14 Disclose.
15 'I' statements.
16 Ownership.
17 Boundaries.
18 Honesty.
19 Don't be afraid to ask questions.
20 Don't be afraid to challenge.
21 Both parties recognized as a resource (sharing).
22 Reliability.
23 Plan to succeed – dare to fail.
24 Valuing diversity.
25 Respecting difference.
26 Equal opportunities.

Example 2

1 Confidentiality, ie assume that the shared material is confidential unless told otherwise.
2 Respect for difference.
3 Openness and risk taking.
4 Being prepared to 'talk it out'.
5 Constructive/supportive criticism.
6 Non-judgemental behaviours and statements: no assumptions.
7 Listening, not interrupting; giving space: active listening.
8 Taking personal responsibility for input and participation and seeking clarification.
9 Sharing tasks.
10 Hold boundaries, ie timekeeping and mobile phones.
11 Mediation approach.
12 Safe environment.
13 Check out assertions.
14 Asking for what you need/want.

Example 3

1 Review the ground rules.
2 Confidentiality – not to share outside the mentoring relationship anything which identifies an individual or their organization.
3 Timekeeping.
4 Attendance.
5 Questions for clarification.
6 Tolerance – right to different opinion.
  Respect for other's right to a different opinion.
7 Listening.
8 Opportunity to speak.
9 Be prepared to disclose.
10 Respecting diversity and learning from diversity.
11 Learning about each other to build trust (differences).
12 Freedom of disclosure – depth at discretion of discloser.
13 Respecting silence.
14 Right to say 'I don't understand'.
15 'I' statements.

Example 4

1 Disclose as much or as little as you feel comfortable with.
2 Safety: freedom to speak.
  Constructive criticism.
3 Willing to be open and honest.
4 Supportive and constructive criticism.
5 Ability to say no or renegotiate.
6 Respect for each other's views.
7 Challenging actions/statements, not the person.
8 To be supported in exploration of attitudes or skills.
9 Being able to be open. Non-judgemental.
10 Timekeeping. Turning up and on time.
11 Following through to a new point of decision.
12 Confidentiality.

APPENDIX 4
Company mentoring

An extract from a mentor manual provided for a corporate programme in the retail industry

What is the mentor's role? The mentor's role is to assist the protégé in identification of learning needs, preparation of learning contracts and review of learning contracts.

Mentoring begins at, or shortly after, induction with a Mentor Meeting where the protégé and mentor study her Management Competences Audit and compare it with the ideal profile for her grade.

Learning needs are identified, a learning contract agreed and a review date arranged.

Mentor meetings will normally last at least one hour and will take place in private, ideally without interruption.

Mentoring is a way of helping by enabling rather than teaching or telling. The mentor's role is to enable the protégé to identify *for herself* the competences which need to be the basis for a learning contract.

The responsibility for identifying learning needs, deciding on the contract and carrying it out lies with the protégé. The mentor is a powerful ally for the protégé, offering her time, her support, and her position in the company to help the protégé to achieve the aims of the company.

Protégés may expect to have meetings with their mentor at least five times during the 12 months of the programme.

Details of how such meetings may proceed appear in section 5 of this handbook.

Job description for mentor

To establish a working relationship with the protégé which will foster learning development.

To enable the protégé to distinguish between individual learning needs and the general objectives of the company.

To prepare for Learning Contract meetings by examining the protégé's competence profile, and to offer support in completion of the Management Competences Audit.

To encourage wide-ranging discussion on possible objectives and enable the protégé to focus on realistic goals.

To ensure that the protégé completes their Learning Contract and to be aware of proposed activities.

To arrange for resources to be provided as required for the protégé to complete their Learning Contract.

To control the Learning Contract Review process, ensuring that criteria are met as agreed.

What does a mentor do? He or she:

- listens;
- makes sense of what is said;
- focuses on the person;
- asks open questions;
- challenges;
- is prepared to be challenged;
- can summarize well;
- nags;
- praises;
- encourages;
- shares his or her life;
- understands the programme;
- uses empathy;
- empowers;
- chooses to be a mentor.

Person specification for mentor

The most important aspect of mentoring is the quality of the relationship. If the relationship is good, mentoring is a success. If it isn't, both parties struggle.

The mentor should:

- be senior to the trainee, typically a store manager, not in a line relationship with the trainee;
- be familiar with the Company and have well-established networks;
- have solid experience to draw on, if necessary;
- know the business and be good at it.

Personal skills required by mentor

- Listening
- Responding
- Waiting
- Asserting
- Challenging
- Questioning
- Confronting
- Feedback
- Managing emotion

What is a mentor like? He or she:

- is senior;
- likes people;
- has credibility;
- has knowledge;
- likes him or herself;
- is not afraid to confront;
- can be impatient;
- has experience;
- can be angry;
- has influence;
- is not afraid to praise;
- is not judgemental;
- understands;
- is not a counsellor;
- wants to be a mentor.

The good news is that it's not a life sentence! The mentoring relationship may exist only for the duration of the programme. However, successful mentor relationships often last longer and become more equal as the protégé develops and progresses.

In the fullness of time the relationship dissolves and both protégé and mentor will need to 'let go'. Mentors have benefited from developing their enabling skills and being associated with a successful protégé. Protégés who have been successfully 'mentored' are very likely to be effective mentors themselves, a clear benefit to the business.

APPENDIX 5
Group dynamics for supervision and team coaching

Group working has inherent characteristics which differ markedly from traditional ways of learning such as lecturing or directive training. When, as a facilitator, you convene a group and facilitate communication within it, group effects, known as group dynamics, affect the individuals in the group and the group as a whole. A group behaves rather like a person, with distinctive and recognizable characteristics, as well as having a significant impact on the individuals within it (Bion, 1961; Egan, 1977; Foulkes, 1975). The facilitator in this document is either a team coach or a group supervisor.

Some of the issues to be aware of are:

- one group or two?
- the facilitator as container – a holding environment;
- providing a secure base;
- defence mechanisms.

One group or two? Bion's two groups

The nature of group dynamics was explored in depth by Wilfred Bion (1961), drawing on his wartime experience where he realized that being in a group could be fearful and the group leader needs to 'remain calm under fire' (Rogers, 2010: 29).

He established that any group operates at two levels, the basic assumption group (unconscious) and the work group (conscious). When operating in the unconscious, basic mode, group members behave as if they hold basic assumptions about the life and purpose of the group, which are quite different from the declared purpose of the work group. There are three basic assumptions which the group may adopt, as follows:

- Dependency: The group believes that security lies in a powerful leader, usually identified as the facilitator or team coach – and failing that, the group will generate a fantasy leader. The effect of this assumption is that group members deny their own competence, preferring to place all their hopes (and therefore blame) on the leader, eg where group members constantly defer to the facilitator with continuous eye contact and nodding.

- Pairing: The group unconsciously shares the assumption that an ideal couple or pairing exists within the group and that this will produce a messiah who will be the group saviour. The effect of this is that group members focus on a fantasy future rather than the present, and may be preoccupied with a potential event such as a new CEO which will solve everything.

- Flight/fight: The shared group assumption is that the group's survival will be achieved if its members fight or flee from someone or something. The effect of this assumption is that group members behave as if the group is being attacked by a fantasy 'enemy'. For example, the group will use battle terms (fight) or members may flee the task by joking, falling asleep or moving their chair out of the circle.

Bion's work, developed by others (de Board, 1978: 37–39), established that any group flips continuously between the basic assumption group (unconscious) and the work group (conscious) throughout its life. Lengthy committee meetings are a mixture of both. How does Bion's work apply to our supervision group or team?

According to Bion, if the group remains strictly in work mode it is deprived of warmth and power, whereas if the group remains strictly in basic assumption mode, group members may not pursue their goals. When the group is in basic assumption mode the effect is revitalizing even if it may feel catastrophic to members. A skilled supervisor or team coach often moves a group into basic assumption mode in order to access its energy, by responding to expressed (but not verbalized) feelings, using primary or advanced empathy. When the emotional charge in the group is put into words by the supervisor or team coach (or indeed a group member), the group is able to access its energy, process the feelings and move on to address their task in work mode.

When a group is able to function effectively in work mode, the members are able to assist each other to achieve their goals, address reality, and develop or change. The same group may operate in basic assumption mode, using its energy to defend itself from fear and anxiety, without achieving any task. The tension between the basic assumption group and the work group is believed to be essential for transformation (de Board, 1978: 44–48; Barnes, Ernst and Hyde, 1999). Effective group work aims to take energy from its basic assumption mode and pursue action within its work group mode and allows the group to move freely between both modes. For example, the speaker may find that her issue uncovers some strong feelings about her work and the group may tap into its basic assumption mode by waiting for the supervisor or team coach (their fantasy leader) to 'rescue' the situation. Where the emotional reality is articulated by the supervisor, team coach, or group members, the group can move off into work mode as the members focus on the task in hand.

The supervisor or team coach does not need to 'work with' these dynamics as an analyst would, but she will feel more confident when she understands what is happening in a group when these unconscious forces are at work. For example, it is quite common, in a group where freedom of expression is granted, for members to attack the perceived leader or authority figure. Indeed, a leaderless group will create such a figure primarily for the purpose. This is an example of Bion's 'dependency' assumption above. The tendency in a group for a speaker to address most of his 'story' to the supervisor or team coach is a sign of their identification of this individual as some sort of leader. A skilled supervisor or team coach will be aware of how this may affect her response, and monitor their own response to the situation. Hence supervisors and team coaches may attract aggression or adulation from group members and these feelings are part of the group dynamic.

A 'holding' environment for team coaching or group supervision

When a group is convened, and members are offered the possibility of being congruent, it is necessary also to protect them from psychological harm. By this we do not mean nervous breakdowns or the like, but we do recognize the potential for group dynamics to trigger the hurt child in every human being (Miller, 1983), and this may include the supervisor or team coach.[1] The effort to 'form' as a group may trigger anxieties from the past. The group can be provided with a 'good enough' environment using the concept of 'holding', ie taking care of group members, through boundaries and ground rules (Winnicott, 1971). In addition, these ground rules provide what has been described as a 'secure base' in which group members can feel safe enough to develop themselves (Bowlby, 1979). Hence when launching a group the supervisor or team coach begins by discussing the model of learning she proposes, gaining agreement to it, and establishing with group members a series of ground rules for group behaviour. These may be agreed when a group is invited to contribute (usually in brainstorming style) to the question: 'What conditions would you want to have in place while working in this group or team?' Examples of ground rules can be found in Appendix 3.

The most dramatic effect experienced by individuals in groups is feelings of fear and lack of safety and the degree of these feelings will vary with membership of the group, and between individuals. This effect exists in everyday social groups, though not articulated, and accounts for some of the discomfort experienced in some social situations, committee meetings and work groups. Some practitioners (often with NLP backgrounds) are intent on denial of any negative feelings in a group and want to focus on positive emotions only. We discuss the impact of this below.

Taking account of this knowledge, in order to facilitate learning using a group format the supervisor or coach may need to accommodate the fears of group members, by establishing an atmosphere of trust and safety very early on, so that learners can contribute and all can benefit. The boundaries and norms in a group go a long way towards providing safety for group members. At an early stage, in order to establish boundaries and establish norms, the group should be invited to agree on ground rules for working in a group.

There is no need to 'work with' any of the psychodynamic issues raised by anxiety; awareness of them is sufficient. When appropriate, the supervisor or coach may use non-technical language to gently point to what is occurring in the group. For example, she may observe that the group is in flight from the task by means of distraction, as they are moving away from the speaker's agenda, or projection, avoiding an uncomfortable feeling of anger or weakness by perceiving it in others. She may note that there is pairing between certain individuals in the group, and open up the issue in the process review. Alternatively, she may simply live with the unconscious behaviours in the group, observing that members are demonstrating dependency by waiting for a lead from her, by offering over-deference or by hostility. The supervisor or coach may deal with her own countertransference (described below) feelings of anger or irritation, internally, without commenting on it. This is described as the supervisor or coach acting as a 'container' for difficult or unacceptable feelings and therefore making them safe (Bion, 1961).

The ideas of a holding environment, containment and defence mechanisms are ideas borrowed from psychodynamic psychology. They inform group working by the need for trust, safety and boundaries to provide a secure base for learning (Stafford-Clark, 1965; Fordham, 1982; Winnicott, 1965; Bowlby, 1979). This means that team coaching must provide for expression of concerns without risk to the individual. The supervision group is a confidential place where client work may be freely discussed, as well as any concerns which arise for coach or mentor practice.

Defences in groups

To facilitate any group activity an understanding of psychodynamic principles is needed, and this applies to group supervision and team coaching. We noted above the impact of group dynamics on the feelings and behaviour of those in the group, as well as the supervisor or team coach. While a full treatment of group dynamics is beyond the scope of this book, we do recognize that group members and supervisors or team coaches may wish to have some idea about the unconscious forces at work in their group and we introduce the basic concepts below. The idea of a part of each person which is unconscious and inaccessible is a key concept in psychodynamic thought, and the unconscious works for the person to maintain an image of self which they find acceptable. Psychodynamic theory maintains that the unconscious uses defence mechanisms to keep the self-image in place, and plays its part in maintaining the psychological health of the individual.

Defensive forms of behaviour in groups are usually triggered by anxieties, either anxiety triggered by being-in-a-group or archaic anxiety with its roots in the past (Heron, 1999). Anxiety about being-in-a-group may take the form of 'self-talk' like: Will I be accepted, wanted, liked? Will I understand what's going on? Will I be able to do what's required? Archaic anxiety is the echo of past distress and comes from the fear of being rejected or overwhelmed. These anxieties are real for anyone who takes part in a group where all members are given voice, as in group supervision or team coaching. The casual comment or joking aside may cause hurt as they can trigger damaging self-talk as described above.

The supervisor or coach needs to be aware of the effects of defences in the group.

The unconscious forces within a group or team, often called defence mechanisms, include:

- projection;
- projective identification;
- transference;
- countertransference.

We define these terms below.

Group members may '*project*' their own feelings onto others, especially if they are uncomfortable feelings like anger or sadness:

> Projection is a process whereby the person defends against threatening and unacceptable feelings and impulses by acting as though these feelings and impulses only exist in other people, not in the person himself or herself.
>
> (McLeod, 1998: 43)

For example, a group member may find themselves feeling angry about the way the speaker is being treated, while the speaker remains as cool as a cucumber! When the projection is 'taken in' by the other person(s), ie they swallow what has been sent unconsciously to them, as the group member did above, and it becomes a recognizable part of self-awareness, this is called *projective identification.*

Projective identification has been defined as a normal psychological process which is a transaction across the boundary between two people, ie between what I am and what you are. Let us look at this idea more closely.

The speaker A, in describing an event where she was landed with extra work, is speaking calmly and without apparent emotion, projecting some feelings of anger about her situation onto another group member, B. A has unconsciously learnt that angry feelings are unacceptable to have and she pushes them away from herself by unconsciously 'seeing' them in others. This means that the speaker is not conscious that her anger is really part of her own self, having learnt in the past that being 'good' was being 'not angry'. The group member B 'takes in' the feeling of anger unconsciously projected at him, experiences it as real, and may feel impelled to express anger about A's colleagues. Hence what group member B is feeling in that moment is really part of the speaker A, but appears to both A and group member B as part of B:

> Projective identification occurs when the person to whom the feelings and impulses are being projected is manipulated into believing that he or she actually has these feelings and impulses.
>
> (McLeod, 1998: 43)

For example, the group member feeling angry above.

What is the benefit for A to project anger onto B and for B to express it? A can allow herself to disapprove of B's anger, and may react strongly. The clue to projection is the strength of feeling which A may now have about the part of herself she perceives in B, as theory suggests that this is how she really feels about her angry self but defends against this knowledge by projection. This is why taking back projections is incredibly illuminating. The perceived aspect of B, being angry, which A reacts to strongly, suggests that anger is something which clearly has importance for A. This is why projection has been called 'a gift in the present from the past', as the clue to your self lies in your reaction to the other (Neumann, 1998).

We must not underestimate the fearful nature of some of our projective material – it is being sent out to another in order to lessen the pain or fear which we would experience if we 'owned' it properly. Hence where projection may be identified by the supervisor, or group members themselves, great care is needed if we call attention to it, and we advocate a careful and non-jargon observation with no pressure on anyone to respond to what is being suggested. Such an observation also releases other group members from 'carrying' the projection without making a huge fuss about it. This frees group members to deal with their own material rather than feeling weak and helpless.

Another form of projection is the defence known as *transference*. Where feelings experienced in the past are 'transferred' unconsciously into present relationships, the term transference is used (Jacoby, 1984). These feelings are not just memories; they are alive and can deeply affect current relationships. 'Transference repeats and relives the love, hatred, aggression and frustration experienced as an infant in relation to his parents' (Jacoby, 1984: 17). In addition, they may not be all negative, and can also take the form of undiluted admiration. The emotions and feelings involved are repetitions of the original ones (de Board, 1978). Transference can be seen as an entirely normal occurrence in any relationship and may have archetypal contents (Jacoby, 1984), ie the ideal father or perfect mother. If this seems a fanciful idea, the concept of projection was applied to everyday living by Ferenczi (1916, cited in de Board, 1978), who suggested that people are continually transferring their own feelings onto other people. For instance, when a speaker focuses all her attention on the supervisor or coach, almost ignoring group members, it may be that the speaker has 'transferred' feelings of undue deference onto the supervisor or coach. On the other hand, the transferred feelings may be resentment and rebellion.

Supervisors or team coaches are type-cast or propelled into the matching pre-prepared script, and may experience two forms of countertransference (a defence which is not fully understood):

- As if they are actually the source of the transferred feelings, and this is called *concordantcountertransference*, as your feelings match those of the speaker. Such countertransference, where emotions are felt in harmony with the projected transference feelings, offers supervisors material for advanced empathy.

- *Complementary countertransference* which, as a response to deference or resentment, may draw on ideal archetypes like the good parent or the punishing god. The speaker's over-deference or resentment, as above, may give rise to corresponding god-like and all-powerful feelings in the supervisor or an impatience with the 'childish behaviour' of the speaker.

These ideas offer supervisors and team coaches useful information in the service of their client group (Jacoby, 1984).

We suggest that when a supervisor or team coach begins to experience such feelings, they may call attention to what is happening by being congruent, eg 'I am feeling rather over-important here – this is your group'. Where the speaker is communicating resentment the supervisor may name the feeling: 'You seem angry with me – what's happening?'

The task for the supervisor or coach or indeed group member is to disentangle what may be their own feelings from what is being unconsciously projected onto them by others. For instance, where the supervisor, coach or group member feels an urge to rescue the speaker – surely not an appropriate feeling between adults – this may alert them to the possibility that the feeling is countertransference. They are feeling the urge to rescue in response to the speaker's feelings of helplessness, transferred and projected onto others. Either group members or supervisor/coach may choose to mention their 'rescue' feeling and discuss whether it is appropriate to the speaker's situation.

The supervisor or team coach will recognize and deal with the defences described above. In humanistic mode, he can help group members to unlock these defences, usually by making possible projections implicit, eg by noting that the speaker is being badly treated at work but it's the group member who is angry about it. The group can be invited to explore why this is occurring and what might change for the speaker if **she** were to be angry for herself. Where the supervisor or team coach is part of the defence, ie countertransference, where group members may project feelings of resentment or anger from the hurt child within, then he needs to resist the temptation to offer a punitive response. Similarly, he may need to resist being carried away by the undiluted admiration given by some group members.

Everyday examples of defence mechanisms

It is important to realize that defence mechanisms are life preserving and therefore part of a healthy and natural human existence. However, one or more particular defence mechanisms may inhibit natural behaviours. You will see how that can happen in the examples below:

Atonement 'Making up for' a previous misdemeanour by performing a socially approved act, eg a member of staff staying late to make up for being slack during the day.

Compensation Anxiety in one area is balanced by achievement in another, eg failure to achieve academically can be compensated for by excessive sociability or obsessive domesticity.

Denial Protection from painful reality by refusing to recognize it, eg believing you're doing OK at work when you are due for a report/final warning.

Displacement Transfer of feelings or actions to another person to reduce anxiety, eg youngsters who are angry with their parents often displace it to teachers, managers etc.

Fantasy Creating an imaginary world to meet a desired goal, eg a manager's belief that things are better than they are.

Identification Trying to 'be' the person we most admire, imitating dress and language. Some youngsters develop this into 'fan worship' of sportspersons or entertainers.

Intellectualization Masking anxious feelings by intellectual and detached discussion, eg discussion of strategy when staff are leaving in droves.

Introjection Adoption of someone else's beliefs or attitudes, eg a young person who believes 'he's no good' because a powerful parent said so.

Projection Putting undesirable characteristics onto someone else, eg accusing another member of staff of incompetence when it's your own.

Rationalization Creating rational but unreal reasons for your own behaviour, eg staff who blame management for their own lack of motivation.

Reaction Formation Disguising real feelings or attitudes by the opposite behaviour, eg expressing disgust with tabloid 'sleaze' but enjoying it.

Regression This is reversion to an earlier stage of development, eg a temper tantrum or sleeping a lot under stress.

Repression Unconscious exclusion of past memories and feelings to prevent pain, anxiety or guilt, eg the person who 'forgets' they have been abused.

Suppression Conscious exclusion of past memories and feelings to prevent pain, anxiety and guilt.

How can you spot defence mechanisms?

Freudian slips are one of the clues to the existence of defence mechanisms.
    For example, someone denying their anger about a colleague's promotion may say, 'I'm so pleased I could hit you' (defence mechanism of denial). Other clues to defence mechanisms are non-verbal behaviour such as false

smiles, twitching limbs or a sarcastic tone of voice. The feelings which are most likely to be 'hidden' by defence mechanisms are anger, anxiety and hurt.

You cannot see your own defence mechanisms because they are unconscious. To bring them into your conscious mind you need to feel very, very safe and that can only happen under special conditions with highly skilled helpers.

Humanistic approach to groups

The *humanistic* principles of abundance in personal resources and experience, rather than deficiency of them and a belief in the human potential to grow and develop as a whole person, provides a positive attitude to human endeavour in groups. These principles inform the structure where, after ground rules are agreed, each group member has protected time, where the group's resources are at their disposal, and group members work without judgement but offer challenge and support in equal measure.

The humanist approach recognizes transference and offers empathy as a response to archaic feelings of anger or adoration. The countertransference experienced in the group, usually by the supervisor or team coach, can be noted by them without intervention, or can be openly articulated through being congruent. The projections in the group can be recognized similarly by group members' congruence. For example, when a group member begins to feel something that doesn't seem to be 'hers', it is possible that the feeling is a projected one from another group member. For instance, if a group member finds herself feeling unaccountably angry and the speaker is talking calmly about exploitation in their role, she may wonder if what she is feeling is projected from the speaker. If she can be congruent about that feeling and say she feels angry but she's not sure why, then the speaker may recognize the feeling as hers and choose to repossess the feeling. Even if the speaker chooses not to own the feeling, our group member has freed herself from the projection by her congruence. All unconscious defences are contained by a humanistic group climate which offers respect and unconditional positive regard, where the ground rules ensure that no one is attacked or over-challenged, so that fears, anxieties and perceived weakness are safely processed within the group.

In humanistic terms, the group dynamic is dominated by feeling, and group behaviour is ruled according to 'habeas emotum' (Luft, 1984: 154), which is a version of the legal term 'habeas corpus'. Habeas corpus means, literally, 'you shall have the body', where the person is protected from illegal custody, having the right to a fair trial. Habeas emotum refers not to physical freedom but the psychological freedom to have emotions and express them. The supervisor or team coach needs to be aware of emotion in the group as potential energy for learning or potential blocks to learning if unexpressed. An effective supervisor or team coach, taking a humanistic approach, will have the ability to observe, identify and, if appropriate, describe such dynamics in a group, through process comments, in simple terms, where appropriate, enabling reflection on that process by articulating it. For instance, calling attention to the group's over-reliance on the supervisor or team coach, noting where group members rather than the speaker feel angry, and mentioning the tendency to 'rescue' in the group. Process comments, if accepted by group members, are the trigger for reflection, and may be the first time the process has been highlighted for them.

Groups in practice

For group supervisors or team coaches we recommend Jenny Rogers' excellent book on facilitating groups (Rogers, 2010), which includes ice-breakers, designs for team coaching, games and exercises. Additional games can be found in Donna Brandes' entertaining *Gamesters Handbooks* 1, 2 and 3 (Brandes, 1979, 1982, 1998).

Note

1 Supervisors or team coaches should have access to supervision for themselves as group dynamics can trigger issues for them.

APPENDIX 6
Evaluation documents for coaches and mentors

Questionnaire for coaching clients

Please tick the appropriate box in response to the statements below about
<u>X</u>

	Strongly disagree	Disagree	Neither agree nor disagree	Agree	Strongly agree
1 X made a clear contract with me at the start of the coaching					
2 In the course of the coaching X established a working relationship with me					
3 X conducted the sessions on the basis of that relationship					
4 X enabled our relationship to end in a satisfactory way					
5 At our final meeting I was enabled to reflect upon our working relationship					
6 As far as I know, X's practice complied with the EMCC and ICF code of ethics					

7 What characteristics of the sessions helped you most?

8 What characteristics of the sessions helped you least?

Thank you for completing this evaluation – please return in SAE.

Learning outcome questionnaire for coaching or mentoring clients

Your responses to this questionnaire provide additional feedback to enhance my practice. Thank you for agreeing to complete it.

Client code:

1 How many sessions did you attend?

2 What brought you to coaching (or mentoring)?

3 What were you hoping to achieve?

4 Describe the experience of coaching (or mentoring):

Claims – what helped/hindered you?

Concerns – what else would you have liked?

Issues – what outstanding issues are you left with?

5 How would you describe the outcome?

6 Please choose one of these two categories to describe your learning outcome and also mark the best phrase (mark as many as you like):

a) Improvement:

– I know more now

– I can do a better job

– I feel more confident that I know what I am doing

– Other .... say what

b) Transformation:

– How I see certain things has changed

– My life has changed

– I am in a different place

– I feel completely different now

– Other .... say what

There is no need to give your name.

Quality assurance questionnaire for coaching clients

Please circle your response – there is no need to give your name.

	Poor				Excellent
1 How easy was it to get/make an appointment?	1	2	3	4	5
2 Were objectives agreed at the first session?	No				Yes
3 Were the number of coaching sessions agreed initially?	No				Yes
4 What is your opinion of the coach?	1	2	3	4	5
5 What is your opinion of the coaching venue?	1	2	3	4	5
6 How effective was the coaching in helping you to solve your difficulties?	1	2	3	4	5
7 At your final session did you discuss the way forward?	No				Yes
8 Would you seek coaching again in the future if necessary?	No				Yes

Thank you for completing this questionnaire.

We offer below a particular exemplar of evaluation currently in use by Two Minds which director Nathalie Tarbuck has kindly shared with us. She can be reached at **info@2mindstogether.co.uk**.

Coaching evaluation form

In order to ensure that I offer a first-rate service, I would like to know how you rate your Coaching experience.

Please **fill box** to indicate score (1 = Strongly disagree, 2 = Disagree, 3 = Neither agree nor disagree, 4 = Agree, 5 = Strongly agree)

1. Coaching Fundamentals Name of coach	1	2	3	4	5
a. Kept to agreed appointments					
b. Allowed me to own and set the agenda for my sessions					
c. Kept a check on the points agreed during my sessions and fed them back to me, including reviewing points from previous sessions					
d. Encouraged me to use a log, journal or reflection note to reflect on learning experiences					

2. Coaching Process Name of coach	1	2	3	4	5
a. Established rapport with me – listened to what I said and displayed empathy with my thoughts and ideas; gave clear responses, summarized and communicated openly with me					
b. Clearly explained concepts, information and techniques, giving clear, concise and constructive feedback					
c. Used questionnaires and/or self-assessment profiles (if appropriate) to help me understand myself better					
d. Ensured I retained responsibility to solve problems and change my behaviour and gained my commitment to agreed to action steps					
e. Asserted herself without being aggressive or passive					
f. Showed that she was knowledgeable, skilful and willing to liaise with other appropriate experts (if applicable)					
g. Demonstrated good time management practices					
h. Communicated a genuine belief in the potential in me to improve my performance					
i. Managed any relevant emotional issues that occurred during the coaching (if appropriate)					
j. Acted as a good role model					

3. Coaching Outcomes	1	2	3	4	5
a. I achieved progress against all my coaching goals					
b. I have higher levels of competence and am more effective at work					
c. My work performance improved as a result of developing specific competencies/behaviours					
d. I have become more aware of myself					
e. I actively use/practise the skills I've learnt					
f. I am able to set myself new development goals or targets and prioritize my development					
g. I can create a personal development plan (if appropriate)					

4. Organizational Benefits as a Result of Coaching	1	2	3	4	5
a. My management/leadership skills have improved					
b. I believe that the coaching I have received has had a tangible impact upon my team, peers and boss					
c. My motivation has increased as a result of the coaching					
d. My coaching has helped me sort out personal issues which may otherwise have affected my performance at work					

Are there any other personal or business benefits you believe have been derived from your coaching?

What suggestion do you have to improve the experience you had?

Would you be willing to recommend Name of coach as a coach?

Thank you for taking the time to complete this questionnaire, I really value your feedback.

Kindest Regards, Name of coach

REFERENCES

Ahern, G (2001) Individual executive development: regulated, structured and ethical, *Occupational Psychologist*, **44**, pp 3–7

Albom, M (1997) *Tuesdays with Morrie*, Doubleday, New York

Amabile, T (2002) Creativity under the gun, *Harvard Business Review* (August), #1571

Anderson, D and Anderson, A (2005) *Coaching that Counts*, Elsevier, Oxford

Anthony, K (2000) Counselling in cyberspace, *Counselling*, **11** (10), pp 625–27

Argyle, M (1975) *Bodily Communication*, Methuen, London

Argyris, C and Schön, D (1996) *Organisational Learning II: Theory, method and practice*, Addison-Wesley, Wokingham

Arkin, A (2005) Hidden talents, *People Management*, 14 July

Auster, D (1984) Mentors and proteges: power-dependent dyads, *Social Inquiry*, **54** (2), pp 142–53

Bachkirova, T and Cox, E (2004) [accessed 4 January 2005] A bridge over troubled water: bringing together coaching and counselling, *International Journal of Mentoring and Coaching*, **2** (1), www.emccouncil.org

Barna, L M (1997) Stumbling blocks in intercultural communication, in *Intercultural Communication: A reader*, 8th edn, ed L A Samovar and R E Porter, pp 337–46, Wadsworth, Belmont, CA

Barnes, B, Ernst, S and Hyde, K (1999) *An Introduction to Groups*, Macmillan, London

Baron-Cohen, S (2011) *Zero Degrees of Empathy: A new theory of human cruelty*, Allen Lane, Penguin Books, London

Baum, H S (1992) Mentoring, *Human Relations*, **45** (3), pp 223–45

Beech, N and Brockbank, A (1999) Guiding blight, *People Management*, IPD, 6 May

Belenky, M F et al (1986) *Women's Ways of Knowing: The development of self, voice and mind*, Basic Books, New York

Berger, P L and Luckmann, T (1966) *The Social Construction of Reality*, Penguin, Harmondsworth

Berglas, S (2002) The very real dangers of executive coaching, *Harvard Business Review*, June, pp 86–92

Bierema, L and Merriam, S B (2002) E-mentoring: using computer mediated communication (CMC) to enhance the mentoring process, *Innovative Higher Education*, **26** (3), pp 214–21

Bion, W (1961) *Experiences in Groups*, Tavistock, London

Blanchard, K and Shula, D (1995) *Everyone's a Coach*, Michigan: Zondervan

Bohm, D (1996) *On Dialogue*, Routledge, London

Boud, D, Keogh, R and Walker, D (1985) *Turning Experience into Learning*, Kogan Page, London

Bowlby, J (1979) *The Making and Breaking of Affectional Bonds*, Tavistock, London

Boyd, E M and Fales, A W (1983) Reflective learning: key to learning from experience, *Journal of Humanistic Psychology*, **23** (2), pp 99–117

Brandes, D (1979) *The New Gamesters Handbook*, Nelson Thornes, Cheltenham

Brandes, D (1982) *The Gamesters Handbook 2*, Nelson Thornes, Cheltenham

Brandes, D (1998) *The Gamesters Handbook 3*, Nelson Thornes, Cheltenham

Brockbank, A (1994) Expectations of mentoring, *Training Officer*, **30** (3), pp 86–88

Brockbank, A (2009) *The Role of Reflective Dialogue in Transformational Reflective Learning*, PhD Thesis, Cass Business School, City University, London

Brockbank, A and Beech, N (1999) Imbalance of power, *Health Management*, July

Brockbank, A and McGill, I (1998) *Facilitating Reflective Learning in Higher Education*, SRHE/Open University Press, Buckingham

Brockbank, A and McGill, I (2007) *Facilitating Reflective Learning in Higher Education*, 2nd edn, SRHE/Open University Press, Buckingham

Brockbank, A, McGill, I and Beech, N (2002) *Reflective Learning in Practice*, Gower, Aldershot

Brookfield, S (1987) *Developing Critical Thinkers*, Open University Press, Buckingham

Brookfield, S and Preskill, S (1999) *Discussion as a Way of Teaching*, Open University Press, Buckingham

Brown, D and Hirsch, W (2011) Performance management: fine intentions, *People Management*, September

Buber, M (1965) *Between Man and Man*, Macmillan, New York

Buber, M (1994) *I and Thou*, T&T Clark, Edinburgh

Bull, P (1983) *Body Movement and Interpersonal Communication*, John Wiley, Chichester

Burgstahler, S and Nourse, S (1999) [accessed 7 August 2002] Opening Doors: Mentoring on the internet, http://www-cod.csun.edu/conf/1999/proceedings/session0032.htm

Burley-Allen, M (1995) *Listening: The forgotten skill*, John Wiley, New York

Burr, V (1995) *An Introduction to Social Constructivism*, Routledge, London

Burrell, G and Morgan, G (1979) *Sociological Paradigms and Organisational Analysis*, Heinemann, London

Bushardt, S C, Fretwell, C and Holdnak, B J (1991) The mentor/protégé relationship, *Human Relations*, **44** (6), pp 619–39

Caplan, J (2003) *Coaching for the Future: How smart companies use coaching and mentoring*, CIPD, London

Cardow, A (1998) Mentoring at light speed, *Mentoring and Tutoring*, 5 (3), pp 32–39

Carroll, M (1996) *Counselling Supervision: Theory skills and practice*, Cassell, London

Carroll, M (2004) Coaching managers to be managers, Private communication

Carruthers, J (1993) The principles and practice of mentoring, Chapter 2 in *The Return of the Mentor: Strategies for workplace learning*, ed B J Caldwell and E M A Carter, Falmer Press, London

Caruso, R (1992) *Mentoring and the Business Environment*, Dartmouth, Aldershot

Caruso, R E (1996) *Who does mentoring?* Paper presented at the Third European Mentoring Conference, London

Chomsky, N (1957) *Syntactic Structures*, Mouton, The Hague

Chomsky, N (1969) *Aspects of the Theory of Syntax*, MIT Press, Cambridge, MA

Cialdini, R (2007) How to get the best solutions for your team, *Harvard Management Update*, **12** (5), pp 2–4

CIPD (2008) [accessed July 2011] Coaching and buying coaching services, http://www.cipd.co.uk/binaries/coaching_buying_services.pdf

CIPD (2009) [accessed July 2011] Employee Engagement in Context, Kingston Business School, CIPD, London, http://www.cipd.co.uk/hr-resources/research/ employee-engagement-context.aspx

CIPD (2010a) [accessed July 2011] Employee Engagement Factsheet, revised by Kathy Daniels, July

CIPD (2010b) [accessed July 2011] Coaching and Mentoring Factsheet, http://www.cipd.co.uk/hr-resources/factsheets/coaching-mentoring.aspx

CIPD (2010c) [accessed July 2011] Creating an Engaged Workforce, Kingston Business School, http://www.cipd.co.uk/binaries/Creating_engaged_workforce.pdf

CIPD (2011a) [accessed July 2011] Learning and Talent Development. Annual Survey Report, http://www.cipd.co.uk/binaries/LandTD%202011%20survey %20report.pdf

CIPD (2011b) [accessed July 2011] Performance Management in Action: Current Trends and practice, http://www.cipd.co.uk/binaries/coaching_buying_services.pdf

CIPD (2011c) [accessed September 2011] The Coaching Climate, http://www.cipd.co.uk/hr-resources/survey-reports/coaching-climate- 2011.aspx

Clarkson, P and Shaw, P (1992) Human relationships at work in organisations, *Management Education and Development*, **23** (1), pp 18–29

Clinchy, B M (1996) Connected and separate knowing: towards a marriage of two minds, in *Knowledge, Difference, and Power*, ed N R Goldberger *et al*, Basic Books, New York

Clutterbuck, D (1991) *Everyone Needs a Mentor*, 2nd edn, Institute of Personnel Management, London

Clutterbuck, D (1998) *Learning Alliances*, IPD, London

Clutterbuck, D and Megginson, D (1999) *Mentoring Executives and Directors*, Butterworth-Heinemann, Oxford

Clutterbuck, D and Ragins, B R (2002) *Mentoring and Diversity*, Butterworth-Heinemann, Oxford

Cohen, N H (1995) *Mentoring Adult Learners: A guide for educators and trainers*, Krieger, Malabar, FL

Colley, H (2003) *Mentoring for Social Inclusion: A critical approach to nurturing mentor relationships*, Routledge-Falmer, London

Cooper, R (1997) Applying emotional intelligence in the workplace, *Training and Development*, December, pp 31–38

Coopey, J (1995) The learning organisation: power, politics and ideology, *Management Learning*, **26** (2), pp 193–213

Cozby, P C (1973) Self-disclosure: a literature review, *Psychological Bulletin*, **79**, pp 73–91

Cramer, P (2000) Defence mechanisms in psychology today, *American Psychologist*, **55** (6), pp 637–46

Cross, S (1999) Roots and wings: mentoring, *Innovation in Education and Training International*, **35** (3), pp 224–30

Crum, A J and Langer, E J (2007) Mind-set matters: exercise and the placebo effect, *Psychological Science*, **18** (2), 165–71

Cunliffe, A and Easterby-Smith, M (2004) From reflection to practical reflexivity: experiential learning as lived experience, in *Organising Reflection*, ed M Reynolds and R Vince, Ashgate, Aldershot

Cunningham, J B and Eberle, T (1993) Characteristics of the mentoring experience: a qualitative study, *Personnel Review*, **22** (4), pp 54–66

Daloz, L (1986) *Effective Teaching and Mentoring: Realizing the transformational power of adult learning experiences*, Jossey-Bass, San Francisco

Damasio, A (1995) *Descartes' Error*, HarperCollins, New York

Darling, L A W (1984) What do nurses want in a mentor? *Journal of Nursing Administration*, **14** (10), pp 42–44

Darling, L A W (1986) What to do about toxic mentors, *Nurse Education*, **11** (2), pp 29–30

Darwin, A (2000) Critical reflections on mentoring in work settings, *Adult Education Quarterly*, **50** (3), May, pp 197–211

Day, C (1993) Reflection: a necessary but not sufficient condition of professional development, *British Educational Research Journal*, **19** (1), pp 83–93

De Board, R (1978) *The Psychoanalysis of Organisations*, Routledge, London

Deci, E L and Ryan, M R (2000) Self-determination theory and the facilitation of intrinsic motivation, social development and well-being, *American Psychologist*, **55** (1), pp 68–78

Downey, M (1999) *Effective Coaching*, Orion Business Books, London

Downey, M (2002) *Effective Coaching*, Orion Business Books, London

Druskat, V U and Wolff, S B (2001) *Building the Emotional Intelligence of Groups*, Harvard Business Review Onpoint enhanced edn, Harvard Business School Publishing, Boston, MA

Dulewicz, V and Higgs, M (1998) Soul researching, *People Management*, 1 October

Egan, G (1976) *Interpersonal Living: A skills/contract approach to human relations training in groups*, Brooks-Cole, Monterey, CA

Egan, G (1977) *You and Me: The skills of being an effective group communicator*, Brooks-Cole, Monterey, CA

Egan, G (1990) *The Skilled Helper: A systematic approach to effective helping*, 4th edn, Brooks-Cole, Pacific Grove, CA

Ekman, P and Freisen, W (1975) *Unmasking the Face*, Prentice Hall, Englewood Cliffs, NJ

Elbow, P (1998) *Writing without Teachers*, 2nd edn, Oxford University Press, New York

Eleftheriadou, Z (1994) *Transcultural Counselling*, Central Book Publishing, London

EMCC (2008) [accessed July 2011] Code of Ethics, http://www.emccouncil.org/src/ultimo/models/Download/4.pdf

EMCC/ICF (2011) [accessed January 2012] Joint Code of Conduct, http://www.aoec.com/downloads/Code%20of%20Conduct.pdf

Ferenzi, S (1916) *Contributions to Psychoanalysis*, Richard Badger, Boston

Fineman, S (1993) (ed) *Emotion in Organisations*, Sage, London

Flaherty, F (1999) *Coaching: Evoking excellence in others*, Butterworth-Heinemann, Oxford

Flood, R and Romm, N (1996) *Diversity Management*, John Wiley, Chichester

Fordham, F (1982) *An Introduction to Jung's Psychology*, Penguin, Harmondsworth

Foulkes, S H (1975) *Group Analytic Psychotherapy: Methods and Principles*, Gordon & Breach, London

French, R and Vince, R (ed) (1999) *Group Relations, Management and Organisation*, Oxford University Press, Oxford

Friedman, M (1985) *The Healing Dialogue in Psychotherapy*, Jason Aronson, New York

Gallup (2010) *Employee Engagement: What's Your Engagement Ratio?* Copyright Gallup Consulting

Gallwey, T (1974) *The Inner Game of Tennis*, Bantam, New York

Geertz, C (1986) The uses of diversity, *Michigan Quarterly Review*, Winter, pp 105–23

Gersick, C J G (1989) Marking time: predictable transitions in task groups, *Academy of Management Journal*, 31, pp 9–41

Giddens, A (1991) *Modernity and Self Identity: Self and society in the late modern age*, Stanford University Press, Stanford, CA

Giddens, A (1992) *The Transformation of Intimacy: Sexuality, love and eroticism in modern societies*, Polity, Cambridge

Giddens, A (1993) *New Rules of Sociological Method: A positive critique of interpretive sociologies*, Stanford University Press, Stanford, CA

Giddens, A (1996) *In Defence of Sociology: Essays, interpretations, and rejoinders*, Polity Press, Cambridge, MA

Goldberger, N R *et al* (ed) (1996) *Knowledge, Difference, and Power*, Basic Books, New York

Goleman, D (1995) *Emotional Intelligence*, Bloomsbury, London

Grant, A M (1999) *Enhancing Performance through Coaching: The Promise of CBT*, Paper presented at the First State Conference of Australian Association of Cognitive Behavioural Therapy, Sydney

Grenfell, M and James, D (1998) *Bourdieu and Education*, Routledge-Falmer, London

Grove, D (1996) And... what kind of a man is David Grove? An interview by Penny Tomkins and James Lawley, *Rapport*, 33, August

Guba, E G and Lincoln, Y S (1989) *Fourth Generation Evaluation*, Sage, London

Hackman, J R (2002) *Leading Teams: Setting the stage for great performances*, Harvard Business School Press, Boston, MA

Hackman, J R and Wageman, R (2005) A theory of team coaching, *Academy of Management Review*, 30 (2), 269–87

Halfpenny, P (1985) Course materials, MSc in Applied Social Research, University of Manchester

Hall, L (2005) IT support, *People Management*, 24 March, pp 34–37

Hammer, M and Stanton, S A (1997) The power of reflection, *Fortune Magazine*, 24 November, pp 291–96

Harris, M and Brockbank, A (2011) *An Integrative Approach to Therapy and Supervision*, Jessica Kingsley, London

Harrison, R (1978) Choosing the depth of organisational interventions, in *Organisation Development and Transformation*, ed W French, C Y Bell and R Zawacki, pp 354–64, McGraw-Hill, Boston, MA

Hart, V, Blattner, J and Leipsic, S (2001) Coaching versus therapy: a perspective, *Consulting Psychology Journal: Practice and Research*, 53, pp 229–37

Harvard (2004) Mentoring and management: developing human assets, in *Coaching and Mentoring: How to develop top talent and achieve stronger performance*, Harvard Business School Press, Boston, MA

Harvard (2007) *Managing Teams for High Performance*, Harvard Business School Publishing, Boston, MA

Hawkins, P (2011) Building emotional, ethical and cognitive capacity in coaches, in *Supervision in Coaching: Supervision, ethics and continuous professional development*, ed J Passmore, Kogan Page, London

Hawkins, P and Shohet, R (1989) *Supervision in the Helping Professions*, Open University Press, Buckingham

Hawkins, P and Shohet, R (2007) *Supervision in the Helping Professions*, 3rd edn, Open University Press, Buckingham

Hawkins, P and Smith, N (2006) *Coaching, Mentoring and Organisational Consultancy*, Open University Press, McGraw-Hill, Maidenhead

Hay, J (1995) *Transformational Mentoring: Creating developmental alliances for changing organisational cultures*, Sherwood Publishing, Watford

Heirs, B and Farrell, P (1986) *The Professional Decision Thinker: Our new management priority*, 2nd edn, Garden City Press, Hertfordshire

Heron, J (1991) *Helping the Client: A creative practical guide*, Sage, London

Heron, J (1993) *Group Facilitation*, Kogan Page, London

Heron, J (1999) *The Complete Facilitator's Handbook*, Kogan Page, London

Holloway, E L (1987) Developmental models of supervision: is it development? *Professional Psychology: Research and Practice*, **18** (3), pp 209–16

Howe, M (2008) Putting down routes, *People Management*, 20 March, CIPD, London

Inskipp, F and Proctor, B (1993) *The Art, Craft and Tasks of Counselling Supervision Part 1: Making the most of supervision*, Cascade Publications, Twickenham

Inskipp, F and Proctor, B (1995) *The Art, Craft and Tasks of Counselling Supervision Part 2: Becoming a supervisor*, Cascade Publications, Twickenham

International Coaching Federation (ICF) (2008) [accessed October 2011] Code of Ethics, http://www.coachfederation.org/icfcredentials/ethics/

International Coaching Federation (ICF) (2011) [accessed October 2011] Core Competences, www.coachfederation.org/icfcredentials/core-competencies/

Isaacs, W (1994) [accessed 1 August 2009] Dialogue Project Report 1993–1994, MIT, http://www.solonline.org/res/wp/8004.html

Isaacs, W (1999) *Dialogue and the Art of Thinking Together: A pioneering approach to communicating in business and in life*, Random House, New York

Jacoby, M (1984) *The Analytic Encounter*, Inner City Books, Toronto

James, K and Baddeley, J (1991) The power of innocence: from politeness to politics, *Management Learning*, **22** (2), pp 106–18

Jarvis, J (2004) *Coaching and Buying Coaching Services*, CIPD, London, http://www.cipd.co.uk

Jensen, E (1995) *Brain Based Learning and Teaching*, Turning Point, Del Mar, CA

Jordan, J (1991) Empathy and self boundaries, in *Women's Growth in Connection: Writings from the Stone Center*, ed J V Jordan *et al*, pp 67–80, Guilford Press, New York

Jowett, B (1953) *The Dialogues of Plato*, vol I, book XVII, Meno, Oxford University Press, Oxford

Kahn, D G (1981) *Fathers as Mentors to Daughters*, Working paper, Radcliffe Institute, Cambridge, MA

Kates, J (1985) In search of professionalism, *City Woman*, **8** (1), pp 34–42

Katzenbach, J and Smith, D (1993) *The Wisdom of Teams: Creating the high performance organisation*, Harper, New York

Keep, E (1992) Corporate training strategies: the vital component?, in *Human Resource Strategies*, ed G Salaman, Sage, London

Kegan, R and Lahey, L L (2009) *Immunity to Change: How to overcome it and unlock the potential in yourself and your organization*, Harvard Business School Publishing, Boston, MA

Kets de Vries, M (1995) *Life and Death in the Executive Fast Lane*, Jossey-Bass, San Francisco

Kim, B (2001) [accessed 8 August 2005] Social constructivism, in *Emerging Perspectives on Learning, Teaching and Technology*, ed M Orey, http://www.coe.uga.edu/epitt/SocialConstructivism.htm

King, M L, Jr (1968) *A Testament of Hope: The essential writings and speeches of Martin Luther King Jr*, ed J M Washington, HarperCollins, New York

Kohn, A (1990) *The Brighter Side of Human Nature: Altruism and empathy in everyday life*, Basic Books, New York

Kohut, H (1991) Empathy and self boundaries, in *Women's Growth in Connection: Writings from the Stone Centre*, ed J Jordan *et al*, pp 67–80, Guilford Press, New York

Kolb, D (1984) *Experiential Learning*, Prentice Hall, Englewood Cliffs, NJ

Kram, K (1988) *Mentoring at Work*, University Pressof America, Lanham, MD

Krantz, J (1989) The managerial couple: superior–subordinate relationships as a unit of analysis, *Human Resource Management*, **28** (2), pp 161–75

Kubler-Ross, E (1991) *On Death and Dying*, Macmillan, London

Kukla, A (2000) *Social Constructivism and the Philosophy of Science*, Routledge, New York

Kushner, S (2000) *Personalising Evaluation*, Sage, London

Landale, M (2005) Working with somatisation, Private communication

Lapierre, L (1989) Mourning potency and power in management, *Human Re-source Management*, **28** (2), pp 177–89

Lehrer, J (2009) *The Decisive Moment: How the Brain makes up its mind*, Canongate, London

Leininger, M M (1987) Transcultural caring: a different way to help people, in *Handbook of Cross-cultural Counselling and Therapy*, ed P Pederson, Praeger, London

Levinson, D J and Levinson, J (1996) *The Seasons of a Woman's Life*, Ballantine Books, New York

Levinson, D J *et al* (1978) *Seasons of a Man's Life*, Alfred A Knopf, New York

London JS International (2005) [accessed 9 June 2005] About NLP, http://www.js-International.com/nlp.html

London, M (1997) *Job Feedback*, Lawrence Erlbaum, Mahwah, NJ

London, M (2003) *Job Feedback*, 2nd edn, Lawrence Erlbaum Associates, Mahwah, NJ

Luft, J (1984) *Group Processes: An introduction to group dynamics*, Mayfield Publishing, Mountain View, CA

Lukes, S (2005) *Power: A radical view*, 2nd edn, Macmillan, London

Magnuson, E (1986) A serious deficiency: the Rogers Commission faults NASA's flawed decision-making process, *Time*, March, pp 40–42

Margulies, A (1989) *The Empathic Imagination*, WW Norton, New York

Marton, F, Dall'Alba, G and Beaty, E (1993) Conceptions of learning, *International Journal of Educational Research*, **19**, pp 277–300

Maslow, A (1969) *The Psychology of Science: A reconnaissance*, Henry Regnery, New York

Mattinson, J (1975) *The Reflection Process in Casework Supervision*, Institute of Marital Studies, Tavistock Institute of Human Relations, London

Maturana, H and Varela, F J (1987) *The Tree of Knowledge*, Shambhala Publications, Boston, MA

Mayer, J (1999) Emotional intelligence, *People Management*, 28 October

McCann, D (1988) *How to Influence Others at Work*, Heinemann, Oxford

McGilchrist, I (2010) *The Master and his Emissary: The divided brain and the making of the Western World*, Yale University Press, New Haven, CT

McGill, I and Brockbank, A (2004) *The Handbook of Action Learning*, Routledge, London

McGuire, G M (1999) Do race and gender affect employees' access to and help from mentors? Insights from the study of a large corporation, in *Mentoring Dilemmas: Developmental relationships within multicultural organisations*, ed A J Murrell, F J Crosby and R J Ely, pp 105–20, Lawrence Erlbaum, Mahwah, NJ

McKeen, C A and Burke, R J (1989) Mentor relationships in organisations: issues, strategies and prospects for women, *Journal of Management Development*, 8 (6), pp 33–42

McKenna, Y A and Bargh, J A (1998) Coming out in the age of the internet: de-marginalisation through virtual group participation, *Journal of Personality and Social Psychology*, 75 (3), pp 681–94

McLeod, A (2003) *Performance Coaching: The handbook for managers, HR professionals and coaches*, Crown House Publishing, Carmarthen, Wales

McLeod, J (1998) *An Introduction to Counselling*, 2nd edn, Open University Press, Buckingham

Mearns, D and Thorne, B (1988) *Person centred counselling in Action*, Sage, London

Megginson, D (1988) Instructor, coach, mentor: three ways of helping for managers, *Management Education and Development*, 19 (1), pp 33–46

Megginson, D and Clutterbuck, D (1995) *Mentoring in Action*, Kogan Page, London

Megginson, D and Clutterbuck, D (2005) *Techniques for Coaching and Mentoring*, Butterworth-Heinemann, Oxford

Megginson, D and Clutterbuck, D (2006) Creating a coaching culture, *Industrial and Commercial Training*, 38 (5), 232–37

Megginson, D and Clutterbuck, D (2009) *Further Techniques for Coaching and Mentoring*, Butterworth-Heinemann, Oxford

Megginson, D and Garvey, B (2004) [accessed 20 February 2005] Odysseus, Telemachus and Mentor: stumbling into, searching for and signposting the road to desire, *International Journal of Mentoring and Coaching*, 2 (1), www.emccouncil.org

Mehrabian, A (1971) *Silent Messages*, Wadsworth, Belmont, CA

Mezirow, J (1994) Understanding transformation theory, *Adult Education Quarterly*, 44 (4), pp 222–44

Miller, A (1983) *For Your Own Good: Hidden cruelty in child-rearing and the roots of violence*, trans H and H Haanum, New American Library, New York

Morris, D (1977) *Manwatching*, Cape, London

Morton-Cooper, A and Palmer, A (1993) *Mentoring and Preceptorship*, Blackwell Science, Oxford (2000) 2nd edn, Blackwell Science, Oxford

Neenan, M and Dryden, W (2002) *Life Coaching*, Brunner-Routledge, Hove

Nelson-Jones, R (1986) *Relationship Skills*, Holt, Rinehart and Winston, London

Neumann, J (1998) *Women's Work: Workshop notes*, Tavistock Institute, Devon

Noddings, N (1984) *Caring*, University of California Press, Berkeley, CA

O'Neill, M B (2000) *Executive Coaching with Backbone and Heart: A systems approach to engaging leaders with their challenges*, Jossey-Bass, San Francisco

Orbach, S (1994) *What's Really Going On Here?* Virago, London

Owen, J M and Rogers, P J (1999) *Programme Evaluation – Forms and Approaches*, Sage, London

Page, S and Wosket, V (1994) *Supervising the Counsellor: A cyclical model*, Routledge, London

Page, S and Wosket, V (2001) *Supervising the Counsellor*, Brunner-Routledge, Hove

Parsloe, E (1995) *The Manager as Coach and Mentor*, IPD, London

Parsloe, E and Wray, M (2000) *Coaching and Mentoring*, Kogan Page, London

Passmore, J (ed) (2010) *Excellence in Coaching: The Industry Guide*, Kogan Page, London

Passmore, J (ed) (2011) *Supervision in Coaching: Supervision, ethics and continuous professional development*, Kogan Page, London

Patterson, E (2011) Presence in coaching supervision, in *Supervision in Coaching: Supervision, ethics and continuous professional development*, ed J Passmore, Kogan Page, London

Paulston, R (1996) *Social Cartography: Mapping ways of seeing social and educational change*, Garland, New York

Pease, A (1981) *Body Language*, Sheldon Press, London

Peltier, B (2001) *The Psychology of Executive Coaching*, Brunner-Routledge, Hove

Perry, W (1970) *Forms of Intellectual and Ethical Development during the College Years: A scheme*, Holt, Rinehart and Winston, New York

Peters, T J and Waterman, R H (1982) *In Search of Excellence*, Harper and Row, New York

Phillips-Jones, L (1982) *Mentors and Protégés: How to establish, strengthen and get the most from a mentor/protégé relationship*, Arbor House, New York

Pointon, C (2003) A life coach in two days? *Counselling and Psychotherapy Journal*, **14** (10), pp 20–23

Purcell, J (2003) *Understanding the People and Performance Link*, CIPD, London

Quinn, Robert (2000) *Change the World*, Jossey-Bass, San Francisco

Reynolds, M (1997) Learning styles: a critique, *Management Learning*, **28** (2), pp 115–33

Reynolds, M and Vince, R (2004) *Organising Reflection*, Ashgate, Aldershot

Ridgeway, N and Manning, J (2008) *Think about Your Thinking to Stop Depression*, West Suffolk CBT Service, Bury St Edmunds, Suffolk

Roberts, A (1998) Androgynous mentor: bridging gender stereotypes in mentoring, *Mentoring and Tutoring*, **6** (1/2), pp 18–29

Roberts, A (2000) Mentoring revisited: a phenomenological reading of the literature, *Mentoring and Tutoring*, **8** (2), pp 145–70

Robinson, D, Perryman, S and Hayday, S (2004) *The Drivers of Employee Engagement*, Institute of Employment Studies, Brighton

Rock, D, based on an interview with Jeffrey M Schwartz, MD (2006) A brain-based approach to coaching, *International Journal of Coaching in Organizations*, **4** (2), pp 32–43

Rogers, C R (1951) *Client-Centered Therapy*, Constable, London

Rogers, C R (1957) The necessary and sufficient conditions for therapeutic personality change, *Journal of Consulting Psychology*, **21**, pp 95–103

Rogers, C R (1961) *On Becoming a Person: A therapist's view of psychotherapy*, Houghton Mifflin, Boston, MA

Rogers, C R (1979) *Carl Rogers on Personal Power*, Constable, London

Rogers, Carl (1983) *Freedom to Learn for the 80s*, Merrill, New York

Rogers, C R (1992) *Client-Centered Therapy*, Constable, London

Rogers, J (2004) *Coaching Skills: A handbook*, Open University Press, New York

Rogers, J (2010) *Facilitating Groups*, Open University Press, Maidenhead

Rooke, D and Torbert, W R (2005) Seven transformations of leadership, *Harvard Business Review*, **83** (4), 67–76

Rose, C and Nicholl, M J (1997) *Accelerated Learning for the 21st Century*, Piatkus, London

Rosinski, P (2003) *Coaching across Cultures*, Nicholas Brealey, London

Ross, J A (2007) Make your good team great, in *Managing Teams for High Performance*, Harvard Business Publishing Newsletters, Harvard Business School Publishing, Boston, MA

Rothschild, B (2000) *The Body Remembers*, WW Norton, New York

Ruddick, S (1984) New combinations: learning from Virginia Woolf, in *Between Women*, ed C Asher, L DeSalvo and S Ruddick, pp 137–59, Beacon Press, Boston, MA

Russell, G (2001) [accessed 8 August 2002] Computer mediated school education and the web, *First Monday*, **6** (11), http://www.firstmonday.org/issues/issue6_11/Russell/index.html

Ryan, M R and Deci, E L (2000) The what and why of goal pursuits: human needs and the self-determination of behaviour, *Psychological Inquiry*, **11** (4), pp 227–68

Ryle, G (1983) *The Concept of Mind*, Penguin, Harmondsworth

Scandura, T A (1998) Dysfunctional mentoring relationships and outcomes, *Journal of Management*, **24**, pp 449–67

Schön, D (1987) *Educating the Reflective Practitioner*, Jossey-Bass, London

Schwaber, E (1983) Construction, reconstruction and the mode of clinical attachment, in *The Future of Psychoanalysis*, ed A Goldberg, pp 273–91, International Universities Press, New York

Sherman, S and Freas, A (2004) The wild west of executive coaching, *Harvard Business Review*, **82** (1), pp 82–90

Siegel, D (2010) *Mindsight*, WW Norton and Co, New York

Silshee, D (2010) *Presence-based Coaching: Cultivating self-generative leaders through mind, body and heart*, Jossey Bass, San Francisco

Silverstone, L (1993) *Art and the Development of the Person*, Autonomy Books, London

Smail, D (2001) *The Nature of Unhappiness*, Constable, London

Stacey, R (1993) *Strategic Management and Organisational Dynamics*, Pitman, London

Stafford-Clark, D (1965) *What Freud Really Said*, Penguin, Harmondsworth

Starr, J (2008) *Brilliant Coaching*, Pearson Education, Harlow

Thomas, K W (1976) Conflict and conflict management, in *Handbook of Industrial and Organisational Psychology*, ed M D Dunnette, Rand McNally, Chicago

Thomson, B (2011) Non-directive supervision of coaching, in *Supervision in Coaching: Supervision, ethics and continuous professional development*, ed J Passmore, Kogan Page, London

Thompson, L, Aranda, E and Robbins, S P (2001) *Tools for Teams: Building effective teams in the workplace*, University of Phoenix, Phoenix, AZ, Pearson Custom Publishing

Warren, C (2005) Quantum leap, *People Management*, 10 March, pp 34–37

Watkins, M (2003) *The First 90 Days*, Harvard Business School Press, Boston, MA

Weafer, S (2001) *The Business Coaching Revolution*, Blackhall, Dublin

Webb, K (2011) [accessed October 2011] The COACH model, www.creativeresultsmanagement.com/resources/coachcard.htm

Weiss, C H (1998) *Evaluation: Methods of studying programs and policies*, 2nd edn, Prentice Hall, Upper Saddle River, NJ

Whitely, W, Dougherty, T W and Dreher, G F (1991) Relationship of career mentoring and socioeconomic origin to managers' and professionals' early career progress, *Academy of Management Journal*, **34** (2), pp 331–51

Whitmore, J (1996) *Coaching for Performance*, Nicholas Brealey, London

Whitworth, L, Kimsey-House, H and Sandhal, P (1998) *Co-active Coaching*, Davies-Black Publishing, Palo Alto, CA

Wikipedia (2005) [accessed 2 June 2005] Coaching, Entry in Wikipedia, http://www.answers.com/coaching

Williams, D and Irving, J (2001) Coaching: an unregulated, unstructured and (potentially) unethical process, *Occupational Psychologist*, **42**, pp 3–7

Winnicott, D W (1965) *The Family and Individual Development*, Routledge, London

Winnicott, D W (1971) *Playing and Reality*, Penguin, Harmondsworth

Worthen, V and McNeill, B W (1996) A phenomenological investigation of 'good' supervision events, *Journal of Counselling Psychology*, **43**, pp 25–34

Wright, R G and Werther, W B (1991) Mentors at work, *Journal of Management Development*, **10** (3), pp 25–32

Zachary, L (2000) *The Mentor's Guide*, Jossey-Bass, San Francisco

Zander, R S and Zander, B (2000) *The Art of Possibility: Transforming professional and personal life*, Harvard Business School Press, Boston, MA

Zinkin, L (1989) Supervision: the impossible profession, in *Clinical Supervision: Issues and Techniques* (papers from the public conference, April 1988), Jungian Training Committee, London

INDEX